Social Life
in Early England

Essays by

J. N. L. MYRES
L. C. LATHAM
ROSE GRAHAM
SIR FRANK STENTON
G. G. COULTON
C. J. FFOULKES
A. HAMILTON THOMPSON
J. N. L. BAKER

Social Life
in Early England

HISTORICAL ASSOCIATION ESSAYS
EDITED BY

Geoffrey Barraclough

GREENWOOD PRESS, PUBLISHERS
WESTPORT, CONNECTICUT

Library of Congress Cataloging in Publication Data

Historical Association, London.
  Social life in early England.

    Reprint of the ed. published by Routledge and Kegan
Paul, London.
    Includes bibliographical references and index.
    1.   England--Social life and customs--Medieval
period, 1066-1485--Addresses, essays, lectures.
2.   Arms and armor--Europe--History--Addresses, essays,
lectures.   3.   Trade routes--Addresses, essays, lectures.
I.   Barraclough, Geoffrey, 1908-   II.   Title.
[DA185.H58   1980]   942   79-16998
ISBN 0-313-21298-8

First published 1960 *by Routledge & Kegan Paul Limited*

Reprinted with the permission of Routledge & Kegan Paul Ltd.

Reprinted in 1980 by Greenwood Press
A division of Congressional Information Service, Inc.
88 Post Road West, Westport, Connecticut 06881

Printed in the United States of America

10 9 8 7 6 5 4 3 2 1

Contents

List of Figures

LIST OF FIGURES

THE ENGLISH HOUSE

MEDIEVAL TRADE ROUTES

Introduction

THE present volume contains a collection of nine essays, originally published by the Historical Association as individual pamphlets; and it is the privilege of the present writer, as Chairman of the Publications Committee, to introduce them to a wider public. I do so the more gladly as their high reputation is already well established. Their authors include some of the most famous names in a long generation of English historians; and the pamphlets themselves have been aptly described as a series of 'short essays on great themes'.

The policy of publishing, year by year, a number of pamphlets on historical subjects of wide general interest was adopted by the Historical Association in the period before the First World War, and there can be few major historical topics which have not been dealt with authoritatively during the course of the subsequent fifty years.[1] Inevitably a number of the pamphlets have gone out of date, or have otherwise been superseded, as the work of historical research has progressed. But a surprisingly large number have retained their value, and the demand for reprints and revisions has been continuous. It is with a view to supplying this demand that the present volume has been compiled; and if it is as successful as there is every reason to hope, the Publications Committee plans to put out further volumes, selected to cover other topics and other periods. Publication in book form, it is thought, may suit the particular needs and requirements of libraries—in the first place, of school libraries—better than paper-backed pamphlets, which it is difficult to preserve in good condition.

The essays in the present volume have been selected with the object of providing an authoritative introduction to the periods of English history usually taught in middle school. They pay particular attention to the broader social aspects of English history on which most teachers today place emphasis, rather than to political developments. They are thus well adapted to picking out the social background and the environment in which English history moved, from the time of the Roman settlement until the close of the Middle Ages. Manor and monasteries, chivalry and castle, and the development of cities and trade, are the backbone of the period; and all these subjects, together with the dwellings which housed the English

[1] Cf. *The Historical Association, 1906–1956*, (London, 1957), pp. 17–18, 41, 52.

people, are represented here. Thus there is something of a conspectus of English life, with side-glances at the European continent, of which England was a part. Since knighthood was a phenomenon common to the whole of Europe, the external trappings of English chivalry, the knight's arms and armour, can no more be considered in isolation from the continent than can the development of English trade, which depended upon the pattern of European trade-routes.

It would be impertinent for me, who am so much less expert than the writers themselves, to attempt an appreciation of the individual contributions to this volume. But a few remarks are not only permissible, but necessary. In the first place, most of the essays are illustrated with plans and drawings, since most of the subjects need to be seen graphically if the student, the schoolboy or the schoolgirl, is to have more than a vague generalized conception of the realities of early life in England. These illustrations are an integral part of the text, and seem to me, from a practical point of view, to be one of its outstanding merits. In the second place, the reader should know that, wherever possible, the essays have been revised and brought up-to-date for inclusion in the present volume. Our thanks are due both to the different authors who have so generously given time and trouble to this end, and also to Professor G. R. Potter and Professor R. F. Treharne, who kindly consented to read and comment on the proofs. We are indebted in particular, to Sir Frank Stenton, whose meticulous revision of his famous essay on 'Norman London' makes this, once again, the only thoroughly up-to-date comprehensive study still available. In other cases, where the authors are no longer alive, such minor changes as seemed desirable, are due to the present writer. The essay on 'The Manor' alone required considerable revision, in which I have benefited from the suggestions of Professor Treharne and Mr. E. B. Fryde. In part, this is a consequence of the close attention given in recent years to English economic history, which has clarified a number of problems and necessitated certain modifications, particularly in regard to the period before and after the Black Death; in part, it is due to the fact that the author, although well aware that the two were not identical, attempted to combine the stories of the manor and of the medieval village in one account. In fact, the coincidence of manor and village, though certainly common, is by no means necessary; while the open-field method of agriculture, which the author makes the basis of village agrarian arrangements, is now known to have been less prevalent than she appears to have believed. The reader who keeps these points in mind, will find, however, that this is a skilful and comprehensive treatment of a difficult subject, and without it the present volume would be less than complete.

It was also decided to abridge the essays on 'European Arms and Armour' and on 'The Meaning of Medieval Moneys'. The former was shortened because, as originally written, it considerably overstepped the limits of the present volume. The latter required revision in the light of the findings of modern economic historians. It might, indeed, be disputed whether Dr. Coulton's essay is still sufficiently authoritative to merit inclusion at all.[1] But in view of the obvious importance of the subject for any understanding of the Middle Ages —and particularly of the life of ordinary people in the Middle Ages—and in view also of the interest and intrinsic value of the information gathered together by Dr. Coulton, it was felt that the loss from its omission would have outweighed any scholarly hesitations as to its finality. Dr. Coulton himself was well aware of the tentative nature of his study; and it retains its importance in so far as it draws attention to a subject which cannot be ignored and to the type of evidence with which investigation has to deal. It is also a characteristic example of the mind and methods of one of England's best known medievalists.

A volume which contains the work of such distinguished historians as Sir Frank Stenton, G. G. Coulton, Rose Graham and Hamilton Thompson, requires little by way of introduction. Here is garnered some of the best work of some of the best historians of an outstanding generation. It is a great gain that it should now be available in durable form, and I am honoured that it should have fallen to me to prepare it for publication and introduce it to a wider public.

G. BARRACLOUGH.

15 September, 1958.

[1] Readers should compare E. Victor Morgan, *The Study of Prices and the Value of Money* (Historical Association, 1950), where the basic assumption of Dr. Coulton's article—that it is possible to establish a general multiplier (in this case, 40) to bring mediaeval money into modern terms—is subjected to criticism.

J. N. L. MYRES

Roman Britain

INTRODUCTION

THE Roman conquest and occupation of Britain has long been taken as the conventional starting point of English history, and there is a conventional justification for so doing. For in the writings of the Roman historians, notably those of Caesar, Tacitus, and Dion Cassius, occur the first literary records of historical events and historical personalities connected with this country. But it is perhaps worth asking whether the accidental preservation of these extremely fragmentary and inadequate records is really a good enough reason for the maintenance of this convention: for, in the first place, the development of archæology and its auxiliary sciences in the last half-century has reduced the contribution made by those records to a very minor one in our present knowledge of the Roman occupation; and, in the second place, we are able by the help of those same sciences to give a much surer account of pre-Roman Britain for centuries, even millennia, before the Christian era than was possible only a very few years ago. At the present time the old distinction between a strictly historic period for which the evidence is literary in character, and a vague pre-history dependent on the guesswork of archæologists, has become quite meaningless. In Britain as elsewhere history and pre-history in this sense meet and mingle over more than a thousand years.

If Roman Britain is to remain the conventional beginning of English history other reasons must be sought. In some ways it might be thought desirable to abandon the old convention altogether. It can always be argued with force that the history of England should

1

begin with the history of the English, and for many purposes that is no doubt an unassailable position. After all, the break between the ancient and the modern world is a far sharper one in this country than it is in most parts of Europe, and no one would venture to place it before rather than after the Roman period. What sense can there be in beginning the story with the last phase of the old world, an old world which in any case left only the slightest cultural influence in Britain on the new, rather than with the first phase of that new world itself? If ever historians are justified in cutting history into sections, they are surely right to make one such cut in British history in the fifth century A.D.

But the cut is one in cultural history only. Roman Britain is the final phase of the old world because it is the climax of a series of movements from the continent to this country, a series of which each successive member, at any rate from the later Stone Age onwards, had brought some addition great or small to the material equipment and culture of the land. The early history of Britain is essentially the history of her invaders[1]; her culture was slowly and patchily built up out of the successive contributions which those invaders brought. The Roman Conquest differed from earlier conquests mainly in the far more emphatic emphasis that it laid on this cultural development and in the greater degree of uniformity which it achieved. For whereas the earlier movements mostly imposed themselves by weight of numbers and more heavily on one part of the land than another, the Romans overcame the Britons by superior military organization and the attractions of a higher standard of life: they made no radical change in the basis of the population in any part. But the Roman Conquest was none the less the cultural climax of British pre-history.

But politically it was not a climax at all. Britain continued to be conquered by successive invaders from the Continent after the Roman occupation as before. The Anglo-Saxons, the Danes, and the Normans carry on the series initiated in the mists of a remote antiquity, and thus prolong the essential political features of the prehistoric period to the end of the eleventh century A.D. If Britain has not been conquered since then it is mainly because the growth of strongly organized forces on the Continent has replaced the political fluidity of prehistoric times, induced a general stability of population, and provided the machinery for a more or less peaceful traffic in ideas. But it is well sometimes to remember that any relapse of Europe into barbarism, indeed any substantial alteration in its political organization or in its cultural basis would be likely on all

[1] *See*, for this whole question, Sir Cyril Fox, *Personality of Britain, its influence on Inhabitant and Invader*, 3rd ed., 1938.

prehistoric analogy to usher in a fresh spate of invasions of these islands.

If on the long view the history of Britain has thus been the history of her invaders, it is desirable to examine the different forms which these invasions may take. It can be argued that a study of Roman Britain is of value as the best example of the imposition of an elaborate highly organized culture on Britain by military conquest, unaccompanied by any great influx of a fresh population: while the Anglo-Saxon settlement which followed it can be regarded as a typical case of quite another sort of conquest, the immigration *en masse* of a new people, culturally and politically backward, but swamping by force of numbers and vitality a civilization technically much higher but deflated by social corruption and economic collapse. The contrast between the two may help to remind us of the infinite variety of influences which have gone to the making of Britain as we know it, and to save us from the historical inadequacy of such a view as is implied in Shakespeare's picture of this country as

> This fortress built by Nature for herself
> Against infection and the hand of war.

It is only against the brief background of eight short centuries that we can attach any significance to such words.

In the pages which follow, a sketch is first given of the political history of Roman Britain, and this is followed by some account of its institutional, economic and social history: finally the problems raised by its collapse are briefly mentioned. In the available space it is impossible to do more than draw attention to the more salient features in each aspect of the subject, and a short bibliography of the more useful books for further reading will be found at the end.[1] No one who writes on this subject at the present time can do so without the feeling that most of what he writes has already been expressed much more felicitously by Prof. R. G. Collingwood, and the first task that must be undertaken by anyone who seeks a balanced introduction to Roman Britain is the study of his works. No originality of standpoint is claimed for the views expressed in this pamphlet: its purpose is merely to focus attention on the essentials of the subject, and its debt to the work of the many scholars who have made those essentials clearer will be obvious to every reader.

[1] There is no room in this pamphlet for separate accounts of Romano-British art and Romano-British religion. Both topics have been admirably discussed by Prof. Collingwood in *Roman Britain and the English Settlements,* chaps. XV and XVI.

POLITICAL HISTORY

THE political connection between Britain and Rome begins half-heartedly with the raids of Julius Caesar in 55 and 54 B.C., and becomes closely knit with the Claudian conquest of A.D. 43. The reasons which prompted the controllers of Roman policy to envisage and finally, after much hesitation, to undertake the military subjugation of the country altered in emphasis in the course of those ninety years. To Julius Caesar the problem of Britain was essentially a military one: its subjection was almost, if not quite, a necessary corollary of the conquest of Gaul, for without the control of southern Britain, the Roman hold on Gaul was believed to be precarious and insecure. There were two main reasons for this, one geographical and one political. Geographically southern Britain is really part of Gaul, the north-western side of the great drowned valley of the English Channel, across which successive invaders of Britain had passed without difficulty for thousands of years: politically too at this time it was almost a part of Gaul, for the last of those invaders, the Belgae, were still pouring across to Britain at the time of Caesar's campaigns in Gaul. It was the Belgic peoples in Gaul who were the spearpoint of resistance to Caesar, and as long as Britain remained untouched their irreconcilable elements had an ideal refuge from Roman invasion, an ideal base from which disaffection could be stirred up in the newly conquered lands.

Cæsar raided Britain in 55 B.C.: in 54 he attempted its conquest, and he failed. Political confusion in Rome and the difficulties attendant on the conversion of the Republic into the Empire deferred fresh attempts and in the course of the next ninety years the position changed. The militancy of Gaulish nationalism died quickly under the beneficent rule of Rome: irreconcilables such as Commius the Atrebate may have found refuge in Britain, and may have contributed with their followers in greater or less degree to the spread of Belgic influence in the south and west, but they constituted no serious danger to the stability of Roman Gaul. In time southern Britain became politically unified under the rule of progressive Belgic princes, amongst whom the descendants of Caesar's enemy Cassivellaunus were the most successful: it provided a market for the products of Gaulish industries now flourishing under the *pax Romana*, and it was in its turn the source of important raw materials, especially corn, cattle, minerals and slaves, the last being the product of continuing Belgic expansion into the hinterland. Although Cunobelin, the most important prince of Cassivellaunus's dynasty, may have held himself politically aloof from Roman alliance, he

4

undoubtedly fostered the spread of Roman standards of living in south-eastern Britain and probably encouraged the investment of Romano-Gaulish capital in British trade.

His death (about A.D. 42) provoked a crisis. The commercial interests, seeing danger in the break-up of the Belgic power among his sons and the emergence of a frankly anti-Roman party, pressed for military intervention. At Rome too there were political reasons which induced Claudius to take the initiative in Britain. The long ignoring of British affairs under Augustus and Tiberius had been given up by the unbalanced and unsuccessful Caligula, but his much advertised preparations for the conquest of Britain had been abandoned at the last moment for obscure reasons which in any case were damaging to the prestige of Roman arms. The circumstances of Claudius's own accession made the early winning of martial successes a matter of the first importance for this most unmilitary of Emperors: the resources and the troops for the enterprise were ready. Everything thus combined to bring about the resumption of the British project: threatened commercial interests, the hope of greater gain from the exploitation of raw materials whose value was magnified by speculative rumour, and the desire to restore the prestige of Roman arms by establishing the Emperor's authority on a firm basis of positive achievement.

With the details of the expedition's history there is no space to deal. It was well led by an able officer, Aulus Plautius, and had little difficulty in attaining its primary objectives. The Emperor was able to appear in Britain at the moment appropriate to the decisive advance, to lay down the main lines of the embryonic provincial organization, and to return to Rome with the necessary materials for the traditional triumph. From this point the political history of Roman Britain, which is essentially the same as its military history, may be conveniently divided into the following periods, on each of which a few words must be said:

    I. 43–84. The attempt to conquer the whole of Britain.
    II. (a) 84–211. The establishment of the northern frontier.
       (b) 211–286. The maintenance of the northern frontier.
    III. 287–410. The breakdown of the *Pax Romana*.

I. 43–84. Whatever the original intentions of the government may have been—it has been argued that in the first place only the tribes of the Belgic south were the direct object of the Roman attack—the struggle quickly turned into an attempt to conquer the whole of Britain. The last Belgic resistance was broken with the capture of Caractacus, son of Cunobelin, in 51: but more than all the Belgic territory had already been occupied four years before, when a diagonal frontier across the midlands from Devonshire to Lincoln had been laid out along the line now known as the Fosse Way by the second governor, Ostorius Scapula. This, however, even with its centre advanced to Wroxeter on the Severn, corresponded to no natural division of the country, and already by 60–61 the fifth governor, Suetonius Paulinus, was attempting by campaigns in North Wales and Anglesey to establish Roman arms on the Irish Sea and to divide the two main centres of anti-Roman feeling, the Silures of South Wales and the Brigantes of Northern England. But the revolt of Boudicca and the Iceni of East Anglia in 61 not only showed that this attempt was premature but very nearly brought the whole enterprise to an inglorious close, for before they were suppressed the rebel forces had pulverized one of the four Roman legions and by destroying the new centres of provincial administration and commerce at Colchester, Verulamium (St. Albans) and London, had effectively paralysed the government and cut the communications of the remaining legions with the Continent.

It took ten years of careful and conciliatory work, after the revolt was over, to pacify the tribes behind the midland frontier once more, and to re-establish the security necessary before the advance could be resumed. This was finally undertaken early in the reign of Vespasian, himself a veteran of the Claudian conquest, by three successive governors of enterprise and ability, Petilius Cerealis, 71–4, Julius Frontius, 74–8, and Julius Agricola, 78–84. Cerealis, who had commanded the Lincoln legion at the time of Boudicca's revolt, concentrated his attention on the Brigantes of the north, who had recently adopted a more hostile attitude to Rome. He was probably the first to conduct effective campaigns beyond the Humber, and to seize the great strategic position which became the legionary fortress of York. Frontinus, who followed him, advanced the left wing of the Roman frontier correspondingly into South Wales and pacified the difficult country of the Silures from his new legionary base at Caerleon-upon-Usk. It was thus possible for Agricola to resume the assault upon the north without fear of troubles in his rear, and to make the conquest of the whole island look for the first time what we know from Tacitus that he himself believed it to be, a practicable proposition.

Tacitus's biography of Agricola has perhaps caused historians to attribute to its hero more than his rightful share of the credit for the great extension of Roman rule in Britain at this period. At least it can be said that he was not the originator of the forward movement and that his work was possible only because secure foundations had been laid by his two predecessors. He was moreover allowed nearly twice as long a term of office as was normal at this time for

6

governors of Britain. But it none the less remains true that Agricola was the only governor who did come within striking distance of a complete conquest of Britain, and if we examine the details of his military dispositions we can see that he had grasped in a remarkable degree the essentials of the problem. He saw the importance both of the Tyne-Solway line, later guarded by Hadrian's Wall, and of the Forth-Clyde isthmus, the site of the Antonine frontier, and he defended both with his own forts. And if, as Professor Collingwood has shown, Agricola had little genuine cause for the resentment which Tacitus attributes to him, at his recall by Domitian in A.D. 84, it cannot be denied that his recall does mark a turning-point in the history of the province. His successors were not encouraged to exploit the possibilities which it was believed at the time that his decisive victory at Mons Graupius had opened up: at the critical moment Rome reduced the army of Britain and refused to pursue the conquest of the north.

II. (a) 84-211. The results were not at first as disastrous as Tacitus's phrase *perdomita Britannia et statim omissa* once led historians to believe. There has of late been some controversy over the extent of Agricola's Scottish conquests and their duration after his recall, but, whatever the detailed story may have been, it seems clear that many of the garrisons which he left north of Brigantia maintained themselves with more or less success at any rate until the end of the first century and in some important instances rather longer. But they could do little more than fight a losing battle against tribesmen increasingly conscious of the ineffectiveness of Roman policy and increasingly prepared to demoralize the isolated garrisons into abandonment of important positions by surprise attacks in overwhelming force. The reign of Trajan (98-117) was marked in Britain by none of the enterprising activity which characterized it in the East. What policy there was may perhaps be described as a 'petrification of the status quo': many forts in Wales and some in northern England hitherto built of earth and timber were now substantially reconstructed in stone: but here and there new forts were built and old ones abandoned, and it seems probable that some attempt was made to check the demoralizing process of enforced withdrawal from Agricola's Scottish fortresses by treating his transverse road from the Tyne to the Solway as a *limes* and fortifying it with a few new posts and the refurbishing of some old ones.

Such half-hearted measures, however, were quite inadequate. We have no knowledge of details, but it is clear that a major military disaster overtook the Roman forces in the north at the end of Trajan's reign or at the beginning of that of his successor, Hadrian (117-38). Not only is there literary evidence that the Britons were

7

in successful revolt at this time, but we know that the York legion and a number of auxiliary units disappeared altogether in these years, and that Hadrian felt it necessary to come to Britain in person and to reinforce the depleted armies with a fresh legion for York, and other less permanent drafts. He also took the opportunity to plan and to initiate the great system of frontier works which bears his name between the Tyne and the Solway, and lies for the most part just north of the Trajanic *limes*. This new complex, with its elaboration of ditch, wall, forts, mile-castles, turrets, and vallum behind, was in construction between 122 and 126 in the governorship of A. Platorius Nepos. Hadrian built a massive frontier on a scale intended to be decisively permanent; but however much we may admire the magnificence of the achievement, his Wall is in reality but the solidest expression of a military panic in European history, and it marks a still more emphatic determination than had been registered hitherto to abandon Agricola's dream of a thoroughly conquered and pacified Britain.

Efficient as Hadrian's frontier system no doubt was in its direct purpose, it did not solve the problem of the unconquered north, and the existence of this problem, which necessitated the continuous maintenance of great armies on the northern frontier, remained henceforward the dominant political fact in Romano-British history. Less than twenty years after its completion, indeed, the construction of the turf wall of Antoninus Pius between the Forth and the Clyde, whatever may have been the purpose which it was built to serve, illustrates official dissatisfaction with the position left by Hadrian. Whether it was intended as a permanent advance to a line which on a superficial view appeared shorter and more defensible, or as a first stage in a belated resumption of Agricola's policy of breaking up the northern tribes into manageable and isolated blocks, or, as Professor Collingwood suggested, as a temporary cover to a systematic deportation of the bellicose Lowlanders to Germany, it emphasized in any case the fundamental weakness of the Hadrianic solution.

And in itself it only made the military situation more alarming. For the existence of the new line did not mean the abandonment of the old, the army of Britain was not augmented to provide for its garrisons, and the latter could thus only be obtained by a drastic withdrawal of troops from Wales, and a dangerous weakening of the forces in occupation of southern Brigantia. This region, though now far behind the official frontier, remained practically unaffected by the emollient penetration of Roman civilian culture, which further south had long since turned the compatriots of Caractacus and Boudicca into peaceful and prosperous provincials.

From the military point of view, in fact, much the same mistake had been made as in the days of Boudicca's revolt, and the results were somewhat similar. In 154, and perhaps more than once in the early years of Marcus Aurelius (161–80), there is both literary and archæological evidence for troubles in Britain which, at any rate on the first occasion, are definitely associated with a revolt of the Brigantes in the rear of the frontier region. After their suppression we hear in the reign of Commodus of the opposite danger—a regular invasion of Caledonians from beyond the Walls, an invasion which at least the northern barrier with its depleted garrisons and inadequate lateral command of the Firths of Forth and Clyde was powerless to withstand. When the situation was retrieved it would appear that the Roman command at last realized that in the existing conditions the double frontier constituted a weaker obstacle than Hadrian's Wall alone would have done, and the Antonine *limes*, after a stormy career of little more than forty years, marked archæologically by at least two major disasters, was deliberately dismantled by its own garrisons, who were thus released for strengthening the more tenable line to the south.

The political disturbances which followed the murder of Commodus in 193 unfortunately deprived this solution of durability. In the confused years that followed, the legions of Britain abandoned the task of frontier defence and were taken over to Gaul in 196 to support the claims of their governor, Clodius Albinus, to the imperial throne, thus providing the first example of a fatal practice whose repetition two centuries later was eventually to deprive Britain of its military protection against barbarian attack. The results on this occasion were disastrous both for Clodius Albinus and for Britain. The former was defeated by Septimius Severus at Lyons in 197 and lost his life: while in Britain the northern tribes took advantage of the deserted frontiers to carry out a deliberate and systematic destruction of Roman military works in the north, the effects of which are archæologically recognizable not only all along Hadrian's Wall but even as far south as the legionary fortresses of York and Chester. The governor sent over by Severus to repair the damage found that he had first to bribe the barbarian horde to return home.

An immense work of reconstruction was then undertaken. The Hadrianic system, wall, forts, and roads, and also the legionary bases at Chester and York, were refortified with a solidity and thoroughness worthy of the earlier period. No pains were spared to complete the work with dispatch. Even cemeteries were sometimes looted for building material as at Chester, and the military drafts were augmented by civilian labour gangs recruited from the southern

British *civitates*, which have left building inscriptions here and there on the Wall itself. By 208 it appears that troops could be spared for a series of punitive expeditions, conducted by the Emperor in person against the tribal centres in the heart of Scotland; these expeditions were designed not so much to effect permanent conquests beyond the fortified zone as to show the barbarians that the restored frontier was to be respected. When Septimius Severus died at York in 211 the problem of the unconquered north, though still unsolved, had no longer the perpetual urgency which had marked it for the previous hundred and thirty years.

(*b*) 211–286. With the final establishment of the Severan frontier a period of unwonted calm falls over British politics. The Caledonian campaigns ended at Severus's death and many bodies of troops, which since the Antonine advance had been employed in the north, were returned to their old quarters in Wales, which in several cases, as at the legionary base at Caerleon itself, they seem to have found grass-grown and ruinous, and in need of complete reconstruction. But after this epilogue to the outburst of Severan building was over, the archæologist and the historian alike have little to record of any substantial moment, until the last quarter of the third century.

This is a fact of some interest. It means not only that Severus's work was so well done that it lasted for three generations, but that Britain as a whole must have escaped much of the political insecurity which characterized Roman history, especially frontier history, during the third century. For a secure frontier and political quiescence were rare enough in any part of the Empire in that troubled time, when Emperor succeeded Emperor in bewildering rapidity, and the incompetent instability of the armies replaced the comparative solidity of middle-class government as the dominant factor in politics. There is of course no reason whatever to believe that Britain was immune from the economic and social upheavals of the age—there is plenty of evidence that she was not—but it would appear that for the best part of a century the hardly-won frontier was held in comparative tranquillity and that Britain enjoyed a period of unusual freedom from the worst political troubles of the time.

III. 287–410. Before the third century was over, however, the characteristics of the final phase of Romano-British history were beginning to appear. The military problem of provincial defence was no longer confined to the maintenance of the northern frontier, for the east and south coasts were coming to demand protection from the increasing menace of Frankish and Saxon pirates, and on the west the tribes of Ireland were on the move, not only raiding the shores of Wales and Dumnonia but pouring across from Ulster into

Scotland and so upsetting in its turn the long stable equilibrium of the north.

Britain experienced only one example of that tendency to political separatism, which nearly broke up the Roman Empire in the third century into a congeries of dynastic monarchies. This came, it appears, directly from the attempt of the central government, now in the capable hands of Diocletian and Maximian, to provide against this new danger of barbarian raids upon the coast. In 286 an officer named Carausius, who had been entrusted with the command of a strengthened naval force in the Channel and the task of suppressing piracy, established himself in Britain as an independent Emperor and successfully defied the forces sent against him. His position was so unassailable that he was for a while acknowledged as a colleague by the reluctant Emperors, and it was not until after his murder by one of his own officers, Allectus, in 293, that the western Caesar, Constantius Chlorus, found himself strong enough to reassert the central authority, a task which he successfully carried through in 296–7.

The brief interlude of Carausius and Allectus is important in Romano-British history as providing the background to a complete reorganization whose military aspect was even more drastic than that which had marked the reign of Septimius Severus. There was certainly every need in Britain for a *Redditor Lucis Aeternae*, the proud phrase with which Constantius described himself on the medal commemorating his victory over Allectus. On the northern frontier for example the latter had apparently removed the garrisons to oppose Constantius and the hostile tribes had poured in as at the end of the second century, once again razing the deserted fortifications as far south as York. Constantius had thus to begin by repeating the wholesale reconstruction effected by Severus a hundred years before, and he had further to meet the new danger of coastal piracy in a way which would not involve the danger of a second Carausius.

An elaborate system of coastal fortification, of which perhaps the outline had already been laid down by Carausius himself, was his solution of this problem. On the east and south coasts nearly every prominent harbour between the Wash and the Isle of Wight was provided with a fortress which served apparently both as a base for the naval patrol and as the headquarters of a military unit, part of the force at the disposal of a new officer, the Count of the Saxon Shore, who was in charge of the whole. The forts conformed in construction to the new tactics of the barbarized Roman army: they were strongly walled and equipped with bastions to resist a siege, but contained a minimum of permanent buildings within, and looked from without more like the lofty defensible castles of the Middle

Ages than the low-built earlier Roman forts, which still retained in the second century features of the marching camps from which they had evolved. The same system was extended in a more half-hearted fashion to Wales, where forts of Saxon Shore type were built at any rate at Cardiff, Caernarvon, and Holyhead, and it would appear that either now or perhaps earlier the native Welsh were permitted or encouraged to refortify for their own defence many of the old hill-forts from which they had been ejected in the first century by the troops of Frontinus or Agricola.

Of the many institutional features of Constantius's reorganization something must be said later. Here it need only be mentioned that the military commands were now divorced from the civil authority, with which under the early Empire they had always been combined, and the legionary legates, hitherto directly responsible to the provincial governors, now gave way, as the chief officers of the army, to regional commanders of whom the Duke of the Britains had responsibility for the northern frontier, and the Count of the Saxon Shore, as already mentioned, took charge of coastal defence.

For more than half a century the system inaugurated by the reforms of Constantius secured the internal peace of Britain, and the landowning classes, if we may judge from the widespread evidence for the extension of unfortified country house life at this time, could live their rather futile lives of sterile virtuosity, untroubled by the alarms of Saxon piracy or the inconvenience of military revolt. Their prosperity, it may be, was only secured by periodic frontier concessions to barbarian settlement, of the type whose negotiation, it seems, brought Constans to Britain in 342, but it was not until after 360 that the military weakness to which such concessions contributed culminated in disaster. In 367 after several years of minor disturbances a concerted assault by Picts and Scots on the north and west and by Franks and Saxons on the south and east coasts overwhelmed the barbarized and partly treacherous forces of the Duke of the Britains and the Count of the Saxon Shore, and with the death of both officers in action there was nothing to prevent the invaders from once again destroying the defences of the north or from looting undefended villas at pleasure up and down the countryside. When Count Theodosius was sent over to restore the situation in 368 he was faced with bands of marauders plundering in Kent.

The Theodosian restoration of Britain was marked by the usual reconstruction of the Wall, though it would seem that attention was now concentrated on the main forts (the mile-castles and turrets being no longer occupied), and by the usual punitive expeditions beyond it. But it had two new features of its own. One was the additional protection afforded to the north-east by the building of coastal signal stations on the Yorkshire cliffs, a system the traces of whose probable employment elsewhere have perhaps been destroyed by subsequent erosion; and the other was the successful incorporation of some undefined frontier district, hitherto occupied by more or less hostile barbarian *foederati*, as the new province of Valentia: this is more likely to have been in Wales than in the north.

The final collapse of effective Roman rule in Britain began within fifteen years of this apparently successful restoration of her power. It was not due to the overthrow of Roman arms by overwhelming barbarian force: still less was it due, as is often carelessly assumed on the basis of an isolated incident reported by a court poet, to the withdrawal of the garrisons of Britain by the central government for the defence of Italy or Rome. It was directly caused, as had been most of the military disasters in Britain since the second century, by the irresponsibility of the Roman forces themselves, and by the increasing tendency of their officers to pay more attention to the possibilities of their own advancement than to the safety of the provincials in their charge. This was perhaps not altogether surprising, for by now the armies were themselves largely barbarian by birth and sentiment and had little reason to feel more sympathy with the effete and oppressive landowning aristocracy which constituted the most Romanized elements of the provincial population, than with their own kinsmen, whom it was their business to keep beyond the frontiers.

The revolt of Maximus, who transferred the bulk of the British garrisons to Gaul in 383, was the beginning of the end, not so much because his exploit differed in kind from others of its type, as because after his failure in 388, and the death of his conqueror Theodosius in 395, the latter's general Stilicho did not find it possible in his patchwork restoration to reoccupy the Wall. This abandonment of the northern frontier, which was apparently followed before 400 by the destruction of the signal stations on the Yorkshire coast, made any future attempt to maintain the internal security of Britain strategically impossible. This being so, it was only a question of time before the final disappearance of effective Roman authority, and it has generally been assumed that this closely followed the next large-scale exodus of troops under the usurper Constantine, who crossed over to Gaul in 407 to repeat the attempt and to meet the fate of Maximus. When the Britons, exasperated at his failure to protect them, returned to the allegiance of the central government, the Emperor Honorius could only reply to their appeals for help by placing the responsibility for the defence of Britain on the civil organization of the *civitates*, thus implying that the last shreds of military organization had gone.

Whether these events represent the effective end of the Roman occupation of Britain, or whether, as some scholars now believe, there was a brief reoccupation of the south-eastern districts under a new official, the Comes Britanniae, for a few years in the second and third decades of the fifth century, the pattern of Romano-British history remains substantially the same. For such a reoccupation cannot have lasted more than fifteen years at the outside, can only have affected a very limited area, and made so little impression on contemporary or later historians that, while none mention it directly, several explicitly or implicitly deny its occurrence. It was in any case a matter of small consequence either in Roman or in British history.

INSTITUTIONAL, ECONOMIC, AND SOCIAL HISTORY

This brief outline of the political history of the province has dealt almost wholly with the creation, maintenance and collapse of the frontier system. The political history of Roman Britain is, in fact, essentially its military history and that history until the last phase is concentrated mainly in the frontier districts. But behind these frontier districts, and protected by them, lay the greater part of the province in area and population, and by far the most important part in wealth and culture. If we seek information about the provincial life behind the frontiers we shall find ourselves discussing not so much political history, as the institutional and economic problems of a complex social organization.

The main reason for this contrast lies in the physical geography of Britain. In the south, east, and over much of the midlands, the countryside was fertile and easy to traverse, capable of supporting a large agricultural population and open, as the Belgic invasions and the Roman conquest itself show, to every sort of continental influence. All this area was conquered in the first stage of the Roman occupation and rapidly pacified: but in the more mountainous, wetter, and more scantily populated country to the north and west of the island, the invaders were up against a different problem, one which in the long run defied even the power of Rome. The legions, it is true, struck deep into the Highland Zone: they conquered and pacified Wales and, less successfully, Brigantia, but they could not civilize either as they civilized the south; and even if Agricola had been successful in conquering the whole island, the contrast between the two halves of Roman Britain would still have remained. But with the Roman frontier established, as it came to be, across the foothills of the Highland Zone, the inevitable contrast was greatly exaggerated. In the north relations between the two peoples remained fundamentally hostile, and interest is concentrated on the political fluctuations of the balance between them. But in the south there was no such basic hostility between Roman and Briton, and the institutional, economic, and social consequences of their co-operation form its main claim on our attention.

1. *The Institutions of Roman Britain*

The main institutional framework of Roman Britain can be very briefly described. Down to the time of Severus it formed a single Imperial province under a legate of the Emperor as governor. Civil and military affairs were alike under his charge, his chief military subordinates being the legates commanding the three legions at Caerleon, Chester, and York, and his chief civilian assistant being the *legatus iuridicus*, of whose work we know little but who presumably controlled the administration of justice. The only part of the governmental machine outside the authority of the governor was the financial department, which was in the hands of procurators directly dependent on the Emperor. Under Severus, and probably with the object of reducing the political power wielded by a single governor with so large an army as that of Britain under his command, the government divided Britain into two provinces, the Upper and the Lower, and the whole machine was presumably doubled. From literary and epigraphic evidence we know that Lincoln and York were in Lower Britain, Chester and Caerleon in Upper Britain, and it has thus been conjectured that the division ran roughly between the Wash and the Mersey, leaving in all probability London as the headquarters of the Upper Province, as York was more certainly the capital of the Lower. As has already been mentioned, the provincial system of Britain was reorganized again a hundred years later, as part of the general administrative rearrangement of the Empire carried out under Diocletian and Constantine. Britain now became one of the new divisions known as Dioceses under a Vicarius responsible to the Pretorian Prefect of the Gauls. It was subdivided into four provinces, Prima, Secunda, Flavia Caesariensis, and Maxima Caesariensis, to which a fifth, Valentia, was added, as already noticed, by Count Theodosius, after 368. We do not know even roughly where these provinces lay, the only safe clue at present being an inscription which records the activities of a governor of Britannia Prima at Cirencester in Gloucestershire.

The reforms of Diocletian and Constantine also involved the separation of civil and military authority. The provincial governors now lost their authority over the troops, and the latter were reorganized into at least two new commands, those of the Duke of

15

the Britains, and the Count of the Saxon Shore, whose functions have been described above. It should also be noticed that the increasing multiplicity of civil posts and military commands which was brought about by these successive alterations was symptomatic of a far-reaching social change which affected the whole character of Imperial government. In earlier times Roman officials had been comparatively few in number, exercising wide and often ill-defined powers with a maximum of individual responsibility and a minimum cost to the tax-paying provincials, who enjoyed a wide measure of self-government; but, after the time of Diocletian, the number of functionaries enormously increased, their individual responsibility and with it their common standard of morality declined, while the chief employment of many was to duplicate one another's activities, and to collect the revenue necessary to their own maintenance. Such a system progressively aggravated its own defects and its increasing top-heaviness and corruption led straight to the disastrous incompetence of later Imperial administration.

So much for the provincial machinery of Britain considered as a unit of the Roman Empire. But there were also the local divisions and loyalties which affected the life of the individual provincial far more than the remote activities of legates and procurators. Foremost among these were the old Celtic and Belgic tribes, which the Romans, with their genius for adapting the institutions of subject peoples to their own purposes, had skilfully converted into self-governing units of local administration. To this end something over a dozen of the larger tribes had been recognized as *civitates*: their royal families, where they were monarchical, were abolished (sometimes with a transition stage in which a Romanophil king might be recognized for his lifetime as a tribal *legatus*), their councils of nobles were turned into local *ordines* or senates, with their own elective annual magistrates, and, to complete the illusion of self-government, they were encouraged and probably assisted to lay out well-planned and finely built tribal capitals of Roman design in which the public buildings would be dedicated to the Emperor by the local senate in carefully worded Latin inscriptions. Here sites for houses and shops would be available on easy terms for all tribesmen anxious to follow the new fashion for urban life. For although in one or two cases in the Belgic districts such towns seem to have grown more or less directly out of a pre-Roman settlement, the sites of most of them were new, as was indeed the whole conception of urban culture which their existence implied. However much we may speak of Belgic cities or trace the origins of town life in Britain back to the Neolithic Age, it remains true that urban life, as a life different in kind from village life and provided with standards and amenities

which the other lacked, was a new and foreign conception introduced into Britain by Rome. As such it was, as we shall see later, perhaps the most important piece of machinery through which Roman
culture came to Britain, and it will thus be of vital significance to
assess the spontaneity of its reception and the extent of its influence.

Here, however, it must be noticed that the tribal capitals, if in
some ways the most interesting, were not the only form which urban
life took in Britain. There were towns more Roman in structure
and therefore more artificial and alien to the British scene: there
were others whose growth was perhaps more spontaneous but which
never achieved the essentials of self-government. Five important
towns at least fall into the former class: there were the four military
colonies, Colchester, Gloucester, Lincoln and York, and the *muni-
cipium* of Verulamium near the present St. Albans. The colonies
were primarily, like all Roman colonies, self-governing settlements
of time-expired legionaries, although Colchester was also, at any rate
at first, the centre of organized Emperor-worship and in some sense
the capital of the province. All four were surrounded by cultivable
lands adequate for the support of their inhabitants, who possessed
full self-governing rights, and thus fell outside the general structure
of the tribal system. In the same way Verulamium, as a *munici-
pium*, would possess the usual *ordo* and magistrates, and a *terri-
torium* which may well have included the bulk of the former lands
of the Catuvellauni whose centre its pre-Roman equivalent had
been. We know less of the status of certain other important places.
London, for example, the largest town and doubtless mainly of
spontaneous commercial growth, was in a class by itself, containing,
as it must have done, the headquarters of many administrative
departments (such as the financial *procuratores*) in addition to a cos-
mopolitan host of traders; it must have been self-governing, but
nothing is known of its position in the provincial structure. The
same is true of Bath, whose existence depended on its hot springs:
it probably won the usual free constitution justified by the possession
of an artificial prosperity like that of many modern watering-places.
The other class includes the smaller towns of Roman Britain, which
were very numerous and doubtless varied a great deal in character:
a good many were walled, which may indicate a certain official
importance, perhaps as the centres of *pagi*, the subdivisions of the
tribes, or the headquarters of imperial estates; but most were no
doubt of natural growth springing up in response to the demands of
trade, or occupying positions of local consequence on the network
of Roman roads.

These roads bound the whole province together much as the railway system bound together Victorian England. Planned in the first

instance to serve the needs of the army and constructed by military engineers as the legions advanced, their primary purpose was to secure rapid transport from the Channel ports and London to the frontier districts of Wales and the north. Once arrived in the military districts, they spread out into an elaborate network linking every fort to its neighbours and to the nearest point on the main arteries from the south. But after the pacification of the civil areas was completed they came to serve more and more the needs of the towns in the regions through which they passed. Branch roads and cross roads of little military significance were built to link the towns together and to ensure rapid communication from every place of any consequence to all its neighbours.

This obvious relationship of the roads to the towns emphasizes, like its counterpart the railway system in the nineteenth century, the contrast between town and country. The chief element of Romanized country life was the *villa*, and the main roads paid no more attention to the convenience of the villas than did the railways to the country houses of a later age. The villas were served, as were the peasant villages, by local tracks and private lanes, many no doubt of prehistoric origin. These, although they may still in some cases exist, are impossible to recognize now as Roman because they lack the characteristic directness and heavy construction of the main roads.

The institutions of the countryside, although more must be said of their economic significance later, deserve notice at this point to complete the picture. Much work, however, needs to be done before the usual division of their material remains into the Villas and Villages of our Romano-British maps can tell us much about the organization of country life. It has already been noticed that we know hardly anything about the administrative geography of the province, the boundaries of the tribal areas or of the territories attributed to the self-governing towns. Nor do we know how much of Britain had been absorbed into the imperial estates, *saltus*, which were characteristic of many provinces and lay for most purposes outside the normal sphere of local government. It has been suggested that the distribution of the villas and villages over the countryside may perhaps provide a clue to some of these uncertainties, for a glance at the maps will show that in some areas villas are very common and villages very rare and vice versa. It can be argued that in the village areas we may have the signs of imperial estates cultivated by tenant small-holders, and certain regions of this type such as the Fenlands, where considerable initial outlay on drainage and regional planning alone made cultivation possible, are perhaps best explained on this hypothesis. On the other hand, the aristocratic structure of British tribal society might be expected to reveal itself architecturally in a countryside dotted with the villas of the upper classes, whose lands were cultivated by dependants, whether slaves or freemen, who were at first often housed on the premises of the villa itself.

All this, however, although offering a profitable field for local study, is at present very speculative, and progress will be slow until more detailed classification of villas and of villages has been carried out. For both terms in fact cover such a variety of architectural remains that it would be most unwise to draw confident conclusions from our present maps. Thus the term *villa* is normally used to cover every type of building from a large country mansion with central heating, elaborate mosaic floors, extensive bathing arrangements, and substantial outbuildings, through every grade of farmhouse, down to the shoddily built bungalows of small-holders or squatters. A countryside such as that of Gloucestershire, where the most luxurious type of villa is fairly common, is likely to have possessed a different social structure from one which is dotted over with villas of the small unheated farmhouse type. Of one fact alone we can be reasonably certain. The villas, large and small, were in the majority of cases the residences of native Romano-Britons of whatever social rank, and the extent to which they display Roman standards of comfort and decoration is indicative both of the degree of native prosperity under Roman rule and of the attractiveness of Roman fashions. If the towns were the chief channels of Romanization for all classes of the population, the villas illustrate in detail the receptiveness of the upper ranks of society to the lessons which Rome taught.

The villages illustrate the same point for the peasant classes. Here there is an even more bewildering variety than among the villas; for under this heading must always have been gathered the great bulk of the population of Roman Britain, even if the material traces of their settlements are far less substantial and far less informative than those of villas, towns and forts. Included among them were not only the descendants of primitive native agriculturalists and many dependent cultivators of the villas and the imperial estates, but also such varied groups as the populous mining communities of the Mendips, or Derbyshire, the half-nomadic charcoal burners of the Weald, the followers of a rural industry like the New Forest potters, and the innkeepers and postboys of a minor halting-place on a main road. Their response to Roman culture varied with their economic position and their accessibility to towns and villas. Rural communities especially in the hills saw in Roman civilization little but the opportunity for obtaining a cheap supply of serviceable household goods to replace the products of primitive domestic industries: others, more ambitious and better off, might attempt to decorate their huts in the classical manner, and to scribble scraps of Latin on their pots and walls. But, apart from such superficialities, the habits and the sentiment of the lower rural classes remained far less touched by Roman institutions than was the case in the upper ranks of native society. To appreciate the significance of this cleavage we must look a little more closely at the economic background to the history of Roman Britain.

2. The Economic Background

The economic basis of pre-Roman Britain was quite simply one of subsistence agriculture. In the highlands of the north and west, and to a less extent on the chalk downs and limestone plateaux of the south, a semi-pastoral existence may have been still followed by many, but the bulk of the population depended for its food supply upon the cultivation of the land, and, its agricultural equipment being for the most part extremely primitive, this cultivation was limited to the lighter and more easily drained soils whether these were found high up on open downland or down on the gravel spreads and terraces which lined the valleys of many rivers in the south and midlands. Thus the pattern of human settlement was strictly conditioned by the distribution of such soils, and the wide regions of heavy land bearing forest or ill-drained marsh and swamp were left practically uninhabited. Only in the south and east, the parts which had been substantially affected by Belgic settlement, had any changes of moment been made in this essentially primitive pattern: there, it is now believed, the newcomers who, partly Teutonic in origin, were more accustomed on the Continent to exploiting forest conditions, had begun to open up some of the heavier lands, with their more efficient tools and implements, and had also developed, alongside the older village agriculture, the system of cultivation based on isolated farmsteads whose broad cornlands so impressed Julius Caesar in Kent.

The Roman conquest made no direct changes in this situation. It was not inspired by any enthusiasm for agricultural pioneering or by the land-hunger which marked, for example, the European settlement of North America. And from first to last the great bulk of the inhabitants of Roman Britain must have been engaged in subsistence agriculture with substantially the same primitive equipment which their ancestors had long possessed. This has been clearly shown by air-photography and field-work in many areas of predominantly light soils, where the Romano-British village populations continued to conform throughout the occupation to the essential pattern of prehistoric times.

But indirectly and unintentionally the balance was altered by the

Roman conquest in a good many ways. Many causes led to an increased demand for the fruits of the earth, and made it worth while to grow more from the land than was wanted for the bare subsistence of its growers. The Roman towns began to spring up, and their non-producing inhabitants had to be fed, and their fires and furnaces supplied with fuel, the demand for which made it worth while to clear good soils of woodland; tax-gatherers came round and officials requisitioning supplies for the army; the new roads made transport easy where before it had been impossible for bulky goods; the imposition of internal peace increased security and minimized the risk of disturbance to growing crops; and, finally, currency was more abundant and it was easier to convert the profits of agriculture into the material comforts supplied by the new industries.

Such causes lay behind the development of the villa system in Roman Britain. It represented no direct importation from Italy to Gaul, but was the natural response of the more progressive British agriculturalists to the new demand for their produce. For Roman villas are but Belgic farmsteads writ large, and the spread of the system means simply adaptation all over the country, by those who could afford the initial outlay, of the progressive methods of cultivation already spreading in the south-east: the centering of broad lands on a house built solidly, *more Romano*, as houses were being built in the new towns, and provided, as taste and resources dictated, with the new decorations and amenities which the towns displayed.

Thus the capital expenditure incurred in the construction of towns and roads stimulated something of an economic revolution in the countryside of Roman Britain, a revolution which, it must be remembered, had its social basis. In pre-Roman times tribal society was no doubt already aristocratic, and the nobility was able to maintain its social prestige mainly by martial prowess, renown won by heroic exploits in intertribal warfare. But if the *Pax Romana* had destroyed the tribal warfare and with it much of the *raison d'être* of the old aristocracy, the latter now won a more durable economic basis for its threatened superiority. For not only were its members recognized by Rome as a governing class by their membership of the tribal senates, but they also were alone in a position to exploit the new demand for corn and cattle, and to adopt the profitable technique of villa agriculture. Hence the momentous economic distinction sprang up between the villa-owning classes, who were able to take full advantage of the new fashion for Roman culture and material comforts and prospered accordingly, and on the other side the bulk of the agricultural peasantry, who remained culturally barbaric and economically backward, and thus became relatively more impoverished than before. This unfortunate distinction developed in time into a social cleavage of the utmost gravity, which eventually threatened the whole stability of Romano-British civilization.

But for perhaps a hundred or a hundred and fifty years all was well. If one may judge from the tremendous output of public and private building which distinguishes the history of almost all Roman towns in the second and third quarters of the second century, there must have been a genuine burst of urban prosperity produced by a wide initial demand for the products of their industries, a demand no doubt fostered by the local nobility, who were equally interested as urban magistrates and as rural landlords in the welfare of town and country alike. It is true that we know little about specifically urban industries. This is in part because so few towns have been adequately excavated, in part because the comparative density of towns in lowland Britain probably confined the products of each to a restricted area, and prevented the development of really large-scale activity. But although the primary function of the towns was to be the centres of culture and administration rather than centres of trade and industry, the facts suggest that for a century or more the initial momentum of their creation lasted, and for a while at least they must have paid their way.

Unfortunately this prosperity was not permanent: it was apparently killed partly by a general change in Imperial economic policy which affected all provinces of the Empire alike, and partly by local factors which operated more strongly in Britain than elsewhere. We may take the latter first. It will be obvious from what has been said that the urban structure of the province was extremely artificial. While its basis still remained a thinly spread rural population engaged mainly in subsistence agriculture, some twenty or thirty towns had sprung up with great rapidity at the bidding of a government primarily concerned with problems of administration and obsessed with the equation between culture and town life. They had not grown naturally as modern towns grow, in response to the demands of industry and commerce. Hence, while their creation played its part, as has been suggested, in producing an initial phase of general prosperity in which they shared, they had in the long run to be fed at the expense of the countryside which could not afford to buy their products in return. The land had neither the wealth nor the population to maintain indefinitely this unnatural burden of a parasitic urban culture.

Just at the time when such factors were probably beginning to make themselves felt a change was coming over Imperial economic policy. The Empire, which had, in a sense, grown out of a federation of Mediterranean city states, had hitherto stimulated and encouraged in its conquered provinces the urban culture which was its own life-blood. But by the beginning of the third century political power had passed from the city bourgeoisie of Italy and Gaul into the hands of the army and its leaders, men trained in the savage realities of frontier defence, who cared little for the amenities of urban civilization. Cities to them were nothing but the sources of wealth from which armies could be maintained, and, whereas in earlier times the towns had grown rich on the conquests of the army, it was now the army which lived on the resources of the towns. Heavy taxation and the imposition of forced services penalized bourgeois industry and, to make matters worse for the trading classes, the currency was ruined by successive inflations which brought commerce and manufacture to a standstill.

The effect of all this is clearly seen in the spectacular dilapidation which seems to have overtaken many towns in the second half of the third century. At Wroxeter, where the forum was burnt before A.D. 300, not only was it never rebuilt but its debris, including ruined columns, and even human bodies, was left where it fell and was worked pell-mell into the improvised road surface formed by the continuing traffic of the surviving inhabitants. At Verulam, the town was ruinous, and its walls and gates in a state of collapse. A great part of the urban population must have melted back into the countryside.

But the countryside itself was strangely unaffected by the tragic breakdown of this artificial urban prosperity, a fact which suggests that the ruin of the towns was brought about more by the disastrous policy of unsympathetic Emperors than by the natural decay which would have resulted from purely economic weakness. For the increase in villa building in the third and fourth centuries suggests that there was still money about but that the moneyed classes, who, as we have seen, had from the first been both urban and rural in their interests, were now deliberately concentrating their resources on their country properties. There are, in fact, all the symptoms of a flight of capital from town to country which can best be explained by the desire of all who could do so to escape from the burdens and services which were now exacted with increasing rigour from the holders of what had once been civic posts of honour and authority. Although stringent legislation was passed to prevent the richer citizens from thus escaping the new and disastrous consequences of their wealth, it is clear that the more influential contrived in many cases to make good their escape, thus leaving the major burdens to be borne by the smaller bourgeois, who had no such means of retreat. Thus, while the towns decayed, the villas prospered and there

23

are many instances in the third and fourth centuries of the building of new ones and of extensions and reconstructions of the old, normally increasing their accommodation and amenities.

The breakdown of the towns was not accompanied by a complete collapse of industry, but rather by its reorganization to suit the new conditions. It is a remarkable fact that the period of their decay is coincident in the pottery industry, about which we know most, with the growth of specialized rural manufactures whose standardized products found a surprisingly wide market. The best-known instances are the New Forest wares of Hampshire, apparently the products of a genuine peasant industry, and the Castor potteries near Peterborough, which, to judge from the very extensive distribution of their output and the number of prosperous villas which surround them, were more heavily capitalized. In the fourth century a similar phenomenon appears in Yorkshire with the Crambeck, Throlam, and Knapton industries, which supplied not only a civilian demand, but the needs of most of the northern garrisons. This curious and rather unexpected development was caused in part, no doubt, by the cessation in the third century of supplies of the better fabrics from the so-called Samian potteries of Gaul, whose wares had hitherto been imported in enormous quantities: in part it was due to the natural increase of specialized industry in a highly capitalized society: but in part too it exemplifies once more the flight of enterprise from town to country, for these late potteries are rarely found in any close relationship with one of the older towns. How the industry was financed in an age when wild fluctuations in price levels were brought about by repeated inflations of an already chaotic currency is far from clear: it may be that the general return to rural conditions assisted the growth of an industry based mainly on barter and other non-monetary expedients. Certain it is that the prosperity of the villas at this time can only be explained on the assumption that their economy rested increasingly on the payments in kind and labour services of the down-trodden peasantry, which gave at any rate greater security to the landlords than an exclusive reliance on the contemporary currency could have done.

At the beginning of the fourth century and no doubt as part of the Constantian overhaul of the whole provincial machinery, a deliberate attempt was made to reverse the trend of the previous hundred years and to pump fresh blood into the arteries of the towns. Verulamium was extensively rebuilt on a scale which certainly implies governmental assistance, and at any rate the defences of many other cities were repaired and brought up to date with the addition of the now fashionable bastions. At the same time the general reformation of the currency must have improved the outlook for

24

urban trade and commerce, although the increasing numbers of the bureaucracy meant heavier taxation and sapped what little remained of local independence.

But, in Britain at any rate, things had gone too far to be easily remedied by assistance from a temporarily benevolent government, and, while the evidence of prosperity in the villas reaches its peak in the first half of the fourth century, a great city like Verulamium had already reverted by 350 to the helpless disrepair and deplorable squalor of a century before. All but a group of streets round about the civic centre of the town seems to have been deserted by its inhabitants, and even in this withered nucleus the municipal theatre was being used as a rubbish tip.

We have thus to think of civilian society in Roman Britain at this time as consisting broadly of three elements whose interests were coming to be ominously divergent: the townsfolk, decadent and impoverished, who were still regarded by government as the natural centres of provincial organization and bore the main burden of its taxation: the rural aristocracy of the villas, who alone maintained the earlier standards of Roman culture and taste, but whose wealth largely depended on the exploitation of the third element, an increasingly barbarous peasantry whose traditional craftsmanship and native culture had long been weakened by dependence on the cheaper products of Roman industry and who now thought of the Empire simply in terms of its tax-collectors and oppressive landlords.

THE END OF ROMAN BRITAIN

It only needed the collapse of the *Pax Romana* to break the feeble ties which bound this society together, and after 360, as we have seen, the countryside was more and more at the mercy of marauding Picts, Scots, and Saxons. Their raids made little difference at first to the towns except perhaps to swell their population with refugees escaping from the insecurity outside their walls; but they fell with shattering effect on the villas, for these not only contained the bulk of the material wealth of the province but were isolated and for the most part entirely unfortified. Thus such early raiding is likely to have endangered the economic and cultural position of the province out of all proportion to the extent of the material damage which it caused: not only did it mean that the most Romanized classes suffered soonest and most severely, but the disorganization of the villas upset the food supply on which the towns still depended, and broke the discipline which bound the reluctant peasantry to their lords. In Gaul a century later it was this menace

of an uprooted peasantry turned brigands which seems to have been
the major terror to the countryside, and no doubt the same was true
of Britain in the last quarter of the fourth century. And, whether we
attribute the general scantiness of coin finds in the villas after 375
to their destruction and desertion, or whether, as has been recently
suggested, we treat it merely as proving their general reversion to a
regime of subsistence agriculture for which currency was not required, it is clear that by 400 the villa-owners had ceased to be the
dominant social class in Britain, and their disappearance marks a
major stage in the collapse of the Roman economy. It must have
been a memory of this collapse of villa agriculture which led Gildas[1]
in his confused summary of the events between 383 and 446 to note
that a moment came when 'the whole province was deprived of
the support of its food supply, except only for the resources of hunting.' Roman Britain was rapidly sinking back to what anthropolo-
gists call a food-gathering economy.

It is rarely wise to use an argument from silence in a Dark Age
context, and an argument from the silence of Gildas is especially
dangerous, but it may none the less be significant that he scarcely
shows any other conscious memory of the days when villa-owners
were the outstanding social aristocracy of Roman Britain: his
apparent ignorance is at least consistent with the view that in his
time the villas had perished so long and so utterly that the part they
had once played in the life of the province had been wholly forgotten.

But the same is not true of the Roman towns. Gildas knew enough
about them to deplore their destruction in one of his purplest passages, and to give the heading *De urbium subversione* to his general
account of what he believed was the most chaotic phase of Anglo-
Saxon settlement, a phase which he places late in the fifth century,
not long before his own birth. His evidence for their survival to
that age is borne out not only by inherent probability, but by other
scraps of literary evidence. Verulamium at least was alive enough
to discuss Pelagianism with St. Germanus in 428, and to offer him
the hospitality of a thatched hut; and an entry in the *Anglo-Saxon
Chronicle* has been held to show that London could still provide
shelter for British refugees from Kent as late as 457. But whether
we take Gildas's account of their entire desertion in his own day at
its face value, and believe with Haverfield that even London 'lay
waste a hundred years' or whether we are convinced that some at
least retained a continuous if diminished population to the days

[1] It is generally agreed that the *De excidio et conquestu Britanniae* is a genuine
work of the British priest Gildas, who lived and wrote in the first half of the sixth
century A.D.

when commerce could revive under the encouragement of settled Saxon dynasties, the entire disappearance of the urban bishoprics, which must have provided in Britain as in Gaul the framework of the Christian organization in Roman times, is clear enough proof that sooner or later they lost the last remnants of that civic consciousness which distinguished the *civitates*, even in the days of Honorius, from the uprooted peasants of the countryside. The institutions of Roman Britain in town and country alike were entirely unsuited to the economic conditions of the age of Anglo-Saxon settlement and, while the British people may have contributed substantially to the blood of our later mongrel population, their long-forgotten villas and depopulated towns had no direct part to play in the slow and painful evolution of the manors and boroughs of medieval England.

SHORT BIBLIOGRAPHY

A full bibliography may be found in R. G. Collingwood and J. N. L. Myres, *Roman Britain and the English Settlements*, ed. 2, 1937, pp. 462–78. The following selection is only intended as an introductory guide.

I. GENERAL HISTORIES, ETC.

J. Horsley, *Britannia Romana*, 1732 (recently described as 'the first and still in many ways the best book on Roman Britain as a whole').

R. G. Collingwood and J. N. L. Myres, *Roman Britain and the English Settlements*, ed. 2, 1937.

R. G. Collingwood, *Roman Britain*, ed. 1934.

F. J. Haverfield and G. Macdonald, *The Roman Occupation of Britain*, 1924.

I. A. Richmond, *Roman Britain*, 1955.

A. R. Burn, *Agricola and Roman Britain*, 1953.

I. D. Margary, *Roman Roads in Britain*, 2 vols., 1955–57.

Ordnance Survey, *Map of Roman Britain* (3rd ed., 1956).

II. REGIONAL STUDIES

Collingwood Bruce, *Handbook to the Roman Wall*, ed. I. A. Richmond, 1947.

G. Macdonald, *The Roman Wall in Scotland*, 1934.

J. Clarke, J. M. Davidson, A. S. Robertson and J. K. St. Joseph, *The Roman Occupation of South-western Scotland*, 1952.

O. G. S. Crawford, *The Topography of Roman Scotland*, 1949.

R. E. M. Wheeler, *Prehistoric and Roman Wales*, 1928, pp. 217–74.

V. E. Nash-Williams, *The Roman Frontier in Wales*, 1954.

III. ECONOMIC HISTORY

R. G. Collingwood in Tenney Frank, *Economic Survey of Rome*, III, 1937, pp. 1–118.

IV. ARCHÆOLOGY

(a) General

R. G. Collingwood, *The Archæology of Roman Britain*, 1930.
British Museum, *Guide to the Antiquities of Roman Britain*, 1922.
R. E. M. Wheeler, *London in Roman Times*, London Museum Guides, 1930.

(b) Coins

C. H. V. Sutherland, *Coinage and Currency in Roman Britain*, 1937.

(c) Excavations

Reports on individual sites are mostly to be found in the general and local archæological periodicals. G. Macdonald, *Roman Britain 1914–28*, 1931, is a good summary of the more important results of excavation for the period it covers. Detailed surveys of each year's work are also published annually in the *Journal of Roman Studies*.

The use of excavation in interpreting the history of some major sites and structures of Roman Britain may be illustrated from the following outstanding examples:

J. Curle, *A Roman Frontier Post and its People* (Newstead), 1911.
Roman London (Royal Commission on Historical Monuments, 1928).
R. E. M. Wheeler and T. V. Wheeler, *Verulamium* (Reports of the Research Committee of the Society of Antiquaries of London, XI, 1936).
J. P. Bushe-Fox, *Excavations at Wroxeter* (ibid., I, II, IV, 1912–16).
J. P. Bushe-Fox, *Excavations at Richborough* (ibid., VI, VII, X, XVI, 1926–49).
C. F. C. Hawkes and M. R. Hull, *Camulodunum* (ibid., XIV, 1947).

L. C. LATHAM

The Manor and the Village[1]

ORIGINS

A MEDIEVAL manuscript displays within an illuminated initial the three characteristic figures of the feudal world—a tonsured clerk, a knight with lowered vizor, and a peasant in homespun, leaning on his spade. The miniature epitomises the mediaeval theory which divided society on lines of function into the classes that respectively maintained Christendom by their prayers, their swords, and their labour; and the very attitude of the peasant, shrinking, and slightly withdrawn from the other two members of the group, seems symbolic of the cultivator's position of despised aloofness from the more honourable callings, although he and his like constituted the broad basis on which society rested in an age when practically every man's status, whatever his occupation, was derived from his relation to, and from the extent of his possession of land.

The relations between these superior and inferior grades in the social hierarchy are to be sought in the economic and manorial aspects of that 'confusion roughly organised' which is medieval feudalism. The manor was at all times something other than a nexus of economic relations between the rustics in a given area and the feudatory who drew from that area the maintenance of his due position in the social order; it was primarily a legal and administrative unit, in which

---

[1] This essay originally appeared under the title 'The Manor'. For reasons explained above, p. x, it seemed desirable to bring the title into line with the contents, and it has been changed accordingly.

29

private landlordly rights implied seignorial jurisdiction. But beneath and behind the medieval manor, there seems to lie a more primitive institution. Over against the lord stands 'a community of share-holders in husbandry,'[1] a community which in its essential economic needs, if not in its particular methods of satisfying them, reaches back into a remote past; which has indeed been compared to the living organism upon which manorial organization is but a shell and an accretion.

The origin of the 'manor'—the term does not appear in England before 1067—and of the township or village is thus distinct, and it is a well known fact that the boundaries of the two need not neces-sarily, and frequently do not, coincide. Nevertheless over almost the whole of England the established village formed a natural unit for the grant of manorial rights, and lords of manors naturally sought to preserve the unity of their manors. Thus there was, in fact, a good deal of overlap; and for this reason modern writers have equated 'manor' with 'township' or 'village', and have used the term 'the medieval manor' to describe not only the jurisdictional and administrative relationships, to which properly it should be confined, but also the agrarian, economic and social arrangements, of which the village, rather than the manor, was the nexus. These arrange-ments, it scarcely needs to be said, ante-date the Norman Conquest, and communal agriculture can be traced back over many generations into the Anglo-Saxon period. Charters of early English kings record gifts of land in such terms as to make it clear that the lands of the single holder in the township fields lay scattered 'acre under acre' among those of his neighbours. Earlier yet, a seventh century 'doom' of the West Saxon Ine,[2] doubtless representing older un-written custom, speaks of the arable 'shareland' and the meadows 'doled' among the peasantry, and gives a glimpse of village disputes over unfenced holdings and cattle straying into the springing corn, as clear as any entry of trespass in a thirteenth-century court roll.

The existence of the 'open-field' system, with its scattered holdings in roughly equivalent grades, still leaves an open question the presence of a lord in whose interests the husbandry of the group is regulated. It was claimed by Seebohm that the very artificiality and inconvenience of such a system necessarily implies a dominating will intent on preserving economic uniformity among a number of dependent cultivators, so that each may remain capable of contri-buting his quota of labour to the maintenance of the domanial 'home-farm', the nucleus of the estate. The same historian sees economic continuity between the 'villa' of Romano-British economy

---

[1] Vinogradoff, P., *Growth of the Manor*, p. 150.

[2] Attenborough, F. L., *Laws of the Earliest English Kings*, p. 49, Ine, 40, 42.

and the 'ham' or 'tun' of Saxon documents,—a continuity broken merely by the irruption of a new set of barbarian lords. In support of this theory parallels are drawn from districts of Rome's continental provinces where the cultivation of large estates by a semi-servile colonate was well developed, and where a considerable Teutonic infiltration and settlement on similar lines of unfree tenure took place before the final overwhelming of Roman rule; where, moreover, renders in kind and labour were imposed on lands occupied by both military and servile colonists. The interchangeability in these frontier regions of the Teutonic place-ending 'heim' with the Latin 'villa' (ville) is further adduced in evidence of continuity, and the argument is then extended to the 'hams' of England.

The reverse of this view of the Roman origin of the manor is that which sees in the English settlements groups of primitive freemen with a theoretic passion for equality and self-government, a theory set forth by J. R. Green, and in a modified form by Stubbs. The historical actuality seems more complex than either view, and Vinogradoff has emphasized the extent to which Roman practices in agriculture must have been modified by, if not abandoned for, pre-existing methods, in regions where the intensive labour and rigidly artificial mensuration of Mediterranean farming would have been inappropriate (although traces of the latter may possibly have survived in the field measurements of south-eastern England). Even if Romano-British territorial arrangements survived the onslaught of the fifth and sixth centuries, these were probably in the nature of rural communities co-operating in tillage with the heavy plough of northern agriculture, rather than of Italian 'villae' or 'latifundia'. The place-names of those regions where the English settlements were densest and earliest, show, however, in their derivations no sign that still earlier units of organized cultivation persisted, while the equality of shares in the arable and meadows is attributable to the settlement of the new-comers in kindred-groups, where reciprocal obligations would demand a rough equivalence between the ' hides', i.e, holdings necessary to support each household in the kindred.

If, however, the origin of the manor may no longer be sought in an estate worked by unfree labour, the significance of the pre-Norman period resides principally in the increasing closeness of connection between lord and land. From their continental homes the English brought social distinctions between the 'eorl' of a noble kindred, and the typical freeman, the 'ceorl' (they brought also domestic slavery, and the Jutes who settled in Kent included a semi-free class comparable to the Roman 'coloni'). The aristocracy by birth tends to be replaced in the early kingdoms by an aristocracy of service, and the king's companion, his 'gesith', his 'thegn' or servingman, at first a member of the war-band attached to his person, receives his guerdon no longer in personal maintenance, but in grants of land which seem to involve obligations to reclaim[1] as well as continued service in the host. Since, in a primitive society, land and its produce are the source of wealth, such a grant would probably carry with it the transference to the grantee of the tribute in kind,—in ale or honey, loaves, eels, or poultry[2]—previously rendered to the king. Since regal jurisdiction involved a complicated system of 'botes' and 'wites' in addition to the 'wer' received by the now disintegrating kindred, the lay or ecclesiastical 'hlaford' might further be endowed with these judicial profits, and would then normally render justice to the population 'seated' on the land; it did not thereby necessarily cease to be free, but a lord was inserted, on territory thus granted by 'land book' or charter, between it and the king.

The Scandinavian invasions of the ninth century, which on the continent resulted in the crystallization of society in feudal units of defence, in England too carried a step further the differentiation between the cultivator 'whose weapons glide out of his hands', and the military thegnhood, which formed the steel spear-point of that otherwise ineffective weapon, the fyrd, and whose ranks it was essential to fill from 'thriving' peasants and chapmen. The great majority of churls in the south-western districts were, however, far from thriving; material devastation and social disintegration must have driven many to dependence on men of superior wealth and status—to personal 'commendation' which involved judicial responsibility and was encouraged by the state,[3] and to direct economic subordination when land and stock were supplied and agricultural service taken in return. The latter practice was known as early as the seventh century for Ine regulates the relations between the tenant of a yardland—one-fourth of a hide—and his lord,[4] but undoubtedly it was extended in the Danish period. On the other hand, the invasions brought to northern and eastern England a considerable influx of Scandinavians who remained racially distinct from the English till at least a century after the Norman Conquest, and who retained their military character as free warriors and consequent superior status as marked in the correspondence of their wergeld to that of the Wessex thegn—sixfold that of the churl,— although economically the thegn of the Danelaw or East Anglia was often a mere peasant, with a holding far removed from the ideal thegnly equipment of five hides.

Evidence which shows how far 'economic feudalism' had pro-

[1] Attenborough, F. L., op. cit., Ine, 64, 66, pp. 57, 58.
[2] Ine, 70, p. 59.
[3] Attenborough, F. L., op. cit., II, Aethelstan, 2, p. 129.
[4] Ine, 67, p. 58.

gressed in southern England fifty years before the Conquest, can be found in treatises on estate-management compiled for use by the steward of some magnate—churchman, earl, or king's thegn. The 'Gerefa'[1] deals principally with the labours of the agricultural year. The 'Rectitudines Singularum Personarum'[2] enumerates from the point of view of their obligations, the various classes 'seated' on the property, from the thegn to whom land is 'loaned', but who yet owes military and garrison service to the king, down to the house-hold and farm servants, probably thralls like the unfree ploughman of the Saxon school-book,[3] though guaranteed certain perquisites by local 'folk-custom' which the steward must not infringe. Inter-mediate grades are 'churlish' in status, free from taint of servitude, since even the occupant of a cotland, smallest and meanest of rural holdings, 'must pay his Hearth-penny on Holy Thursday as all free men should'. It is this freedom of status which chiefly differentiates the eleventh-century 'geneat', 'gebur' and 'cottar' from their manor-ial descendants, since counterparts to the 'customary services' of a later date are being exacted, and the 'gebur's' outfit and probably his dwelling are the property of his lord.

The Domesday Survey proves, however, that manorialism was not ubiquitous on the eve of the Conquest. Predominantly in regions settled by Scandinavians, though in other districts as well, there existed in 1065, a considerable number of cultivators who are described as 'freemen' or 'sokemen', the former term apparently referring less to status than to the bearer's right to alienate or sell his land,—'to go with it where he will', the latter to one who is more tenurially dependent on a superior; the sokeman might in many cases be bound to 'seek' his lord's jurisdiction, and, when of lowly economic position, he might owe predial 'customs', e.g. the folding of his flock not on his own but on his lord's fallow, yet he was not involved to any great extent in the quasi-manorial system which brought villeins with their plough teams to provide regular labour on the home-farm that was the economic and directing centre of the estate.

The Norman occupation profoundly affected the English land system, but on its legal and tenurial rather than on its agrarian side. There was a sweeping dispossession of over 90 per cent of the upper class of Saxon lay landholders, and replacement by a military alien aristocracy whose intrusion entailed for the cultivator, not dis-possession—since he was needed to work and to pay—but inevitable

[1] Translated W. Cunningham, *Growth of English Industry and Commerce*, Vol. I (ed. 1910), Appendix B., p. 571–6.
[2] Translated D. C. Douglas and G. W. Greenaway, *English Historical Docu-ments*, Vol. II (1092–1189), pp. 813–816.
[3] Aelfric, *Colloquies*.

depression. The Norman monarchy was based on right by conquest, and there could be no check on its exactions; the terrible geld of 1083, which Maitland thinks may have amounted to nearly one-third of the annual value of land,[1] must have fallen crushingly on poorer folk, and acted, as the Danish inroads had done, in driving them into deeper dependence on those wealthier and more powerful. In 1086 villeins—dependent rustics—appear everywhere in place of the earlier sokemen, freemen, and even lesser thegns; Domesday's great value to the economic historian lies in the fact that it shows a society in movement—a movement violently accelerated by the political changes of twenty years. How great that change and consequent degradation might be, can be gauged when the Bedfordshire Domesday records that 'there are one villein and seven bordars and a slave . . . nine thegns held this manor'.[2]

The conquest further entailed the importation into inchoate Saxon relationships of a legal theory whereby service in war was straitly bound to the tenure of land—a theory which left no place for the man who 'could carry his land where he would', since all land must now have a lord who had granted it upon terms of suit and service. Again the Norman lawyer, with views on servitude borrowed from Roman jurisprudence, combined with the Norman feudatory to thrust the churl to the wrong side of the line that marked the distinction between free and servile status. By the time the first century of English feudalism was completed the term 'villein', at first the designation of a villager, was coming to imply servitude, and the chattel 'servi' mingled with the once personally free peasantry to form a class of serfs tied to manorial soil.[3]

THE ORGANISATION OF THE MANOR

The 150 or 200 years that followed the importation of developed political feudalism, witnessed the crystallization of economic feudalism into the manorial form that is so familiar an aspect of mediaeval society. It is essential, however, to recognize that in the thirteenth century (and probably earlier) elements are discernible in the manorial records now beginning to be universally kept, whose development was bound eventually to disrupt manorial economy. There is, in fact, no 'typical manor' of any one mediaeval century; at any given date local variations will be wide; and only with this reservation does it become safe to generalize on certain broad features

[1] Maitland, F. W., *Domesday Book and Beyond*, p. 4.
[2] Vinogradoff, P., *English Society in the Eleventh Century*, p. 410, note 3.
[3] The most recent short account of the progress towards legal serfdom is in Poole, A. L., *Obligations of Society in the Twelfth and Thirteenth Centuries* (1946).

of manorial organization, classifying these for the sake of a rather artificial convenience, as they belong to the manor as an agricultural unit, frequently, though not always, coinciding with a village community in husbandry, or to the manor as a politico-legal unit, feudal in origin, but to some extent utilized by the crown for purposes of local government and justice.

(a) *The Manorialized Village as an Economic Unit.*—The best known feature of manorial and pre-manorial agriculture is its open-field system, whose origin has been traced to the consequences of the co-operative technique of communal farming adopted by the English settlers at the time of the Anglo-Saxon conquest of Britain, and to the assertion of the superior rights of the community over the possible wishes and interests of the individual farmer. These rights were valid against the lord himself, when his demesne—far from being the physical as it was the institutional centre of the manor—lay parcelled among his tenants' holdings, and was accordingly liable to the same routine of husbandry. On about two-thirds of English soil the open fields of a manor were two or three in number, each containing about the same acreage, and each holder's bundle of acre or half-acre strips being apportioned between them. It has been suggested that the arable of the earlier village was divided into two fields only, and that when increased population necessitated an increased food supply, more fertile regions, e.g. the midland plain, found it possible to fallow once in three instead of once in two years, thus adding one-third to the area under crops in any one season. Further deviations in the direction of more intensive cultivation sometimes appear from the thirteenth century onwards, usually on demesne land withdrawn from the common fields and farmed in separate consolidated 'furlongs'.[1]

Although the system of strip-holding seems cumbrous and uneconomic by modern agrarian standards, judged by the criteria of a primitive age which knew little or nothing of production for market, and had to be content with a highly localized subsistence economy seeking only to keep alive the members of a single village community, the open-field method of agriculture was adequate to its purpose. It effected a balance between the need for arable land to produce grain and other human food crops, the need for rough pasture for the village stock (whether plough-oxen, sheep, pigs or other animals bred for meat or milk), and the need for meadow to provide winter fodder for the animals which were not killed off for food. Pasture was as essential as arable to manorial or village economy, in certain regions perhaps more so; thus rights of common

[1]For this and the subsequent paragraph, cf. Gray, H. L., *English Field Systems* (1915), and Orwin, C. S., *The Open Fields* (1938).

over the 'waste' were indissolubly connected with tenure in the fields round which lay that area of woodland and rough grazing. It was an absolute necessity to use the fallow field, the stubble on the cultivated fields after the harvest, the rough grass on the roads giving access to the cultivated fields, and every uncultivable 'sike' of rough grass, too wet, too stony or too steep for the plough, to graze the village stock, and especially the plough-oxen, which must be pastured close to the strips which they had to plough. In certain regions the utilization of vast extents of pasture led to peculiar manorial or extra-manorial developments; in the Kentish weald the 'denns' or units of swine-pasture might lie within the forest at a considerable distance from the villages to which they appertained, and only gradually became transformed into manorialized settlements—discrete parts of remote lordships.[1] In Lincolnshire the rights of groups of vills to regulate intercommoning arrangements on the fens—arrangements that may reach back to the English settlement—persist under a seignorial regime, as shown in the need for the vills' assent to fresh partitions and in their share of fines for trespass.[2]

Meadow was the most valuable type of land in a husbandry that looked to hay as its only winter fodder, and meadow had from early times been parcelled among the holders of strips. Unlike the plough-land, there was often yearly redistribution by lot or in rotation, while after hay harvest it passed from several to common use, although the lord's share probably fell early into his undivided occupation.

Although there were exceptions to which F. W. Maitland and others have drawn attention, it is decidedly unusual to find a manor which did not possess demesne land worked by servile labour, and the organization of these villein or customary services was as essential a part of estate-management, as their character and incidence was inextricably connected with villeinage in its legal aspect. In legal theory the villein was one who did 'base' services (notably the heavy 'week-work' that occupied three or even more of the virgater's days), whose kind and amount rested on the lord's will. Actually the peasant knew well enough that the sheep that he was bound to shear, the cartloads that his horse must draw, and the amount of bread, beer and herrings that he consumed at the lord's expense on boon-days were accurately determined for him and his fellows by 'custom time out of mind', and that the most over-bearing bailiff would hesitate to disregard them. The tendency in a feudal period was for service of all kinds to attach itself to land rather than to persons; it was the holding that must provide the

[1] Neilson, N., *Terrier of Bilsington.*
[2] Neilson, N., *Terrier of Fleet.*

36

stipulated 'opera', and even were it to be subdivided among seven or eight tenants, the repartition of its obligations rested rather with these than with the manorial authority. Just as certain peasant tenements might send men to represent the vill at the communal Hundred Court, so specified holdings might entail for their occupants manorial service as reeve[1] or beadle, hayward, carter, or ploughman. A man personally free, who occupied 'native' land, was bound to conform to the conditions of servile tenure. The obligation of the freeholder might, of course, include service as well as the more distinctive payment of rent, but such service was a matter of individual contract rather than of collective obligation, and consisted of boonworks at special seasons, and possibly of supervisory functions, rather than of regular weekly toil.

On most manors there was a unit of tenure, a standard holding to which all villein land tended to conform. Though this norm varied in acreage and in nomenclature, the virgate is its commonest form, and is usually taken to imply about thirty acres scattered in the arable fields; it represented one-fourth of the hide—the original land of a Saxon household, tilled by a full team of eight oxen; and the shrinkage which dates from before the Conquest, witnesses increase of population, or economic depression, or both. Actually there are districts where the virgate is unknown, other where the semi-virgate or bovate is the average holding, while 'virgate' is useless as a term of field measurement, since it may vary from fifteen to eighty acres, and represents a complex of customary obligations and economic claims rather than a fixed area.

Besides predial service the tenant was liable to a variety of dues in kind, or payments representing such dues and tending to replace them, which varied infinitely in different districts and on different estates. Thus the peasantry, collectively or as individuals, might render 'larder silver' at Christmas, eggs and capons, pannage for the right to graze swine, house- and heybote for gathering timber; while the unfree was also liable to the personally degrading incidents of tallage—a tax whose amount was decided by the lord—merchet, levied on the marriages of bond-women and sometimes men, and chevage for leave to live off the manor—all legally recognized marks of villeinage.

But if the foregoing picture is broadly true of the manor on Wessex and Mercian soil, it is important to remember that varying land-systems and more significant differences in tenurial and social arrangements prevailed in other districts, whether these varieties arose out of geographical peculiarities (as in the fens and the weald) or from distinctive racial elements in the population.

[1] Bennett, H. S., *Life on the English Manor* (1937), pp. 166 sqq.

Dr. H. L. Gray has traced the boundaries of the area within which the two- and three-field systems prevailed.[1] In the northern and western districts he finds the influence of the Celtic land-system which was connected with the predominance of pasture and was based on the family group of tribesmen, rather than on 'the manorial community, with its pyramidal structure of lord and graded dependents'.[2] In Northumberland, the four north-western counties, and the Devonian peninsula, the normal manorial structure co-exists with a distribution of the population in scattered hamlets—a Celtic trait—rather than in concentrated village settlements, and fields of equal size undergoing recurrent fallowing are absent. There seems evidence that here the original system was the Celtic one of concentrated tillage of an 'inland' of small extent, and periodical reclamation of a larger 'outfield' from the waste, whose inexhaustibility obviated the need for common pasture rights over the fallow.

The Thames basin is another region where the field-system, though not the other characteristics of the midland manor, is lacking, and Gray finds the cause both in the large woodlands from which 'assarting' for tillage took place late and irregularly and in the proximity and influence of Kent and East Anglia. In the former county the unit of tenure is not the scattered virgate but a compact holding, often in the shape of a rectangular block, which may indicate an original derivation from Roman land-measurements. These 'juga', once the holdings of family groups whose names they continued to bear, in course of time became infinitely subdivided owing to the peculiar Kentish custom of gavelkind or equal inheritance, itself connected with the free status of the peasantry of Kent, where legal villeinage was absent. The sokemen tenure of Kent may be ascribable to the original settlement by Jutes, whose wergeld system set a relatively high value on the churl; to the early formulation and assertion of Saxon custom against the depressing influence of Norman manorialism; finally, to the situation of the county on the main highway of continental trade, resulting in an early money economy which rendered obsolete the more rigid tenurial arrangements of the manor.[3]

In East Anglia both tenurial and social conditions are unique, and have usually been ascribed to the influx of free Scandinavians (in 1086 the proportion of freeman and sokeman in the district to

[1] Orwin, in the book cited above, p. 35, n. 1, showed, however, that the problem of drawing boundaries was more complicated than Gray had supposed.
[2] Vinogradoff, P., *Survey of Denbigh*, Introduction, p. 87.
[3] For conditions in Kent, cf. Jolliffe, J. E. A., *Pre-Feudal England: the Jutes* (1933), with which should be compared Muhlfeld, H. E., *A Survey of the Manor of Wye*.

the whole population was 36 per cent).[1] They brought with them a land-system based on a holding of about twelve acres, which lies at the basis of an elaborate fiscal system. 'Nowhere was the failure of the manor to comprise the agricultural and tenurial arrangements of society more noticeable.'[2] The vill and manor markedly fail to coincide, the older institution is correspondingly independent in its economic arrangements, notably in those relating to intercommunal pasturage. The population of one village might be tenurially related to a number of different lords, and in post-Conquest times the relation persists as a jurisdictional one rather than as involving economic dependence, despite 'manorializing' pressure by great ecclesiastical landholders. Personal freedom carried with it, as in Kent, a movement towards a cash economy and the unrestricted disposal of land, and already in the twelfth century there was an active land market, and consequently a rapid disintegration and redistribution of holdings, which contrasts strongly with the uniformity and unpartitioned descent of the midland villein's virgate. Here, too, equal distribution of parcels over the fields of a vill is absent, and a more individualized use of the flock for manuring the tenant's arable is followed.

The neighbouring Danelaw was another 'region full of small landholders with a power of alienating their tenements'[3] by charter —a legal impossibility to the bondman. As in East Anglia, the village and the territorial soke, and not the manor, represented 'the essential form of rural organization'.[4] Here, too, the freedom from seignorial control of a large body of the peasantry (whose personal names in Lincolnshire argue an unassimilated Danish element in the late twelfth century) resulted in holdings of irregular size, and in an early circulation of ready money. In contrast to Norfolk and Suffolk, the greater part of the Danelaw counties apparently fell within the area of two-field husbandry, but the latter seems to have been to some extent disturbed by the break-up and reconstitution of holdings.

(b) *Manorial Jurisdiction.*—The classical exposition of manorial jurisdiction as exercised in the later thirteenth century, when a strenuous, and on the whole successful, attempt had been made by the crown to limit and define it, is, of course, that of Maitland in the essay introductory to 'Select Pleas in Manorial Courts'. He emphasizes the fact that while there was but one court—the

[1] More recently, other explanations have been advanced by Davis, R. H. C., 'East Anglia and the Danelaw', *Trans. R. Hist. Society*, 5th Ser., vol. 5.
[2] Douglas, D. C., *Social Structure of Medieval East Anglia*, p. 3.
[3] Stenton, F. M., *Social and Economic Conditions in the Danelaw*, Introduction, p. 48.
[4] Ibid., p. 62.

halimote—held under the presidency of the steward, that court was yet wielding powers derived from two different sources of authority: the *feudal* right of every lord to demand suit from his tenants, and the *franchisal* rights or 'regalia', in theory emanating from royal delegation, but actually in many cases acquired at an earlier stage, and confirmed or withdrawn by the first Edward as a result of the Quo Warranto enquiry.

The most common franchises exercised by lords of manors were the view of frankpledge—itself in origin a public, not a seignorial, organization—and the assize of bread and ale. The former is rendered in Court Rolls by the Latin 'Visus Franci Plegii' and the vernacular 'lawday'; the word 'leet', which, as Professor Hearnshaw points out,[1] 'is not so much a court as a jurisdiction', was not universally applied to the view and concurrent manorial jurisdictions till the fourteenth century, but it originates at an early date in East Anglia where it implied not merely a jurisdictional area intermediate between the hundred and the vill, but also an economic one connected with inter-village pasturage, and a unit in the partition of geld liabilities.[2]

There must have been remarkable vitality about a system of mutual responsibility and affixing of police duties, which originated in some form in the tenth century,[3] and was by no means moribund five hundred years later. Maitland has traced the utilization by Henry II of this older police unit of ten or twelve men—the tithing—for the jurisdictional purpose of 'telling tales'—making collective presentment of crime, at the sheriff's tourn or session in the Hundred Court twice yearly, with which the view of frankpledge held by the steward was co-ordinate. The two yearly inspections of these groups is the one obligation common to every one of the various statutory and private lists of 'articuli visus franci plegii' of the thirteenth and fourteenth centuries; the chief pledge's presentments of various offences as recorded in manorial court rolls can, however, all be discovered in one or other of them. On Saxon soil the tithing becomes territorial, i.e. it includes the male inhabitants of an entire vill or hamlet, of which one or several might lie within the manor after it tends to become tenurial; landless men on the manor are allowed to escape enrolment by a small payment; the office of tithingman (like that of reeve) becomes attached to certain holdings, and hence may fall to a woman, or to a free tenant holding villein land. In districts with Scandinavian affinities, the tithing persists in its earlier 'personal' form of ten or twelve men.

[1] Hearnshaw, F. J. C., *Leet Jurisdiction*, p. 72.
[2] Douglas, D. C., op. cit., pp. 55–8, 193–202.
[3] Attenborough, F. L., op. cit., VI, Aethelstan, 3, 4, 8, pp. 159, 163. Morris, W. A., *The Frankpledge System* (1910), has dealt with the whole subject.

The tithingman's presentments fall into certain fairly definite categories. He makes accusations of brawls and disorder punishable by the lord; he is responsible for arresting and conveying to prison felons whom the ordinary manorial court was not competent to try; the upkeep of bridges and repair of highways was incumbent on the tithing, and purely 'manorial' nuisances—undrained ditches, obstructed paths and polluted wells—naturally tend also to fall within the tithingman's survey at the view. In the absence of a specifically appointed aletaster, he reports breaches of regulations of the prices, measures, and quality of ale and bread, and of victuals standardized in later statutes, although lords derived a regular income from petty fines instead of administering the corporal punishment legally incurred; he proclaimed the retention of strays in the lord's pound till redeemed by their owners.

Some lords possessed feudal jurisdiction only, though even so two 'magnae curiae' tend to differentiate themselves, in imitation of the Hocktide and Autumn views, from the 'parvae' or three-weekly courts, and business concentrates itself on the former sessions; indeed, by the fourteenth century the latter are dwindling in number, or disappearing as burdensome to both lord and suitors; and manorial business may be done outside the court and merely ratified when it meets.

The halimote, like the manor whose organ it was, has a two-fold aspect. On the one hand, perhaps as representing the pre-seignorial 'tunmote', it defends and administers manorial custom; the suitors, though unfree, are in practice if not in law judgment-finders as well as justiciable; manorial juries may be appointed as repositories of traditional knowledge, to trace bounds or declare custom. Mr. Ault, in a discussion of those byelaws which by the late thirteenth century were being committed to writing,[1] points out how rarely they are couched in the form of seignorial injunction, how often their formulation implies the necessity of the tenants' assent, and bears witness to the lord's inclusion under the restrictions of co-operative agriculture. On the other hand the lord utilized the court to subserve his economic and fiscal interests; he derived profit from his jurisdiction in cases of village litigation over debt and trespass, as well as from his power to punish village misdemeanours. Land transfer and the taking up of customary holdings must take place through the lord or his minister, since the villein holds at his lord's will, and against his lord is rightless, so far as his tenement is concerned, in courts where the king's justice is administered to free-holders.

Not infrequently the distinction between seignorial and delegated

[1] *English Historical Review,* Vol. 45, p. 208.

justice might be ignored, and a tithingman complain of ill-performed villein services or transgression of communal regulations. Indeed, where the 'homage' or collective body of tenants, who presented purely manorial cases, was identical with the tithing, the peasants who composed both probably drew but little distinction between their respective actions in these two capacities. It is in fact surprising that where a unitary court performs two sets of functions so much attempt at a systematic grouping of business under the heads of 'Visus' and 'Curia' was actually made.

Just as the separate Court Leet is an institution of the future, when manorial jurisdiction had been emptied of real importance, so are the Court Baron and Court Customary which appear in Tudor and Jacobean Court Keepers' Guides. Both villeins holding at the lord's will by the custom of the manor, and his free tenants, were bound to do suit at the one undifferentiated court, although it was obviously more difficult to enforce the latters' attendance. In later manorial history, when personal villeinage was dying out, the earlier distinction in status seems also on the wane, and the jury of 'liberi tenentes', who in imitation of procedure in the public courts received or confirmed the tithingman's presentments, were often drawn from the manorial copyholders 'though villeinage was the pit from which copyhold tenure was digged.'[1]

TRANSFORMATION AND DECAY

(a) *Before 1348.*—The economic basis of the manorial system was at no period an entirely natural one; some accumulation and circulation of money there must have been from an early time, not only in regions with exceptional economic conditions and an exceptionally emancipated peasantry, but also in districts whose manorial structure conformed more closely to the normal type, and the tendency among economic historians is to emphasize the early appearance of a money economy.[2] Vinogradoff[3] has pointed to the 'molmen' as a peasant group which, while counted unfree, yet rendered a money rent and not service; more significant is, however, the invariable payment by the ordinary working 'customer' of a rent for his holding—the 'rent of assize', which figures first among seignorial receipts when yearly accounts begin to be kept. Under this payment were probably consolidated a variety of earlier dues and obligations

[1] Tawney, R. H., *Agrarian Problem in the Sixteenth Century*, p. 53.
[2] 'Money rents played a far more prominent part than has generally been assumed in the manorial system of the thirteenth century.' Kosminsky, *Economic History Review*, Vol. I, p. 223.
[3] *Villeinage in England*, p. 183.

—food rents and other gifts in kind of pre-Conquest origin; commuted services, like the carting, paid for on some estates by tenants not owning horses, with 'horsgabulum'; possibly public and royal taxation, for Mr. Douglas suggests[1] that in the eastern counties customary rent may represent the peasants' geld converted into a seignorial exaction. Within the manor, this assized rent might vary with the size of the holding, the full virgate paying, for example, 5s., the semi-virgate 2s. 6d.; but that rent is as yet fixed by custom, and not by economic demand, is proved by its variations on different manors, while it is possible for all classes of tenement on one manor, from virgate to cotcetland, to pay roughly equivalent sums, showing that rent was regarded rather as a tax paid for license to dwell upon the lord's land, than as an economic payment proportioned to acreage.

A money-rent presupposes a money income, and the peasant's accumulation might be derived from various sources,—from the practice of a village craft; from the sale of surplus grain, not hampered like that of his stock by a possible seignorial veto, in the local market which the growth of town life opened to him; from the wage-earnings, if not of the virgater himself, then of members of his household—brothers or grown sons—who provided a supply of labour additional to that required on the holding, or absorbed by compulsory services.

From the lord's point of view his manor was eminently a profit and loss concern which provided income as well as maintenance, and its successful working involved not only transport of grain, stock, wool, and dairy-produce to a centre of consumption and management, but also the marketing of surplus produce, together with the purchase of necessaries, e.g. fresh beasts and seed corn, unless these were supplied from another unit of the same manorial group. A striking feature of manorial book-keeping in the thirteenth and fourteenth centuries is the wide margin of annual profits over expenditure.[2]

The complete transition to a money economy was bound in the long run to disintegrate a system characterized by 'social stability resting on a wasteful uniformity of custom',[3] and it is important to note that the transition had begun fully a century before the pestilence of 1348, which economic historians are tending less and less to regard as the cause of a process whose latter stages it did at most but accelerate. The combined factors of an increased population,

---

[1] Op. cit., pp. 99–113.

[2] Levett, A. E., 'Financial Organization of the Manor', *Economic History Review*, Vol. I, No. 1, pp. 78–83. This essay has been reprinted in the same author's *Studies in Manorial History*, pp. 63–68.

[3] Unwin, G., *Victoria County History, Suffolk*, I, p. 653.

an increased cash circulation, and rising prices, were already in the thirteenth century reacting on the economic organization of the manor, and, more indirectly, on the social condition of the peasant. Nevertheless it would be erroneous to regard the process as a steady progress towards commutation. It is generally accepted that, already in the twelfth century, there had been a marked trend towards commutation of some services and the leasing of domanial estates, but that in England this process was arrested and even reversed in the thirteenth century.[1] Profitability and price levels were doubtless the operative factors. On the other hand, where the customary holdings became unable to support the population, two results might be expected: on the one hand the creation of a wage-earning class detached from the obligation of bond tenure though not from personal bondage, on the other the throwing of fresh land into peasant holdings. The Statute of Merton (1236) which recognizes the lord's right to 'approve' from the manorial waste, while it safeguards the tenants' interests in pasture rights, witnesses to the land hunger from which the lord profited by appeasing with 'assarts' and 'purprestures', leased as a rule for a money rent, and often to men already occupying customary holdings. Outlying parcels of demesne were also being let, and instances of the stock and land lease to individual or collective farmers anticipate the estate-management of the fifteenth century. Meanwhile individual peasants were leasing and exchanging strips and plots through the manorial court which afforded a cheap means of land-conveyancing; and this redistribution marked the first steps away from the old uniformity of holdings in manorialized areas, towards a growing economic inequality between tenants of the same legal status.

A question often debated and studied in groups of manorial documents[2] or in the records of single manors,[3] is the extent to which the commutation of customary services had progressed during the thirteenth and earlier fourteenth centuries. Apparently while the process had begun, it had reached very different lengths on different manors, as determined by local conditions, or by the estate policy of different lords, and there was no universal tendency to replace any one type of service with hired labour, unless it was that of the manorial servants—carters, shepherds, and the rest—who

[1] Cf. Postan, M. M., 'The Chronology of Labour Services', *Trans. R. Hist. Society*, 4th Ser., Vol. 20 (1937). There is further discussion in Miller, E., *The Abbey and Bishopric of Ely* (1951), and in the economic chapters in Knowles, D. M., *The Religious Orders in England* (Vols, I and II, 1948, 1955).

[2] Page, T. W., *End of Villeinage in England*. Gray, H. L., *Commutation of Villein Services*, E.H.R., Vol. 29.

[3] Davenport, F. G., *The Economic Development of a Norfolk Manor*. Feiling, K., *An Essex Manor in the Fourteenth Century*, E.H.R., Vol. 26. Maitland, F. W., *History of a Cambridgeshire Manor*, E.H.R., Vol. 9.

now often appear as permanent employees in receipt of a small money wage, and of their 'livery' in the form of grain allowances and sometimes clothing. The lord's motive here was probably the efficiency of hired as compared to compulsory service; the rise of prices would be a factor operating towards the discontinuance of 'boon works', when the hire of day-labour was less expensive than the villein's customary meal; on the other hand, customary ploughing was often retained as well as those 'precariae' required at seasons when a good deal of labour was likely to be needed within a limited period. It must always be borne in mind that on most manors there was a reserve of customary labour not drawn upon every year, and hence that the 'sale of works' as set out in account-rolls, is evidence *not* of permanent commutation, but of the lord's option of taking the equivalent in cash, varying perhaps from ½d. to 6d., at which every type of work was assessed; hence the fluctuation from year to year in the number actually performed.

(*b*) *1348–1381.*—As it is impossible to generalize about the stage reached before 1348 in manorial evolution, so the incidence of the Black Death itself seems to have been capricious. It was not an isolated visitation. Plague was endemic for most of the fourteenth century,[1] and its economic results varied widely from district to district, and even from one manor to another. There is no doubt that the demographic effects were serious and produced a prolonged labour crisis; but it seems that such consequences as the leasing of domanial manors did not become widespread until after approximately 1370. Such an intensive and analytical study as that by Professor Levett of 'The Black Death on the estates of the See of Winchester',[2] in southern England, shows that while there might be temporary difficulties (and possibly a permanent legacy of unrest), there was in these manors no breakdown of administration nor of communal husbandry. Surplus population apparently provided tenants for holdings left vacant by death; the immediate effect of the mortality was to swell the revenue from heriots and fines; and when the prices of commodities and labour rose, manorial receipts left a margin amply sufficient to cover increased outlay. Neither was there on these estates or elsewhere, any reversal of the earlier movement from predial service to commutation, though customary work was naturally heavier for the survivors of a population which in some places had diminished by over one-third.[3] On the other hand, it was exceptional for the pestilence to be followed

[1] Cf. Saltmarsh J., 'Plague and Economic Decline in England in the later Middle Ages', *Cambridge Hist. Journal*, Vol. 7 (1941).
[2] In *Oxford Studies in Social and Legal History*, ed. Sir P. Vinogradoff, Vol. 5.
[3] Robo, E., *The Black Death in the Hundred of Farnham*, E.H.R., Vol. 44, p. 648.

directly by the wholesale abandonment of the tenants' services and the inauguration of a new system of leases for life or for a term of years, although on certain estates, e.g. those of the Bishopric of Durham,[1] the latter did take place.

Broadly speaking, the existing economic changes continued to work themselves out after as before the pestilence, but the cultivator's attitude had become consciously aggressive. His acquiescence in the place assigned to him by mediaeval social theory had been shaken; he resented the continuance of, and still more attempts to re-impose, the older system with its restrictions and disabilities, and court rolls show him taking refuge in flight, while his fellow-villeins ignored or resisted the injunction to recover him. The conflagration of 1381 throws a fierce light upon the grievances, smouldering through a generation, of the manorial population that rose to march upon London or to create local anarchy. The villein tenant demanded emancipation from the stigma and burden of un-freedom in the name of a crude Christian democracy, and destroyed the rolls which at once recorded and limited his bondage. The wage-earner vented his resentment on the lawyer class which in the persons of the justices administered the Statutes of Labourers, and which, as supplying an important element in those seignorial councils with whose assistance landowners were by this time administering their estates,[2] may have been disliked for its tendency to overrule by a stricter legalism the manorial custom which the peasant rightly felt to be protective.

It is apparently not altogether easy to determine the extent to which fourteenth century labour legislation was actually successful in checking a rise in wages. Many presentments of offenders were made, and many fines levied on rural and urban employers, work-men, and traders; but the proportion of convictions to unrecorded transgressions is undiscoverable. Among those who offended by giving excess wages there may well have been, not only manorial lords, but prosperous villeins whose families could not supply all the labour required on the two or three virgates concentrated in one man's tenure; the poet who in 'Piers Ploughman' idealizes the land-holding peasant, has little love for the landless and thriftless labourer who may have worked for hire on the former's half-acre. But even if the rise in wages was a phenomenon in origin independent of the pestilence, and if the statutory wage-rates had in some districts been reached during the years preceding it, the intervention of the state must to some degree have led indirectly to the undermining of

---

[1] Bradshaw, F., V.C.H., Durham, Vol. II.
[2] Levett, A. E., 'Baronial Council and their Relation to Manorial Courts', in *Mélanges d'histoire du Moyen Age offertes à M. Ferdinand Lot.*

seignorial discipline, and have 'meant for the villein a relaxation of his personal dependence as the justices of the peace and other courts of common law were placed between the lord and the serf '.[1]

(c) *From 1381*.—The revolt of the commons had ended in rout and failure, but the wave of which it was the breaking crest swept on, and in the end carried away most of the old landmarks of manorialism. The latter part of the fourteenth century and first half of the fifteenth was probably the period when the manor underwent its most rapid transformation. By 1450 the lord's demesne had usually passed from direct exploitation by his ministers to the occupation of a rent-paying farmer; to an ever-increasing degree, the cash nexus—at least in southern England—was replacing all the older tenurial relations. The essence of the manorial system was gone.

It appears that the lease of the demesne first became general on lay manors. Ecclesiastical tradition was more conservative in its estate-management, the undying corporation kept a tighter hold upon its dependent peasantry. Yet there are notable exceptions in the fourteenth century,[2] and the middle of the fifteenth century saw a widespread practice of leases for short terms of years on episcopal and monastic lands, the lessee being, as a rule, on south midland manors at all events, a copyholder or even a villein, who might be paying a yearly rent of from £4 to £40, and be acting in addition as a 'liveried' bailiff, or rent-collector. The tendency was to extend the terms of the lease so as to include not merely the demesne lands, but also the tenants' rents, and profits of the court, so that even if the steward continued to hold the latter, the lord's financial motives for controlling his tenants were to a great extent removed.

Although great sheepruns were no new economic phenomenon[3] sheep-farming was of course developing at this time in the hands of both lords and farmers. The former might lease part only of the demesne arable, retaining the residue, together with some permanent pasture, for the upkeep of the manorial flock of several thousand beasts. On other manors the farmer was the sheep-master; and small men as well as great profited by the rise in wool prices; the 'small flocks of thirty to forty sheep which had long been run upon the

---

[1] Savine, A., Review of *Wat Tyler's Rebellion*, by Petrushevshky, E.H.R., Vol. 17, p. 781. Cf. Putnam, B. H., *Enforcement of the Statutes of Labourers*, p. 223.

[2] For example, by leasing between 1391 and 1396 all the estates of Christ Church, Canterbury, Prior Chillenden nearly doubled the income of the cathedral priory, and this high income from rents (much larger than Canterbury's income from direct farming in the 1320s and 1330s) was maintained for some decades. Cf. Smith, R. A. L., *Canterbury Cathedral Priory: a study in monastic administration* (1943).

[3] Cf. Page, F. M., 'Bidentes Hoylandie', *Economic Journal*, Economic History Series, No. 4, 1929.

common wastes and meadow'[1] were in some cases increasing from tens to hundreds.

Economically, the peasant of the last mediaeval century was in a strong position. If the lord had found it difficult and unprofitable to exact predial services, the farmer of rustic stock was in a still worse position for securing them when leased with the land. The line of least resistance was to allow commutation or simple lapse. While services were turned into payments, or tacitly dropped,[2] the old assized rents (still accounted for separately) were rarely raised from their amount in the thirteenth century, custom operating to prevent their rising to an economic level, despite 'the healthy land-hunger' and active land market among the peasantry described by Mr. Tawney as characteristic of the period,[3] and as marking a spontaneous movement to consolidation of holdings and cultivation in severalty. The rate of entry fines was also falling rather than rising after 1400, except where migration of industry to a rural centre had greatly increased circulating capital, and the lord was powerful enough to exact his share.

Meanwhile villein tenure was being transformed wholesale into copyhold, and to the latter the protection of the Equity Courts and even of the common law was extended at least from the middle of the fifteenth century.[4] The process is connected with the decay of services, though customary boon works survived in some places down to Tudor, and even Stuart times.[5] Of the disappearance of villeinage as a legal status whose disabilities were yet more galling than its obligations were onerous, it is hard to generalize. Savine[6] has traced some five hundred bondmen families in the sixteenth century, but their existence, like that of the manor itself, had become a social anomaly, and this retention by the few of the weight of unfreedom from which the many had shaken themselves free, characterizes manorial conditions a century before Elizabeth. While fifteenth century manors in close geographical proximity are in quite different stages as regards the abandonment of personal villeinage, it is broadly true that small groups of villein households are—illogically—becoming marked off not merely as of old from the freeholders, but from the bulk of 'customary' tenants, by their continued liability to servile incidents and payments; and it has been suggested that their unfreedom rested more heavily than ever

[1] Tawney, R. H., op. cit., p. 115.
[2] Levett, A. E., op. cit., p. 157.
[3] Tawney, R. H., op. cit., p. 60.
[4] Leadam, I. S., *The Security of Copyholders*, E.H.R., Vol. 8. Cf. Transactions Royal Historical Society, New Series, Vol. 6.
[5] Peyton, S. S., Review of *Court Rolls of Clitheroe*, translated by Farrer, W., E.H.R., Vol. 22, p. 129.
[6] Savine, A., *Bondmen Under the Tudors*, Trans. R.H.S., New Series, Vol. 10.

before on these survivors of what had been 'the most numerous class of the nation', who were now 'few and isolated, an undesirable reminder of the past'.

The processes by which the mass of the manorial population became emancipated are as obscure as the causes for the minority's continued servitude. In strict law manumission was the only door to freedom, but the number of recorded manumissions is too scanty to account for the emancipation of a class.[1] Flight was fairly common in the troubled fourteenth century, and on some manors doubtless caused a large displacement of the former villein population,[2] while a villein was no villein save to his own lord. This may account for the greater survival of unfreedom on upland manors remote from riverine arteries of communication and from the towns which might receive escaping bondmen. In the fifteenth century, however, the notices in court rolls of fugitives decrease, and in any case flight, like manumission, could only have freed occasional persons. It is more probable that as with the services so with the personal disabilities of bondage, in most cases they simply ceased to be exacted, as seignorial discipline relaxed, 'because the growth of a commercial organization of agriculture made its maintenance both useless and unprofitable.'[3]

SHORT BIBLIOGRAPHY

SECTION I

P. Vinogradoff, *The Growth of the Manor.*
English Society in the Eleventh Century.
F. W. Maitland, *Domesday Book and Beyond.*
F. Seebohm, *The English Village Community.*
C. S. and C. S. Orwin, *The Open Fields.*
H. L. Gray, *English Field Systems.*

SECTION II (a)

P. Vinogradoff, *Villeinage in England.*
Survey of the Honour of Denbigh, 1334.
H. L. Gray, *English Field Systems.*
D. C. Douglas, *The Social and Economic Structure of Mediæval East Anglia.*
F. M. Stenton, *Types of Manorial Structure in the Northern Danelaw.*
Documents Illustrative of Social and Economic Conditions in the Danelaw.
E. A. Kosminsky, *Studies in the Agrarian History of England in the Thirteenth Century.*

[1] Cheyney, E. P. *Disappearance of English Serfdom*, E.H.R., Vol. 15.
[2] As at Forncett, cf. Davenport, op. cit., p. 140.
[3] Tawney, R. H., op. cit., p. 46.

N. Neilson, *A Terrier of Fleet, Lincolnshire.*
Cartulary and Terrier of the Priory of Bilsington, Kent.
Economic Conditions on the Manors of Ramsey Abbey.
Customary Rents.
Lord Ernle (R. E. Prothero), *British Farming Past and Present.*
N. Hone, *The Manor and Manorial Records.*
N. S. B. Gras, *The Evolution of the English Corn-market.*
The Economic and Social History of an English Village.
Sir H. Hall, *The Pipe Roll of the Bishopric of Winchester 1208–9.*
G. C. Homans, *English Villagers in the Thirteenth Century.*
H. S. Bennett, *Life on the English Manor.*
E. Miller, *The Abbey and Bishopric of Ely.*
R. A. C. Smith, *Canterbury Cathedral Priory.*
Collected Papers.
F. M. Page. *The Estates of Crowland Abbey.*

SECTION II (*b*)

F. W. Maitland, *Select Pleas in Manorial and other Seignorial Courts.*
F. W. Maitland and W. P. Baildon, *The Court Baron.*
F. Pollock and F. W. Maitland, *History of English Law.*
F. J. C. Hearnshaw, *Leet Jurisdiction in England.*
W. A. Morris, *The Frankpledge System.*

SECTION III

A. E. Levett, *The Black Death on the Estates of the See of Winchester.*
B. H. Putnam, *The Enforcement of the Statutes of Labourers, 1349–1359.*
T. W. Page, *The End of Villeinage in England.*
F. G. Davenport, *The Economic Development of a Norfolk Manor.*
C. Petit-Dutaillis, *Studies and Notes Supplementary to Stubbs' Constitutional History,* Vol. II ('Causes and general characteristics of the rising of 1381').
A. Réville, *Le Soulèvement des Travailleurs d'Angleterre en 1381.*
R. H. Tawney, *The Agrarian Problem in the Sixteenth Century.*
P. Vinogradoff, *Collected Papers,* Vol. I.
A. E. Levett, *Studies in Manorial History.*
R. H. Hilton, *The Economic Development of some Leicestershire Estates in the Fourteenth and Fifteenth Centuries.*
G. Holmes, *The Estates of the English Nobility in the Fourteenth Century.*

ROSE GRAHAM

An Essay on
English Monasteries

IN an essay on so vast a subject as English monasteries, it is only
possible to write upon certain aspects of their history within a fixed
period. An attempt has been made in the following pages to throw
some light on the work of monks and Regular Canons as historians
and as builders, to define the differences in their architecture and
art, and to comment on the way in which they managed their
revenues, mainly from 1066 to the middle of the fourteenth century.

THE ORIGINS OF THE MONASTIC ORDERS

At the time of the Norman Conquest the English monasteries
were served by monks who professed to keep the Rule of St.
Benedict, but in the opinion of William of Malmesbury and other
historians, zeal for religion and learning had grown cold many
years before. In his famous Rule 'to institute a school of the service
of God' for the monks of Monte Cassino, halfway between Rome
and Naples, St. Benedict of Nursia (*ob.* 543) wrote that 'the whole
observance of perfection' was not contained therein, it was 'a little
Rule written for beginners.' He introduced the vow of stability
by which the monk bound himself for life to the monastery in which
he made his profession. He dealt with the spiritual life of the monk,
the *Opus Dei* or the daily services of the Church, the organization

51

of the monastery, the duties of the abbot and other officers, the reception of novices and guests. He left the abbot a large discretion in regard to the diet and dress of the monks, the training of the novices, the number and duties of the officers. Wherever the Rule was adopted, a body of customs concerning liturgical observance and the details of the daily life and administration was gradually drawn up to supplement it. Although St. Benedict insisted on the absolute renunciation of personal property, since no monk might possess anything of his own, he assumed that monasteries must hold property as communities. He had no intention of founding an order, i.e., a number of monasteries knit together by a system of government. A Benedictine monastery was an independent unit. The successful creation of a monastic order was the work of the first abbots of Cluny, who drew their inspiration from an earlier reformer, St. Benedict of Aniane (*ob*. 823).

In 910, William, Duke of Aquitaine founded a monastery at Cluny in Burgundy, for monks who should live a regular life according to the Rule of St. Benedict. In his charter the duke set forth his ideal for the community. 'With a full heart and mind the monks shall build an exceeding pleasant place, so far as they can and know how. We will also, that in our time and those of our successors, works of mercy shall be shown daily to the poor and needy, to travellers and pilgrims, so far as the opportunity and ability of the place shall allow.' The monks of Cluny observed the customs which St. Benedict of Aniane had instituted and gradually made many additions to them. Early in the second half of the eleventh century a monk named Bernard wrote a most complete and detailed account of everyday life in the monastery.

The ideal of the Order of Cluny was the right use of wealth in the service of God, and of man, an ideal indeed of individual Benedictine monasteries so far back as we have records to the seventh century. The founder of Cluny exempted the monastery from the control of all earthly powers and placed it under the protection, not the sovereignty of the Papal See. In the next two centuries Cluny was the centre of a great reform. Many monasteries, not only in France, but in other lands, were founded and made subject to Cluny, and were so closely dependent on the mother house that even their heads were nominated by the abbot of Cluny. Other Benedictine monasteries did not become members of the Order of Cluny, but they adopted Cluniac customs. These were introduced into the monasteries of Normandy by William of Dijon and his followers in the earlier years of the eleventh century.

In the reigns of King Edgar and his sons, the English monasteries came indirectly under the influence of Cluny through the monastery of Fleury-sur-Loire which had been reformed by Odo of Cluny about 930. However, the brief but brilliant revival associated with the names of St. Dunstan, St. Ethelwold and St. Oswald, was checked, and from the time of the fresh Danish invasions the impetus of reform decreased.

Under the influence of Lanfranc and the Norman abbots, who came to rule over the English monasteries, customs closely related to those of Cluny were adopted in many places. There was a strong monastic revival, and many new houses were founded by William the Conqueror and the Norman barons, among them Battle, Malvern, Shrewsbury, and St. John's, Colchester.

William the Conqueror offered Abbot Hugh of Cluny a large sum of money if he would give him twelve monks to be abbots in England, but the abbot refused and said his monks were not for sale. William de Warenne who had come from Normandy with William the Conqueror to England was more successful. After a visit to Cluny with his wife Gundreda they requested that monks might be sent to the monastery which they intended to found at Lewes, and in 1077 four monks arrived from Cluny to serve a little stone church in the valley below Lewes castle. At the request of other Norman lords Cluniac monks from the great priory of La Charité-sur-Loire came to Wenlock in Shropshire and St. Andrew's outside Northampton. In 1082 a citizen of London, Alwin Child took the first steps towards founding Bermondsey priory.

In the twelfth century monasteries were founded for several new orders. The first in point of time was that of the Augustinian Canons. The earliest house in England was the priory of St. Julian and St. Botulph at Colchester, which became a monastery of Augustinian Canons between 1093 and 1099. Unlike other orders the Augustinian Canons had no one great founder, and the early history of Regular Canons is an obscure and difficult subject. Attempts were made in the Frankish empire, in the eighth and ninth centuries, to induce the clergy who served the greater churches to live a common life, and a rule was drawn up for them by Chrode-gang, Bishop of Metz (*ob.* 766). There was a fresh movement in the middle of the eleventh century, which spread gradually in Italy, France, England and Germany. Bishop Frere has pointed out that there were two lines of development.[1] In the greater churches bodies of clergy, or of secular canons, sought a reform which would bring them under corporate discipline; they adopted a rule and drew up customs, and obtained a confirmation of these from pope, king or bishop. Secondly, great landowners sometimes gave the churches

---

[1] *Fasciculus J. W. Clark dicatus*, pp. 186–216.

of their estates to be served by a body of Regular Canons whom they established at a central church. There is some doubt as to the time in the eleventh century when houses of Regular Canons adopted the Rule of St. Augustine, but it is clear that they were already widely spread. The Rule of St. Augustine was adapted for men from a letter written by him to a convent of nuns in his diocese of Hippo in North Africa. It was very brief, consisting only of seven short chapters, and touches the spirit of monastic life rather than its details, but it served the Regular Canons as a principle of unity and gave them a status comparable with that of the sons of St. Benedict. The customs which were compiled in famous houses to supplement the Rule of St. Augustine were gradually adopted in others, in which they were varied as necessity arose. It is not easy to draw a sharp distinction between Regular Canons and monks, because the organization of community life was already accomplished by the Benedictines and Cluniacs before the Regular Canons of St. Augustine came into existence. One distinction was that the canons became priests, whereas it was not until 1311 that the obligation to take priest's orders was imposed on all monks. Augustinian houses of both the types of development noted by Bishop Frere were founded in England in the twelfth century, but out of a total of 254 over 200 were purely conventual; although a number of houses were endowed by founders with groups of neighbouring churches, in the hope that these would be served by the canons, before the reign of Henry I was over Regular Canons were no longer supposed, even in theory, to serve the churches handed over to them. Almost all the English houses of Augustinian Canons were independent units like Benedictine monasteries. A few English houses belonged to the small Order of Arrouaise in Picardy, and a few others to the Order of St. Victor of Paris.

In 1098 a small monastery was founded at Cîteaux in Burgundy. It became the mother house of an Order which spread so rapidly that at the end of fifty-four years there were 330 houses scattered over France, Germany, Italy, Spain and England. The first monks who settled at Cîteaux left the Benedictine monastery of Molesme in the company of its abbot, Robert, to live strictly according to the Rule of St. Benedict. They contrasted the customs of other monasteries with the Rule and resolved to keep it in the letter without the snare of using discretion, and to abandon everything which they did not find either in the Rule or in the life of St. Benedict. The new community had a hard struggle for existence, and at first failed to attract men; but in 1112 St. Bernard, then a very young man, arrived with thirty companions who wished to join them, and the success of the order was assured. Within a few years several daughter-houses were founded. Robert of Torigny, a monk of the Benedictine monastery of Mont St. Michel observed that many noble rich and learned men were attracted to the Cistercian Order by its peculiar novelty. William of Malmesbury, himself a Benedictine monk of that monastery, wrote that the Cistercian way of life was the surest road to heaven.

Among the first monks of Cîteaux was Stephen Harding, an Englishman, who became abbot in 1109. Shortly afterwards a book of customs, known as the *Liber Usuum* was compiled, and the famous constitution of the order, the Carta Caritatis, was drawn up to maintain absolute uniformity in all the houses and confirmed by Pope Calixtus II in 1119. A system of mutual visitation was devised, and the abbots of all the houses were bound to assemble at the yearly general chapter at Cîteaux at which, as need arose, other statutes were passed. Each Cistercian house elected its abbot and recruited its own novices. The distinctive features of the Order were insistence on manual labour and simplicity in all the details of life, i.e., dress, food, beds, building, the worship of God and the use of ornaments for the services. The monasteries were founded on sites remote from the dwellings of men, and their land was farmed by lay brothers who lived in granges. The first foundation of the Cistercians in England was at Waverley, in Surrey, in 1128, Rievaulx followed in 1131, Fountains in 1132, and twenty years later there were more than fifty houses; of these thirteen originally belonged to the austere Order of Savigny, which was founded in Normandy by Vitalis of Mortain about 1105, and incorporated into the Cistercian Order in 1147.

A decree of the Lateran Council of 1215 enforced the holding of general chapters every three years by other orders, according to provinces or kingdoms, and also a system of internal visitation. In obedience to this decree, the Benedictines and Augustinian Canons of the southern and northern provinces of Canterbury and York began to hold triennial chapters, and to appoint visitors among themselves.

The Premonstratensian Order of Regular Canons was founded by St. Norbert in 1121. Having failed to induce the canons of Xanten to lead a strict life, he withdrew from them, and with the papal sanction he became a wandering preacher in France and Flanders. At the Council of Rheims in 1119 he met Bartholomew, Bishop of Laon, and at last consented to stay in his diocese. He chose a desolate valley in the forest of Coucy, about two miles from Laon, which received the name of Prémontré, and promised that if God should give him companions he would settle there. Meanwhile he again went forth to preach. At Easter he had thirteen followers, who lived in huts round a chapel of St. John the Baptist at Prémontré; at Christmas there were nearly forty clerks and many laymen. St. Norbert was perplexed by much conflicting advice from bishops and abbots: some suggested that the community should live as anchorites, others that they should follow the Cistercian way of life. He sent for a copy of the Rule of St. Augustine, and approved of it so strongly that all agreed to adopt it. He added many precepts for a strict life. Within a few years several monasteries were founded, and in 1125 Honorius III confirmed the statutes and possessions of the order. In 1126 Norbert became Archbishop of Magdeburg. Not long afterwards the abbots of the different houses met together, and to attain outward uniformity in all things they drew up a Book of Customs. They borrowed the provision for a yearly general chapter and the arrangements concerning the daily life and the officers of the monastery almost verbatim from the Cistercian customs and statutes. But they adopted a different system of visitation. The order was divided into provinces, and two abbots were appointed each year as circators, to visit all the houses in their province and to report to the general chapter. The first English monastery of the order was founded at Newhouse, in Lincolnshire, in 1143, and in all there were thirty-four houses, of which two were for women.

The one purely English order was founded by St. Gilbert of Sempringham in 1131. It has a peculiar interest, because he revived the institution of the double monastery, which was common in England in the seventh century. It arose out of the practical needs of a small number of women, for whom St. Gilbert founded a nunnery against the north wall of the parish church of Sempringham, which he served as rector. First, he added lay sisters for household service, and then lay brothers to work on the land, giving to all a rule of life. The little community grew in numbers, and in 1139 St. Gilbert accepted land from Gilbert of Ghent, his feudal lord. Sempringham Priory with its double church, cloisters, and other buildings, was erected on the new site, close to the parish church, and St. Gilbert was offered lands elsewhere for new houses. In 1147 he set out with some of his Cistercian friends for the general chapter of Cîteaux, to ask if the order would take over the charge of his foundations. But his request was refused, and Eugenius III laid upon him the care of his order. St. Bernard invited him to Clairvaux, and there helped him to draw up the Institutes of Sempringham, after a study of the rules and customs of divers churches and monasteries. It was most probably in imitation of the double Order of Fontevrault, founded fifty years earlier by Robert of Arbrissel, that St. Gilbert enrolled men in holy orders as canons, to serve the whole community as priests and to help him in the work of administration. St. Gilbert gave the Rule of St. Benedict to his nuns, but, like St. Norbert, he chose the Rule of St. Augustine for his canons. He supplemented both by his provision for a very strict observance of monastic life for the whole community. These he adapted from the Cistercian Charter of Charity, Book of Uses and Institutes, more especially with regard to the lay brothers and the yearly general chapter. Other provisions were borrowed from the Rule of Fontevrault, and from the customs of both Augustinian and Premonstratensian canons. Of the twenty-six houses of the Order of Sempringham, eleven were double; but most of those founded after the death of St. Gilbert were for men only.

Another austere order was founded by a young canon of Rheims who set out with six companions in search of a life of solitude, and the bishop of Grenoble gave them a home among the mountains near his cathedral city. There in 1084 they founded the monastery of La Chartreuse which gave its name to the Carthusian Order. The monks were isolated from the world as well as from one another, and lived in two-roomed houses, each with a little garden, built around the great cloister. There they ate, slept, said their services and worked, except on Sundays, and a certain number of feast days, when they went to the great church for all services, listened to a sermon in the chapter-house, took a common meal in the refectory, and conversed with their fellows afterwards. They kept the Rule of St. Benedict. The written Customs of the Carthusians were compiled under Guigo, prior of the Grande Chartreuse, who died in 1137. The number prescribed for each monastery was thirteen monks and sixteen lay brothers; the latter were responsible for the secular business of the house and lived apart from the monks. The austere life of silence did not attract men, and the Order spread slowly. The first English Charterhouse was founded at Witham in Somerset, about 1173, the second a few miles away at Hinton in 1232. There were no more until the middle of the fourteenth century, when the utter sincerity of their religious life made a strong appeal, and seven Charterhouses were founded in seventy years, between 1343 and 1414, among them those in London, Hull and Coventry, for the idea of life in a solitude was giving place to the enclosed life.

In the wars between England and France from 1295 until 1413 some monasteries were designated as alien priories, because their priors and sometimes the monks also, were nominated by the heads of the French mother houses, and because they sent money abroad to the mother houses, either a fixed annual due called an *apport* in recognition of subjection, or much larger sums when the priories were only manors in which two or three monks were sent to live and collect revenues from the English properties for the mother house. The alien priories included the Cluniac houses, the Benedictine priories dependent on monasteries in Normandy and Anjou, the few priories of the Orders of Tiron and Grandmont. The Cistercian, Premonstratensian and Carthusian monasteries were not reckoned as alien priories. Owing to the financial difficulties of the alien priories in the Hundred Years' War, and to the fact that many of the monks in the conventual priories were English, the more important conventual priories bought charters of denization from the Crown and were thus released from excessive taxation and the disabilities of aliens. The majority of the alien priories were taken into the King's hands in 1414, and most of them were subsequently granted away for the endowment of colleges and schools.

HISTORICAL WRITINGS AND RECORDS OF ENGLISH MONKS

The spirit of learning followed closely in the wake of the revivals of monasticism, and William of Malmesbury wrote that without the study of letters other reforms were vain. Throughout a great part of the Middle Ages in England, that is to say until the end of the thirteenth century, the Benedictine monks and Augustinian Canons were the chief historians. It is almost impossible to realize what limits would be set to our knowledge of English history if the chronicles had perished at the dissolution of the monasteries. Moreover, it would be infinitely more difficult to interpret the vast official collections in the Public Record Office, such as the Pipe, Charter, Patent, Close Rolls, and other documents without the narratives and comments of contemporary writers. Yet no systematic effort was made to save the books in the monastic libraries.[1] John Leland, a royal chaplain and the keeper of the king's library, was made the king's antiquary in 1533, and in the same year he was granted a commission to make a search for English antiquities in the libraries of all cathedrals, abbeys, priories and colleges, and all places where records, writings, and secrets of antiquity were deposited. For six or seven years he travelled on his quest throughout the length and breadth of England. The spoiling of the libraries greatly distressed him, and on July 16th, 1536, he appealed to Cromwell to extend his commission so that he might collect manuscripts for the king's library. 'It would be a great profit to students and honour to this realm,' he wrote, 'whereas now the Germans, perceiving our desidiousness and negligence, do

[1] M. R. James, *Ancient Libraries of Canterbury and Dover*, pp. lxxxi, lxxxii.

daily send young scholars hither that spoileth them and cutteth them out of their own libraries, returning home and putting them abroad as monuments of their own country.' In 1537 Leland sent some valuable manuscripts to London, of which some came from St. Augustine's, Canterbury. But usually the manuscripts were dispersed and sold for what they would fetch, and it is almost entirely owing to the zeal of private collectors like Archbishop Parker and Sir Robert Cotton that so many manuscripts, once in monastic libraries, are now found in the British Museum, the Public Record Office, the Lambeth Library, the Bodleian Library, Cambridge University Library, the libraries of the Oxford and Cambridge Colleges, and also in private collections.

One of the greatest of English medieval historians was Bede (672–734) who spent his life in the Northumbrian monasteries of Jarrow and Monkwearmouth. In the *Ecclesiastical History of the English People*, he told the story of the spread of Christianity in England, of the growth of the Church, and of life in the monasteries, with a singular charm of simplicity and truthfulness. 'Thus much . . .' he wrote in his preface, 'I . . . have, with the Lord's help, composed, so far as I could gather it either from ancient documents, or from the traditions of the elders, or from my own knowledge,'[1] The *Ecclesiastical History* was not, as Bishop Stubbs has noted, the earliest historical work in England, 'the life of Wilfrid, by Eddius takes precedence in date, but it is the basis of all that follow. No one dreamed of superseding or improving upon it; with a wonderful rapidity it circulated throughout western Christendom, and drew for a time the eyes of the learned world on the monasteries of Deira. The schools of York were the result of the general learned movement originated by Bede, and the schools of York produced Alcuin.'[2]

The Saxon Chronicle was begun in the cathedral monastery of the royal city of Winchester, under Alfred's care and supervision, and copies were sent to other monasteries. Up to 892 it was compiled from earlier materials, among them from annals written at Canterbury and in Northumbria, which no longer exist. For the reigns of Alfred and Edward the Elder it is 'a national and contemporary record of the finest and most authentic kind.'[3]

Asser, a monk of St. David's, and afterwards Bishop of Sherborne, wrote the first biography of a layman, the famous life' of King Alfred. The most recent editor, Mr. W. H. Stevenson, writes: 'Probably no work of similar extent has contributed so much to English history. At an early period it was transcribed almost entirely

---

[1] *Historia Ecclesiastica*, ed. C. Plummer, I, p. ix.
[2] *Chronica Rogeri de Hovedene*, Rolls Series, I, pp. ix, x.
[3] *Two of the Saxon Chronicles*, ed. C. Plummer, II, pp. civ, cv.

into the continuous chronicles of Florence of Worcester and Simeon of Durham, and by their means it descended to Roger of Hoveden and the St. Albans school of historians.'

The monastic revival in the tenth century had a strong intellectual influence. Some of the contemporary lives of the great churchmen, e.g., that of Oswald, Bishop of Worcester and Archbishop of York, which was written by a monk of Ramsey between 995 and 1005, are valuable authorities for the history of the reigns of King Edgar and his sons. The Saxon Chronicle was continued at Winchester, Abingdon, Peterborough and elsewhere.

The Norman Conquest gave a great impetus to the study of history.[1] The cultured Norman abbots and monks and their English brethren wished to have some account of the history of their monasteries, the lives of their special saints and benefactors, and a record of their possessions and privileges. While a monk at Ely, the Norman Goscelin wrote the life of St. Etheldreda, at Ramsey that of St. Ivo, and afterwards, at Canterbury, the lives of St. Augustine and his first six successors. Hermann of Bury wrote the miracles of St. Edmund at the request of Abbot Baldwin. Folcard, Abbot of Thorney, wrote the lives of St. Adulf, St. Botulf and St. John of Beverley. At Canterbury an Englishman, Osbern the precentor, wrote the lives of St. Dunstan and St. Elphege at Lanfranc's request. His successor and fellow countryman, Eadmer, added another life of St. Dunstan and lives of St. Odo, St. Wilfrid and St. Oswald.

The Normans continued the practice of chronicling monastic and national events, but they used the Latin language; at Peterborough alone, after 1075 and only until 1154, the chronicle was continued in Saxon. In the twelfth century most of the Benedictine monasteries appear to have kept chronicles. The provenance of some of these is difficult to trace, for the chronicle of one monastery was incorporated into that of another, without any acknowledgement, and interpolations were freely made. Abbots showed much zeal in increasing their libraries; at St. Albans, Abbot Paul (1077–93) assigned the tithes of Hatfield and Redbourn for the writing of books, and built a scriptorium or writing-room in which hired scribes copied the manuscripts lent by Lanfranc. Manuscripts were freely lent from one monastery to another; William of Malmesbury visited both Canterbury and Bury St. Edmunds on literary errands, and he seems to have presented an autograph copy of his own work, the *Gesta Pontificum*, to Bury.[2] The monastic chroniclers suffered from no lack of books. For local events their works are first-hand authorities of great value, and for national history they

1 Graham, *English Ecclesiastical Studies*, pp. 177–82.
1 R. James, *The Abbey of St. Edmund at Bury*, p. 7.

are faithful reproductions of independent authorities. Some chroniclers, like Florence of Worcester, were chiefly concerned with national history; others again, like Gervase of Canterbury and the chroniclers of Ramsey and Abingdon, found their chief sources in their own archives, and used general history only as a setting for local events.

Most of the ecclesiastical biographies were written in the Benedictine monasteries. Milo Crispin, a monk of Westminster, wrote the life of Lanfranc; Eadmer that of Anselm; Coleman, a monk of Worcester, a Saxon life of Wulfstan, from which William of Malmesbury drew his materials. Several of the Canterbury monks contributed lives of Thomas, their murdered Archbishop.

At Bury St. Edmunds, Jocelin revealed the inner life of the monastery in a book which Mr. J. R. Green declared to be worth a thousand chronicles. Jocelin wrote what he had seen and heard from the time when he became a monk during the last years of Abbot Hugh (ob. 1180) until 1203, when he breaks off abruptly, eight years before the death of Abbot Samson. In his simple and amusing record he tells first how, under the rule of Abbot Hugh, worldly affairs were badly managed and debts were recklessly piled up, while any who attempted to oppose the abbot were punished. Next follows the story of Samson's election and of the previous discussions among the monks of the manner of man whom they would like to rule over them, whether it were not better to choose a king log, whether he should be a man of learning or a good manager. Within four months Jocelin became Abbot Samson's chaplain, and for six years he was constantly with him by day and by night. Samson showed great administrative capacity, paid off the debts, and increased the revenues, yet with all his admiration for him Jocelin shows in many a vivid touch how Samson bore down all opposition within the monastery and without.

The monks had a high conception of the value of their historical studies. Eadmer wrote the story of the struggles of Anselm with William II and Henry I, to afford precedents for future generations. William of Malmesbury deemed it shameful to be ignorant of the history of England, and showed a due appreciation of the connection between literature and politics; the Augustinian canon, William of Newburgh, wrote to increase knowledge, and to warn posterity by the lessons of history. Many of the canons of modern historical teaching are duly set forth in their pages. They carefully weighed their authorities. Internal evidence proved the veracity of Gildas and Bede to William of Newburgh, while a skilful analysis of the contents of the *Historia Britonum*, a comparison with other authorities, and an appeal to reason, led him to reject Geoffrey of

Monmouth. In writing of contemporary events he showed equal care and judgment in sifting evidence. He urged that style was no criterion of historical accuracy, for Gildas wrote execrably and Geoffrey of Monmouth with marvellous fascination. William of Malmesbury justified his life of St. Dunstan on the ground that the older writers lacked grace, and therefore remained unread, while Osbern, on the other hand, had used rhetoric to cover his lack of truth. Nevertheless, the graceful style of Eadmer, the forcible simplicity of William of Malmesbury, and the neatly finished periods of William of New-burgh were admirable models.

The greatest of English mediæval historians was Matthew Paris, a monk of St. Albans from 1217 to 1259, who is described in the fourteenth-century book of benefactors of St. Albans as an incom-parable chronographer and a painter of supreme excellence. His chief work was the *Chronica Majora*, which fills seven volumes of the Rolls Series. In the earlier portion he revised a compilation from the creation to 1188 of which the portion from 1154–89 was the work of Abbot John of Cell (1195–1214), and following upon it the chronicle of the monk, Roger of Wendover, who died in 1235.[1] From that year until his death in 1259, the chronicle was his own original work. He had correspondents in many lands, he sought every opportunity of gathering fresh information from the many distinguished visitors who came to St. Albans, and was him-self an eye-witness of much that he describes. He was a fearless critic and a vivid writer. Dr. Jessopp has written a charming sketch of Brother Matthew, in an essay entitled *St. Albans and her Historian*,[2] and the *Chronica Majora* have been translated into English by Dr. Giles. His work contains the full texts of papal bulls, royal letters and many other documents. The chief merit of other monastic writers of the thirteenth century is that they recognized the value of documents, and have preserved them for us by copying them into their work. The *Annals of Burton*, from 1211 to 1263, consist mainly of a collection of documents connected by short notices of events concerning Burton and the kingdom; some of the documents are also found in Matthew Paris, but the greater part of them only survive in these Annals. In editing the manuscript for the Rolls Series, Dr. Luard recognized it to be one of the most valuable collections of materials for the time that we possess. The *Historia Anglicana* of Bartholomew Cotton, a monk of Norwich from 1291 to 1298, also contains an important series of documents. Indeed, with the conspicuous exception of St. Albans, which had a succession of chroniclers of very inferior merit until 1461, and of a few others

---

[1] C. Jenkins, *The Monastic Chronicler*, pp. 64, 77–90.
[2] There is also a fuller biography by R. Vaughan, *Matthew Paris* (1958).

of less value, the chief contribution of the monasteries to history in the later centuries was the preservation of documents for the use of future historians.

The monks took a keen interest in the custody of their records. Their claims to their possessions, rights and privileges were often called in question. Charters and deeds were needed as evidence in lawsuits, bishops insisted on the production of evidences by which the monks held parish churches, or claimed exemption from their visitation. A register at Canterbury contains a catalogue of the principal muniments and of the places in which they were kept stored in chests, hampers, lettered bundles and sacks. They were examined and endorsed in the twelfth century, and again in the thirteenth century. A great number of original charters and deeds are found in the British Museum, the Record Office, and other public and private collections. Another most important class of records consists of the monastic cartularies and registers, in which were entered papal bulls, royal and other charters, accounts, rentals, and surveys of their estates, leases, records of judicial proceedings, injunctions issued at papal and episcopal visitations, the procedure at the election of abbots, and agreements between abbots and their convents. The Reports of the Historical Manuscripts Commission on the muniments now in the custody of the Dean and Chapter of Canterbury, give some idea of the varied contents of monastic archives.

Chroniclers noted the destruction of charters in disastrous fires in which the church and monastic buildings were burnt. Many monastic charters are now recognized to be spurious, but they often contain facts that are substantially correct. The evidence of Domesday Book proves that the monks of Battle Abbey possessed the lands which subsequently they claimed to hold by a spurious charter of William the Conqueror, which was fabricated at Battle in the later years of Stephen's reign for use in lawsuits. On the chancery rolls there are many monastic charters of confirmation reciting spurious charters which the king had inspected, and which he confirmed and strengthened by his own authority. Professor Tout has explained that if there had never been an original or if it was lost or destroyed by fire, the applicant for the charter made a false original, and cut the seal off another document, but he was often betrayed by the fact that he was unaware that such documents had particular forms and technicalities in different periods.[1]

The monks of Crowland had a strong motive for the forgeries of their charters. For two hundred and fifty years the abbot and convent had been dragged at intervals into a series of costly lawsuits in

[1] *Medieval Forgers and Forgeries*, pp. 12–14.

defence of their rights in the marsh of Crowland.[1] In 1413 there was another most serious case of trespass, and the prior went to London to prosecute the men of Spalding and others, taking with him the charters of Ethelbald, Edred and Edgar. It is significant that they were then produced for the first time as evidence in a lawsuit. The charters of Ethelbald and Edred were inspected and confirmed in 1393, and again in 1399, but they had not been officially recognized by any previous kings. The conclusion is that these and other Saxon charters were forged soon after the middle of the fourteenth century. The writers showed ignorance of the language of an old English diploma and of the history of the rights which were claimed, but their ignorance was shared by all who afterwards accepted them. About the same time, before 1360, a history of Crowland was compiled and ascribed, with a stroke of genius, to Ingulf, the first Norman abbot. The object of the writer seems to have been to provide a setting for the Saxon charters and a defence of the rights of the monastery. With vivid imagination and keen insight he wrote a delightful story, weaving into it traditions which at that time may well have gained acceptance as history among the monks of Crowland. Until the first quarter of the nineteenth century was passed, it was accepted as a genuine and valuable chronicle, but later scholarship has rejected it.

BUILDING ACTIVITY

The vast amount of building which was undertaken in the Middle Ages is apparent to the student who travels in England with open eyes. One of the most conspicuous results of the Norman Conquest was the speed with which new buildings were begun and completed. Before the end of the eleventh century every one of the Saxon cathedrals was being destroyed to make way for rebuilding on a larger scale. Lanfranc rebuilt the cathedral church of Canterbury in seven years, yet before twenty years had elapsed the east end was pulled down, the new choir of far greater splendour was begun by Prior Ernulf (1096–1107) and completed by Prior Conrad (1108–26). In 1079 Walkelin, Bishop of Winchester, began to rebuild the cathedral from the foundation, and it is said to have been completed in 1093. In 1093 the foundation stone was laid of the new cathedral church at Durham. The Bishop, William of St. Carileph, had been accumulating money, and before his death, in 1096, he appears to have completed the work from the east end of the choir as far as the first bay of the nave, and possibly the outside wall throughout

[1] V. C. H., *Lincoln*, II, p. 113.

its whole extent.[1] Three years elapsed before the election of Ralph Flambard, and during that time the monks built the west side of the transept, and vaulted the north transept. It has been suggested that the smaller funds at their disposal account for the plainer character of their work. Flambard completed the nave as far as the vaulting, and the progress of the work then depended on the altar offerings, and on burial fees received by the sacrist. On his death the monks completed the vaulting of the nave.

Similar activity was shown in the greater abbeys. At St. Albans Abbot Paul rebuilt the church in eleven years, from 1077 to 1088. At Gloucester the foundation stone was laid in 1089, and the church was dedicated in 1100. So much of it was then built as would be used for the monks' services, probably the presbytery, choir and transepts, and one or two bays of the nave, and the other parts would be in various stages of erection. At Bury St. Edmunds, Abbot Baldwin and his sacrists built the choir as far as the two piers east of the central tower, the crypt with twenty-four pillars, and laid the foundations of the whole of the rest of the church, and raised the walls to some height.

The great number of new monastic foundations added to the vast amount of building. As the result of a rough calculation, it has been estimated that out of a total of 697 dated foundations, 247 were built before the reign of Stephen, 115 during the nineteen turbulent years of his reign, and 113 during the thirty-five years of Henry II's reign.[2] Of this total 68 were in Yorkshire and 20 were founded in the reign of Stephen, 50 were in Lincolnshire, and 19 were founded in that reign. Maps in *Medieval England*[3] show how thickly some counties were studded with monasteries. In commenting on 'the true proportion of all this activity in architecture to the social life of the time,' Professor E. S. Prior noted that the population of all England and Wales in the twelfth century was under two millions. 'Yet in that century between four and five hundred large collegiate and monastic buildings were erected, and in nearly every parish in England there is evidence of a twelfth-century rebuilding of the church.'[4]

The ways and means by which building went on is a very interesting question. The few instances in which actual figures of costs can be given are very precious. It is extremely difficult to estimate

---

[1] *Trans. Architect and Archæol. Soc., Durham and Northumberland*, 1869–75, pp. 175–88.

[2] *Chronicles of Stephen, Henry II, Richard I*, Ed. R. Howlett, Rolls Series, I, p. xiii.

[3] Ed. H. W. C. Davis, pp. 377–9; cf. also the Ordnance Survey *Map of Monastic Britain* (2 sheets, 1954–55).

[4] *Gothic Art in England*, p. 41.

the exact value of these in money at the present time, and economists have arrived at varying conclusions. Dr. Coulton has suggested that between 1300 and 1348 sums of money should be multiplied by forty to arrive at the value in 1931 before Great Britain went off the gold standard.[1]

In the monastic cathedrals the bishops often shouldered a great part of the burden of building the great church. This was not an obligation, but a matter of arrangement. The monastic cathedral is almost peculiar to England. Its origin and later history have been written by Bishop Stubbs. 'The missionary bishop, himself a monk, accompanied by a staff of priests who were also monks, settled in the chief city of a kingdom or province. He built his church, his staff of missionary monks became the clergy of that church; the church itself was called a monastery.' Later sees were served by secular clerks who afterwards received the name of canons. During the period covered in this essay the seven cathedrals of Canterbury, Rochester, Winchester, Worcester, Norwich, Ely and Durham were served by Benedictine monks, but five of them were served by secular canons during some portion of their history before the Norman Conquest, and the bishoprics of Norwich and Ely were not created until after that date. The cathedral church of Carlisle was served by Augustinian Canons. In these cathedral monasteries the bishop nominally filled the place of abbot, but after the division of the estates of the bishop from those of the prior and convent soon after the Norman Conquest, the prior in many respects filled the place of an abbot in another monastery. Nevertheless the bishop retained certain rights which sometimes led to conflicts between him and his monastic chapter.

In 1393 William of Wykeham held a visitation at Winchester as the fabric of the cathedral was greatly out of repair, and the estates allotted to it were insufficient.[2] The bishop enjoined that the prior should contribute £100 for the next seven years and the sub-prior and convent 100 marks out of their common fund for the same time. Not long afterwards he relieved them of the charge and undertook to bear the cost himself. The prior and convent acquitted the bishop of all obligation, and recognized that he acted from his mere liberality and zeal for the honour of God. For their part they gave the bishop free leave to dig and carry away chalk and sand from any of their lands . . . and they allowed the whole materials of the old building to be used for the new, i.e., stones, lead, ironwork, timber, glass, etc., and agreed to provide the scaffolding. This work of transforming the nave from a Norman building into Perpendicular had

[1] Cf. below, pp. 208–222.
[2] *Proceedings of Archæol. Institute, Winchester,* 1845, pp. 55–9.

been undertaken by Wykeham's predecessor, Bishop Edingdon (1346–66). Wykeham's work on it was begun in 1394, and was not complete when he made his will, dated July 24th, 1403, fifteen months before his death. He ordered his executors to continue the work and to find 2,500 marks if so much were needed, and he gave a further sum of 500 marks towards the glazing of the windows.

The six eastern bays of the choir at Ely were built between 1244 and 1251 at a cost of £5,040 18s. 7d.; the greater part of it was found by the bishop, Hugh of Northwold, but small sums were contributed by the prior and convent and other persons. After the fall of the central tower in 1322, the three western bays of the choir were rebuilt at a cost of £2,034 12s. 8¾d., which was defrayed by Bishop Hotham. The new tower, known as the octagon, was completed in 1342 at a cost of £2,046 6s. 11d.; with the exception of £206 12s. 0¼d., the whole sum was found by the prior and convent.

The cost of the rebuilding of the choir of Westminster Abbey by Henry III amounted to £17,933 during the first 8 years of the work, from 1245 to 1253. The nave was 150 years in building, from 1376 to 1528. The story of the work has been told by the Rev. R. B. Rackham in a most interesting paper published in the *Proceedings of the British Academy* for 1909–10. As the result of a very careful study of the records and accounts, he has shown that the total cost of the building was £24,211. Of this sum £6,066 8s. 4d. were contributed by the kings; gifts from other secular persons, including legacies, amounted to £349 19s. 8d.; indulgences brought in £70 4s. 5d.; offerings in the new pyx £7 14s. 4d.; the abbots gave £1,232 4s. 7d., the brethren £2,079, and the convent revenues supplied the remainder, £14,416 8s. 8d.

Even in the richer monasteries building charges were often a very heavy item of expenditure. The chroniclers record numerous instances of terrible destruction by fire in churches and monastic buildings. On April 1st, 1301, the vigil of Easter, the church of the monastery of Llanthony by Gloucester, with its four bell towers was burnt and only the bare walls were left standing. In 1305 lightning set fire to the wooden belfry of Milton Abbey in Dorset in the middle of the night, the flames spread rapidly for the church had a wooden vault, liquid lead poured down, the bells, books, vestments, common seal, and all the muniments were destroyed. Although gilds provided against losses by fire for their own members, there was no system of insurance until after the middle of the seventeenth century, and the first company was founded in 1680. The whole cost of restoration and rebuilding of the monastic churches had to be defrayed by some means. In 1305 the Bishop of Salisbury granted an indulgence of forty days to those who contributed to the re-building of Milton Abbey. In 1308 the Bishop of Winchester appropriated the revenues of the parish church of Barton Stacy to Llanthony in aid of the heavy financial losses and burdens of the canons. Bad foundations and the unskilled work of early masons perhaps explain a not uncommon statement that the fabric of a church 'threatened ruin.'

But the most frequent motive seems to have been a passion for building. In 1237 and 1267 the papal legates, Cardinals Otto and Ottoboni, forbade abbots to pull down old churches on the pretext of building a larger or more beautiful fabric, without first securing the consent of the bishop who was bound to consider carefully whether it was expedient to grant or refuse the licence. The prohibition had no effect.

The undertaking of 'new work' was a most serious matter and made heavy demands on the business ability of the monks. Unlike a dean and chapter at the present day, who accept a contract on the advice of an architect, the abbots and their convents provided all the materials, building stone, timber, iron and nails, lead, sand, chalk, canvas, glass, oil and colour materials, etc., and engaged masons, carpenters, painters, glaziers, and labourers at a fixed wage to do the work. The possession of quarries was eagerly sought after and the abbeys of Ramsey, Crowland, Bury St. Edmunds, Sawtry, Spalding and Peterborough had quarries at Barnack, in Northamptonshire, and the famous stone was easily carried thence by water or by land along the Ermine Street. Immense quantities of stone were imported from Caen. The Crown was often generous in granting timber from the royal forests. Iron and nails were bought at fairs. In 1278 the abbot and convent of Winchcombe made an agreement with Walter, the mason of Hereford, who bound himself to serve the abbot and his successors all his life, to finish the new work as well as he knew how, and to undertake no other building, except for the king. He was allowed to build a chamber for himself next the granary, for which the abbot was to find the stone and timber. He boarded with the abbot's chief servants, but if he were ill and confined to his room he was to have an allowance of two monk's loaves, two noggins of ale and two dishes from the abbot's kitchen.[1] Food, clothes and provender were provided for his two servants and two horses. Each year he was promised a robe for himself like that of the steward, and if incapacitated by continuous sickness or old age he was to have the same allowance, but to content himself with one servant and one horse. Thirty years later he was still in the service of the house, and paid the costs of the

[1] V. C. H., *Glouc.*, II, p. 67.

appropriation of the church of Enstone. In 1329 it was ordained that ten marks should be set aside for the keeping of his anniversary.

Though stone, timber, sand and chalk might be found on the estates of a monastery, ready money in the treasury was at no time plentiful. When the tower of Evesham was being built, about 1200, the monks gave up the rents, which were used to provide pittances or additional food beyond the bare allowance. At St. Albans during the rule of John of Cell (1195–1214) the convent gave up their wine for fifteen years to find funds for building.

Many choirs were extended eastwards as a splendid setting for the shrines of saints whose relics were treasured in the abbey church, and attracted pilgrims whose offerings went towards the cost of building. On the great occasion of the translation of St. Thomas of Canterbury in 1220, the offerings reached the high figure of £1,074 13s. 1d. The murder, near Rochester, of a native of Perth when he was on his way to the Holy Land, proved most profitable to the Benedictines of the cathedral monastery of Rochester. He was speedily canonized as St. William of Perth, and the offerings at his shrine in the church provided all the funds which were needed for the rebuilding of the choir. The case of Gloucester is even more striking. After the murder of Edward II at Berkeley Castle, the abbots of Bristol, Kingswood and Malmesbury feared the vengeance of Roger Mortimer and Queen Isabella if they gave the king burial in their churches.[1] Abbot Thoky of Gloucester had known the king well, and he sent an escort to Berkeley to bring the body of the king to Gloucester, where it was buried with great honour near the high altar on the north side of the choir. In spite of the misgovernance of the king and the general unrest throughout the couhtry during his reign, his tomb at once became an object for a pilgrimage. According to the Gloucester chronicler, the crowds which flocked thither were so great that the town of Gloucester could scarcely contain them, and the offerings were so numerous and costly that the new work in the south transept was completed in 1335, and the vaulting of the choir during the rule of Adam of Staunton (1337–51) was also paid for out of them. There were certainly fashions in pilgrimages, for very trifling sums were contributed at the shrine of St. Etheldreda at Ely towards the rebuilding in the fourteenth century.

The history of some of the early Cistercian monasteries in England reveals the circumstances under which their churches and other buildings were erected. Men and women who wished to found abbeys sent petitions to the general chapter which issued instructions to two abbots of the country to visit the site and report on

[1] V. C. H., *Glouc.*, II, p. 57.

its suitability to the next general chapter, and their consent was needed before the next steps were taken. According to the Cistercian Customs a community consisting of an abbot and twelve could not be sent to take possession until the necessary buildings were provided, viz., a church or oratory, a refectory, dormitory, guest-house, and a porter's lodge. Sir William Hope noted that at Woburn, Newminster and Louth Park, these were provided by the founder and were often of a temporary character, being built of wood, or even wattle and daub. In *The Architectural History of Kirkstall Abbey* (Thoresby Society) he has told the story of the building. It was founded by Henry de Lacy in fulfilment of a vow when he recovered from a serious illness. He offered the vill of Barnoldswick to the Abbot of Fountains, and, sending brethren, the abbot built humble offices according to the form of the order. On May 19th, 1147, Alexander, the prior of Fountains, went forth as abbot of the new foundation, with twelve monks and ten lay brothers. The site proved quite unsuitable, and after a stay of more than six years, during which the convent suffered from unbroken poverty, lack of food and clothing, floods and robber raids, Alexander determined to seek another spot. Henry de Lacy prevailed upon William of Poitou to grant a site which the abbot wanted in the valley of Airedale. There Alexander built a church and humble offices according to order, and the convent removed thither from Barnoldswick on May 19th, 1152. Sir William Hope continued: 'The site is described as covered with woods and unproductive of crops, a place well-nigh destitute of good things, save timber and stone, and a pleasant valley with the Aire flowing through the middle of it. . . . By the industry of the monks space was soon cleared for the new buildings, while the convent itself was increased in the number of brethren and the tale of its possessions. For the abbot, being a man of piety and prudence, watched with unwearying sagacity over the progress of his house in every direction, and increased it as far as possible with just claims. And throughout Henry de Lacy, the founder of the monastery, stood by him, now providing the fruits of harvest, now supplying money as the needs of the establishment required. He had part in providing the buildings, laid with his own hand the foundations of the church, and himself completed the fabric at his own cost. The date of Henry de Lacy's death is uncertain, but he apparently survived Abbot Alexander, who, after ruling the house for thirty-five years, died in 1182. In his days "the buildings of Kirkstall were erected of stone and wood brought there, that is the church and both dorters to wit, of the monks and of the lay brothers, both their fraters and the cloister, the chapter house and other offices necessary within the abbey, and all these were covered excellently with tiles. . . ." The infirmary hall, with the chapel block to the south, and the guest-house west of the church, were not erected until about 1220.'

The ways in which the Benedictines raised money for building were not open to the Cistercians; they were forbidden by the general chapter to preach sermons and appeal for that purpose, and in 1204 collecting-boxes in churches and the institution of confraternities were likewise forbidden.

MONASTIC FINANCES

It has been suggested that building on a large scale could not have been undertaken by some of the Cistercian monasteries without the help of money borrowed from the Jews, since Christians were forbidden by the Church to engage in the business of money-lending.[1] It is a significant fact that when the great financier, Aaron of Lincoln, died in 1189, the sum of £4,800 was due to him from the Cistercian abbeys of Rievaulx, Newminster, Kirkstead, Louth Park, Revesby, Rufford, Kirkstall, Roche and Biddlesden, all of which were founded between 1140 and 1152. The Jews in England were under the special protection of the Crown, which claimed their chattels at their death. Richard I, as universal legatee of Aaron of Lincoln, allowed the abbot and convents of these monasteries to clear themselves for the sum of £666 13s. 4d. so the loan proved a very profitable one to them.

Even before the Jews were expelled from England, in 1290, the Italian merchants who came to England to act as collectors of the pope's moneys began to compete with them as money-lenders, and numerous entries on the Patent and Close Rolls prove that many of the monasteries were heavily in debt to them in the fourteenth century. The rate of interest was very high; the Jews seldom charged less than 40 per cent, and sometimes as much as 80 per cent. The Italian merchants were no cheaper. They demanded interest nominally for expenses incurred in sending for the money again and again, and thus evaded the canons and enactments of the Church about taking interest. Matthew Paris mentions an instance in which their charge was 60 per cent. When, in the course of the fourteenth century, the English merchants superseded the Italians, they were not less guilty of extortion.

Like other landowners, the monks and Regular Canons felt the effects of the Black Death very severely, and their revenues were greatly diminished. But even before the middle of the fourteenth

[1] *Jewish Quarterly Review*, X, pp. 633–7.

century there is plenty of evidence to show that the financial condition of the monasteries, both great and small, was often very unstable. It is very difficult to discover any figures which reveal the exact income of the monasteries. The Taxation of Pope Nicholas was merely an assessment made for the purpose of taxation, and for various reasons it is impossible to determine the exact relation between that assessment and income.[1]

Soon after the Norman Conquest the property of the Benedictine house appears to have been divided between the abbot and his convent.[2] It seems probable that the division was due to the influence of the Cluniac Customs. The abbot and chapter also allotted certain estates and revenues to the several obedientiars. Though calculated to insure efficient management, these arrangements proved a fertile source of strife: the abbot sometimes granted away his estates to his kinsfolk, and disputed with his monks about the incidence of fresh burdens and the expenses of hospitality. The convent had the utmost difficulty in exercising any real check upon the abbot, for he rid himself of his critics and opponents by banishing them to distant cells. Though the departmental system worked admirably in many Benedictine houses, in others it was a source of danger. The obedientiars were in reality too much emancipated from the control of the chapter, and at times contracted debts wtihout the knowledge of the convent. They were at the same time receivers, treasurers, and administrators of the funds, and they kept their own money chests. Such property as remained unallotted constituted the common fund under one or more treasurers, and out of it the revenues of the obedientiars were supplemented in some houses. In the thirteenth century papal legates and bishops pressed for changes in the financial management of Benedictine houses. They enjoined that an annual balance-sheet should be drawn up, and strict accounts kept and presented at stated intervals. In the houses of the newer orders there was one common treasury, and their customs provided for a divided control over receipts and expenditure and a detailed system of account keeping. However, they were no more successful than the Benedictines in keeping free of debt. The general chapter of the Cistercians feared that the destruction of many of their houses was imminent; between 1240 and 1256 a statute was passed forbidding any abbot whose debts amounted to 100 marks to buy lands or to build, unless some special alms were received or some sale had been effected for that purpose; and even then he was restrained unless the house grew plenty of corn. Yet the debts of Meaux in 1280 amounted to more than £3,678 3s. 11d.; of Kirkstall in 1284

[1] R. Graham, *English Ecclesiastical Studies*, pp. 271–301.
[2] Ibid., p. 251.

to £5,248 15s. 7d., besides five sacks of wool; of Fountains in 1290 to £6,373.

The monasteries derived the greater part of their revenue from their estates. Until after the Black Death, when the system broke down for lack of labour, the monks kept almost the whole of their estates in their own hands, and thus their revenues depended principally, not on a rent-roll, but on the success of their farming, which often provided them with their food supplies.

The profits of farming were subject to very great fluctuations. The amount of destruction and loss from flooded rivers and inundations of the sea was enormous, when vast tracts of the country were undrained and the flood waters of rivers were not controlled by means of locks and weirs. In the Tewkesbury Annals it is noted that after great storms of rain, about June 20th, 1257, the Severn was in high flood from Shrewsbury to Bristol; the crops were ruined, and many men, women and children were drowned. Matthew Paris records that in the same year continuous rain from February to May had turned the country into a marsh. It was a year of great dearth, 'apples were rare, pears still rarer, figs, acorns, cherries and plums were completely destroyed.' Corn rose to the price of 13s. 4d. a quarter, and many died of hunger throughout the country.

Droughts were most disastrous. Owing to a drought of nearly four months in 1251, the hay crop was reduced by one half and there was a great loss of cattle. Even in ordinary seasons there was great difficulty in keeping the cattle alive during the winter months; there was no feeding stuff, and even carrots and parsnips were unknown. Thomas Walsingham, a monk of St. Albans, records that in 1353 no rain fell from March to July; all the crops failed, and food was imported from other lands. Murrains among sheep were ruinous to the Cistercians and the Gilbertines, who derived the greater part of their income from the wool trade. The Gilbertine canons of Malton received £5,224 9s. 3d. from the sale of wool in fourteen years, from 1244 to 1257, and during the same time they spent £2,099 12s 10½d. on food and ale for the house and for the maintenance of the lay brothers and servants at the granges.

The monasteries suffered immense losses in times of war and civil disturbance. A schedule of the losses in the manors of St. Albans during the struggle between King John and the barons shows that the total reached the high figure of £2,555. In 1318, after the Scotch war, it was necessary to make a new assessment of Church property in part of the province of York; so great was the devastation that taxes could not be levied upon the Taxation of Pope Nicholas of 1290. Wars on the Welsh borderland seriously affected the revenues of Gloucester, Tewkesbury and other monasteries, which had been endowed with lands and churches by the Lords Marchers. Some monasteries received lands in Ireland. In 1224 the abbot and convent of Tewkesbury sold their lands at Dungarthan, the gift of King John, to the Bishop of Dublin for £80, because they brought no profit. In the thirteenth century the prior and convent of Christ Church, Canterbury, made over their Irish lands to the Irish monastery of Tintern for 625 marks and a yearly rent of 10 marks. The prior and convent of the Augustinian house of Llanthony by Gloucester, sent one or two of their canons to live at the grange of Dulek, in East Meath, and in one year during the rule of Prior Walter (1283–1300) they received from them £81 5s. 7d. A few years later, when they drew up a lamentable petition to Adam of Orleton, Bishop of Worcester, for the appropriation of the church of Tytherington, they put forward the frequent ravages of their Irish lands as one of the reasons for their poverty.

In several of the towns which had grown up around monasteries there was a serious uprising of the townsfolk in 1327.[1] At Bury St. Edmunds agitators from London stirred up the townsfolk and the villeins on the neighbouring manors, and about 3,000 of them broke into the monastery and did an enormous amount of damage. In the autumn there was a further outbreak, and the rioters set fire to the abbey gates, and afterwards to all the monastic buildings. They also ravaged twenty-two manors belonging to the monastery, and burnt buildings upon them. A record of the losses of cattle and crops in each case has been preserved, and the total was computed at £1,118 6s. 9d.; but it was impossible to estimate the value of the buildings burnt and destroyed, of the silver and gold, jewels and books which were stolen. The town was afterwards cast in damages and costs for the immense sum of £140,000. In 1331 the abbot and convent remitted all but a small part of it, and recovered some of their treasures and bonds.

While the revenues of the monasteries were subject to great fluctuations, there were heavy charges upon them. One of the greatest and most constant was the cost of hospitality. In his Rule St. Benedict wrote: 'Let all guests who come to the monastery be entertained like Christ Himself, because he will say, "I was a stranger and ye took me in."' He willed that the guest-house should stand apart, 'so that the guests, who are never wanting in a monastery, may not disquiet the brethren by their untimely arrivals.' A monk of Battle Abbey chronicled that in the early years of the twelfth century 'there was such an abundance of all good things and such great attention paid to hospitality, that guests and strangers came

[1] Cf. N. M. Trenholme, *American Hist. Review*, July, 1901.

not so much like passing visitors as to remain a longer time at their pleasure as if they had come to their own homes.'

An officer, called the hospitarius or hostillarius, was in charge of the guest-house, and in Benedictine monasteries certain revenues were assigned to him for the provision of beds, linen, plate and vessels for the table. Some account rolls of the hostillarius have survived, as at Durham, but it is impossible to calculate the cost of hospitality, because bread and food were obtained from the cellarer, who sent them out of his store. At Durham the hostillarius added oysters, fish, both fresh and dried, and sugar. In the larger monasteries the guest-house was often a splendid building. The author of the *Rites of Durham* describes this hall as 'a goodly brave place, much like unto the body of a church, with very fair pillars supporting it on either side, and in the midst of the hall a most large range for the fire. The chambers and lodgings belonging to it were sweetly kept, and so richly furnished that they were not unpleasant to lie in, especially one chamber, called the king's chamber, deserving that name in that the king himself might very well have lain in it for the princely linen thereof.' A Durham roll for 1454 mentions also the knights' chamber, 'Barry,' the water-chamber, the new chamber and the clerks' chamber, the summer hall and the winter hall. At St. Albans there was stabling for 300 horses, and at Abingdon there was a special endowment to meet the cost of new shoes for the guests' horses. It was usual to give free hospitality for two days, but the custom was much abused by the rich and powerful. Soon after his coronation King John went to the monastery of Bury St. Edmunds, and Jocelin of Brakelond writes: 'We indeed believed that he was come to make offering of some great matter: but all that he offered was one silken cloth, which his servants had borrowed from our sacrist and to this day have not paid for. He availed himself of the hospitality of St. Edmund, which was attended with enormous expense, and upon his departure bestowed nothing at all, either of honour or profit, upon the saint, save thirteen pence sterling, which he offered at his mass on the day of his departure.'[1]

In striking contrast was the liberality of his son, Henry III, who was at the monastery on March 14th, 1251, and gave orders for the sacrist to have forty marks to carry thirty oaks which the king gave him in the distant forest of Inglewood, in Cumberland, for the repair of a belfry in the church, and forty-four marks to buy candlesticks of silver to be placed around the shrine of St. Edmund and thirty marks to complete the new altar front there. The burden of hospitality became so oppressive that Edward I forbade anyone to venture to eat or lodge in a religious house unless he had been

[1] *Chronicle of Jocelin of Brakelond*, ed. Sir Ernest Clarke, p. 178.

formally invited, or was the founder, and even then his consumption should be moderate.[1] The poor only might be lodged free, 'for the king intendeth not that the grace of hospitality should be withdrawn from the destitute.' The statute continued to be more honoured in the breach than in the observance. Queen Isabella left her pack of hounds at Canterbury for two years towards the end of the reign of Edward II.

The costs of litigation were extremely heavy and the delays of justice were very great. If the monasteries did not submit to encroachments on their rights and property, or to letting judgment go by default, they were bound to take legal action. There is evidence from the fourteenth century onwards that the greater monasteries retained a standing counsel. In the cartularies there are numerous instances in which heirs disputed the titles to lands which had been granted away by their relations, and often the result was a compromise by which the heir secured a rent charge on the property. The Abbey of Crowland was engaged in a series of great lawsuits from the twelfth century onwards about the marshes of the monastery, which were very profitable. Some of these had already been drained, and the lords and men of neighbouring manors attempted to secure rights of common by violent occupation. Disputes continued at intervals until the end of the fifteenth century. One lawsuit, arising out of a trespass, in which great damage was done, in 1413, dragged on for two years, and the costs exceeded £500. Between 1243 and 1257 the law expenses of Malton Priory amounted to £170 11s. 4½d., when the income varied from £500 to £600 a year.

The monasteries had to pay still heavier costs when appeals were made to the papal curia. Thomas of Marlborough, a monk of Evesham, was obliged to spend a year and a half at Rome or elsewhere in Italy in defence of the claim of his house to be exempt from the visitation of the Bishop of Worcester. In January, 1206, he was in danger of being arrested for debt by Roman merchants, from whom Roger Norreys, the abbot of Evesham, had borrowed 440 marks during his stay in the city. Thomas himself had got through fifty marks, which he had borrowed, and poverty then forced him to plead in person instead of employing an advocate. The abbey was publicly declared exempt on April 16th, 1206, but, with the pope's permission, the Roman merchants seized the Evesham documents as a pledge for the money owing to them, and set out for England. Thomas went off secretly, without leave, because he had no money to give the usual presents to the pope and cardinals. The creditors were not finally paid until 1214.

When money was scarce the monks sold corrodies, binding them-

[1] Jusserand, *English Wayfaring Life*, pp. 120, 121.

selves to provide food and drink, and sometimes clothes and lodging as well, to individuals for the rest of their lives. The financial results were often disastrous and both papal legates and bishops attempted to regulate the practice, but in vain. In the later years of the thirteenth century, and in the fourteenth century, the Crown made frequent demands upon the monasteries to grant corrodies to their old servants and other persons, i.e. board, lodging, and clothing. Edward II sent Hugh de la Chaumbre to St. Catherine's outside Lincoln, in place of Matthew le Ussher, received by the request of the late king, and Christiana de Hauville, whose husband and three sons were slain by the Scotch rebels, and her goods and lands totally destroyed and wasted by them, 'until she be able to live of her own again.' Men-at-arms who had grown old fighting in the king's wars thus ended their days in monastic precincts. In 1317 Richard de Whitchurch, arblaster, was sent to Malton; Robert de Tadcaster, footman, to Watton. In granting a corrody the religious sometimes stated that the case should not be made a precedent, but their protests were always ineffectual.

Taxation was sometimes very heavy. Throughout the thirteenth century it is clear that it was regarded as an unjust exaction and not as a charge for which money should be set aside each year. In consequence there was often difficulty in paying the taxes. In the fourteenth century, owing to great financial embarrassment, some of the poorer monasteries, not ordinarily exempt, were excused from payment for some years.

With all these charges upon their income the monasteries made great efforts to increase their annual revenues by buying land and by securing the appropriation of churches, which usually gave them the great tithes of a parish. Their success or failure depended largely on the business capacity of their heads. Henry of Eastry, Prior of Christ Church, Canterbury (1284–1313) discharged debts amounting to £4924 18s. 4d., bought real property with a yearly rental of £87 15s. 0d., and spent immense sums on the buildings of the monastery and its manors; during his rule twenty-one law-suits were settled favourably for the convent. John, Prior of Bermondsey (1266–72) was caught in the toils of the most notorious money-lender of the age, Adam of Stratton, who became enormously rich by fraud, and Edward I intervened to save the monastery from ruin.[1] Reckless speculation which led to a very serious financial crisis was not infrequent. When hopelessly overwhelmed with debt, the abbots and convents appealed to the Crown, for in default of payment creditors were entitled to take possession of lands by a summary process: they might either sell them after a year's possession

[1] R. Graham, *English Ecclesiastical Studies*, pp. 102–5.

77

or hold them until they had satisfied themselves out of the profits. In these cases the king took the monastery under his special protection, which prevented creditors from distraining, and gave it in custody to commissioners. They were bound to collect the revenues, provide for the maintenance of the convent and servants and for almsgiving, and set aside the residue for the payment of debts. Of the Gloucestershire monasteries, St. Peter at Gloucester was entrusted to a royal commissioner in 1273, Winchcombe in 1353, St. Augustine's, Bristol, in 1366. All of these had large revenues. The poor Cistercian house of Flaxley, in the Forest of Dean, was several times in great straits, and in 1277, 1281 and 1283, Edward I appointed commissioners, of whom the last was Thomas de Basing, a citizen of London.

The study of the financial condition of a monastery gives a valuable clue to its history. The monastic chronicler records with approval the deeds of abbots who were skilled administrators, while his praise is faint for the men who were ignorant of the affairs of this world, however great their zeal for the spiritual life. Jocelin of Brakelond described Abbot Hugh of Bury St. Edmunds as 'a pious and kind man, a good and religious monk; yet not wise or far-sighted in worldly affairs; one who relied too much on his officers and put faith in them, rather taking counsel of others than abiding by his own judgment. To be sure, the Rule and the religious life and all pertaining thereto were healthy enough in the cloister, but outdoor affairs were badly managed, inasmuch as everyone serving under a simple and already aged lord did what he would, not what he should. The townships of the abbot and all the hundreds were set to farm, the forests were destroyed, the manor-houses threatened to fall, everything daily got worse and worse. One resource only the abbot had, and that was to take up moneys on interest, so that thereby he might be able in some measure to keep up the dignity of his house. There befel not a term of Easter or St. Michael for eight years before his decease, but that one or two hundred pounds at least increased in principal debt; the securities were always renewed, and the interest which accrued was converted into principal. This laxity descended from the head to the members, from the superior to the subjects. Hence it came to pass that every official of the house had a seal of his own, and bound himself in debt at his own pleasure to Jews as well as to Christians.'[1] In the discussions which took place in the monastery about the choice of Hugh's successor Jocelin's opinion was that 'no one should be made abbot unless he knew somewhat of dialectics, and knew how to discern truth from falsehood.' As an older man he wrote: 'If I should live so long as to see the abbacy

[1] *Chronicle of Jocelin of Brakelond*, ed. Sir Ernest Clarke, pp. 1, 2.

vacant . . . I shall then advise . . . that we choose not too good a monk, nor yet an overwise clerk, neither one too simple nor too weak.'

MONASTIC ART AND ARCHITECTURE

In the conflicting ideals of Cluny and Cîteaux in the first half of the twelfth century, the late Abbot Cabrol saw another phase of the recurring conflict between Christian humanism and Christian asceticism in the religious life.[1] The ascetic outlook on art and architecture is most forcibly expressed in St. Bernard's well-known criticism of the churches and ornaments of the older monastic orders: 'I will not speak of the immense height of the churches, of their immoderate length, of their superfluous breadth, costly polishing, and strange designs, which, while they attract the eyes of the worshipper, hinder the soul's devotion and somehow remind me of the old Jewish ritual. However, let all this pass; we will suppose it is done as we are told, for the glory of God. But, a monk myself, I do ask other monks . . . " Tell me, O ye professors of poverty, what does gold do in a holy place? . . ." By the right of wonderful and costly vanities men are prompted to give rather than to pray. Some beautiful picture of a saint is exhibited, and the brighter the colours the greater the holiness attributed to it. Men run, eager to kiss; they are invited to give, and the beautiful is more admired than the sacred is revered. In the churches are suspended not coronae, but wheels studded with gems, and surrounded by lights, which are scarcely brighter than the precious stones which are near them. Instead of candlesticks we behold great trees of brass, fashioned with wonderful skill and glittering as much through their jewels as their lights. . . . If we cannot do without the images, why can we not spare the brilliant colours?'

The great church of the monastery of Cluny, begun in 1088, had double aisles, double transepts, an ambulatory with radiating chapels and a nave of sixteen bays. There were three towers at the crossing between the nave and the greater transept, another tower at the crossing of the choir and the eastern transept, and two towers at the western end of the narthex or galilee which was not finished until 1220. The total length was then over 520 feet. It was the largest church in Western Europe after St. Peter's at Rome. In the semidome of the apse on a gold background, a great seated figure of Christ was painted, his right hand raised in blessing, his left resting on a sealed book, his throne being on the clouds between

[1] *Association Bourguignonne des Sociétés Savantes, Congrès de 1927*, pp. 19–28.

the symbols of the four evangelists. There were gold and silver shrines, gold crosses, candlesticks, thuribles and chalices. The great seven-branched candlestick, which stood before the high altar was eighteen and a half feet high; it was made of coppergilt of marvellous workmanship in imitation of the candlestick which Moses commanded Bezaleel to make for the Tabernacle. At least five great chandeliers called coronae or light-towers hung in the church.

In England as in France the Benedictines and Cluniacs were zealous in building great churches to the glory of God and in using the arts of sculpture and painting and the crafts of the goldsmith and metal worker in His service. The church of the Cluniac monastery of Lewes had the same plan as that of Cluny, and it was owing to Cluniac influence that when the choir of Canterbury was extended under Prior Ernulf (1096–1107) it was planned with a double transept and the eastern transept had a pair of apsidal chapels in each arm.[1] The richness of the decoration of the Benedictine churches of the twelfth century was due to Cluniac influence; Cluniac monks were elected abbots of Evesham, Abingdon, Glastonbury and Ramsey. Henry I chose Cluniac monks from Lewes for the Benedictine monastery which he refounded at Reading. Stephen took Cluniac monks from Bermondsey for the new Benedictine monastery of Faversham. The walls of the churches were plastered and painted, sometimes in imitation of masonry, sometimes with ornaments copied from manuscripts. The fine representation of St. Paul and the viper in St. Anselm's chapel in Canterbury cathedral was painted in the middle of the twelfth century; the splendid figure of St. Faith and the newly discovered SS. Thomas and Christopher in Westminster Abbey in the thirteenth century. Medallions containing figures were painted about 1250 on the vaulted roof of the chapter-house of the Augustinian Canons of St. Frideswide's, since 1546 the cathedral of Christ Church, Oxford.[2] At the east end of the south choir aisle of the church in the subdivisions of the vaulting are four angels, the two westernmost are dancing, and below one of them on the north side, a young girl plays a stringed instrument with a bow. Windows were filled with painted glass; in the cathedral church of Canterbury about 1184 there were twelve medallion-windows of New Testament subjects and their Old Testament types, in others the long series of ancestors of Christ were represented.[3] The twelve windows of the retro-choir were all once filled with medallions depicting miracles worked by the intercession of St. Thomas of Canterbury inserted early in the thirteenth century.

[1] A. W. Clapham, *English Romanesque Architecture after the Conquest*, pp. 71–4.
[2] *Walpole Society*, Vol. XVI, pp. 1–8.
[3] J. D. Le Couteur, *English Medieval Painted Glass*, pp. 60, 61, 69.

Pavements in choirs and chapels were of patterned or of pictured tiles. The paving of the abbey church of Chertsey consisted of many varieties of tiles of very fine quality made in a tile kiln in the precincts which was discovered in 1923. The story of the Romance of Tristram was depicted on a long series of tiles of which some are exhibited in the new medieval room in the British Museum; in Professor Lethaby's judgment they were drawn by one of the ablest masters of the second half of the thirteenth century.[1] Other series at Chertsey represented the signs of the Zodiac and the labours of the months. On the floor of the chapter house of Westminster Abbey there are patterned and pictured tiles from designs by the same artist as those at Chertsey.

Costly shrines were made for the relics of the saints, gold and silver chalices and other vessels for the altars, magnificent vestments and copes were provided: the wealth of the treasures of the cathedral church of Canterbury is revealed in the inventories of the monastery.[2] Great seven-branched candlesticks stood before the high altars of Winchester, Christ Church and St. Augustine's, Canterbury, Bury St. Edmunds and Durham. Splendid illuminated service books were produced in the monasteries of St. Albans, Christ Church and St. Augustine's, Canterbury, Bury St. Edmunds, Winchester and Durham.[3] In 1315 Christ Church, Canterbury, possessed twenty-two books of the Gospels with jewelled or metalled covers.

Dr. John Bilson has written an admirable description of the origin and development of the Cistercian church plan which was evolved between 1120 and 1139.[4] This was a cruciform church with a short presbytery or sanctuary east of the crossing, westward of the crossing a long nave, the eastern part of which formed the choir of the monks, the western part the choir of the lay brothers; chapels on the east side of each arm of the transept and an aisle on each side of the nave made it easy to pass between the different parts of the church. Subsequently the eastern arm was extended to provide a greater number of chapels contrived with an ambulatory, either rectangular or semi-circular in plan. The simplicity of detail is striking. The walls were uncoloured, the glass in the windows was ordered to be white without crosses or pictures. Sculptures and pictures, except the image of the Redeemer, were forbidden, likewise elaborate pavements. Crosses on altars were to be of painted wood, the use of gold and silver was forbidden, only the

---

[1] *Walpole Society*, Vol. II, pp. 69–80.
[2] *Inventories of Christchurch, Canterbury*, ed. J. Wickham Legg and W. H. St. John Hope.
[3] E. G. Millar, *English Illuminated Manuscripts from the Tenth to the Thirteenth Century*.
[4] W. H. St. John Hope and John Bilson, *Kirkstall Abbey*, pp. 84–100.

chalice and pyx for communion were to be made of silver. The capital letters of service books were to be of one colour and not painted. Stone masonry bell-towers were forbidden, but in England, as Mr. Clapham has noted, 'building tradition was too strong to be resisted, though there is no provision for one in the first church at Rievaulx.' Fountains, Kirkstall and Buildwas, built rather later, all had the four arches to the crossing and a low central tower. Bells might not exceed 500 lb in weight, so that one person might ring them, and two bells might not be rung together. The significance of this prohibition can be appreciated by remembering that 'Prior Conrad (1108–26) gave Canterbury Cathedral five large bells which required respectively ten, ten, eleven, eight and twenty-four men to ring.'[1]

Although many of the buildings have been destroyed which Leland saw and noted in the book of *The Laboriouse Journey and Serche for Englandes Antiquitees*, given as his New Year's gift to Henry VIII in 1546, much still remains, and the traveller to-day will find that a visit to monastic sites opens up a most fascinating study. The first essential is an understanding of the plan of monastic buildings. A charming description of the buildings of Durham and their uses before the dissolution was written in 1593. There can be no more delightful way of grasping the monastic plan than to stay at Durham and to read *The Rites of Durham* in the cathedral cloister and other buildings.

THE MONASTIC PLAN[2]

Benedictines, Cluniacs and Augustinian Canons.

'In choosing the site of a monastery, the first consideration . . . was the water supply. The domestic needs of the house, the mill, and the sanitary arrangements all depended on this, and the whole disposition of the buildings was regulated by the relative positions of water and site.'[3]

'The usual plan of a monastery consisted of a square cloister enclosed on all sides by buildings, the church always forming one side and the frater (or refectory) the opposite one. The east side was bounded by the dorter (or dormitory) and the west by the cellarer's buildings for guests and stores. When the site permitted,

[1] H. B. Walters, *Church Bells of England*, p. 14.
[2] The following description of the monastic plan is taken mainly from papers contributed to archæological journals by the late Sir William Hope and quoted by his kind permission.
[3] *Derbyshire Archæol. Soc. Journal*, VI, p. 87.

the church occupied the north side of the cloister, so that the north walk of the latter, which formed the living-room of the inmates, might have the benefit of the midday sun, and shelter from the north winds. If, however, the water supply lay to the north, the church formed the south range, and the frater the north. . . . The church was always cruciform, and the cloister square invariably joined the nave. The only exception known is Rochester Cathedral Priory, where it is on the south side of the choir, and even this is probably a later alteration. The cloister was an open court, enclosed round its four sides by covered alleys which served different purposes. The alley next the nave was the living-room of the brethren, and furnished with book-cases against the church wall, and reading-desks or 'carols' in the window recesses looking out on the central area. The western alley seems to have been used for the novices and the other two were passages. The eastern side of the cloister was bounded by one arm of the transept of the church, next to which was the chapter house, and beyond that the calefactorium, or common-house, as it was called at Durham: a long vaulted apartment with a fireplace. Between these three buildings were often placed other smaller apartments or passages, such as the vestry and the regular parlour; the latter being a place where necessary conversation might be carried on, for the statutes of most of the Orders forbade speaking in the church, cloister, frater and dorter. Over all these apartments was the dorter. It usually had two staircases, one descending directly into the transept to enable the brethren to go to matins at midnight without going through the cold cloister, the other communicating with the cloister itself. At the end of the dorter was the necessarium, or rere-dorter, a building always of considerable size, and most admirably contrived for its purpose. It was well ventilated, and the waste water of the monastery, or the mill race, constantly ran through it, and effectually flushed it. On the opposite side of the cloister to the nave was the refectorium, or frater, a long and lofty hall, usually in canons' houses raised upon an undercroft. In the side wall was a pulpit from which portions of pious works were read every day during meals. There was often a passage from the cloister between the east end of the frater and the dorter range. At the west end of the frater was the buttery and kitchen, the latter being sometimes semi-detached. The whole of the western block of buildings pertained to the cellarer, who had charge of the stores, and upon whom devolved the care of guests. His range was, therefore, always two, and sometimes three, stories high, the lowest being cellars for provisions, etc., and the first floor a long hall where guests might eat and sleep. The sick and infirm brethren had a separate dwelling called the infirmitorium, or farmery . . . . It usually stood on the east of the monastery, so as to secure peace and quiet. The bakehouse and brewhouse and other offices were placed in the outer court, which was entered by a gatehouse, with porter's lodge and almonry adjoining and a lodging-house for tramps, etc. There was, sometimes, a small chapel nigh the gate.'[1]

'The monastic infirmaries in this country, like the houses for the accommodation of guests, were purely domestic buildings, and therefore followed more or less closely in plan and arrangement the ordinary dwelling-house of the period. In the larger monasteries the infirmary took the form of a great hall as may have formed the house of a Saxon thane, or the quarters of a castle guard, or the hall of a king's palace, like the great hall of William Rufus at Westminster, but as befitted an adjunct to a house of religion, it differed from these in having attached to it a chapel. We find accordingly at Christ Church, Canterbury, at Gloucester, Ely, Peterborough, Fountains and elsewhere, a great hall divided by pillars into a nave and aisles like the body of a church, with a chapel opening out of it on the east. The addition of a kitchen and other necessary offices made the building complete in itself. As these infirmaries were not only for the sick and infirm, but also for the temporary lodging of the *minuti*, or those who had been blooded, and for any other of the brethren who were released from strict observance of the rule, the great halls were none too large when the monastic fervour was at its height. Moreover, since most of the inmates lived a common life, these halls were used in a similar manner to the domestic halls from which they were copied; that is, the hall itself served for exercise and for meals, and had a fire in the middle in cold weather, while the beds were laid along the aisles against the walls. In later days the aisles were fitted with cubicles, and finally became converted into sets of chambers, but the hall continued its original use more or less to the end. In the lesser monasteries the roominess of the hall-type of infirmary was not needed, and a building on the lines of an ordinary manor house, of which a chapel also formed part, served all purposes.'[2]

'The arrangement of a Cluniac house seems to differ in no important point from the regular Benedictine plan.'[3]

The buildings of the Augustinian Canons conformed closely to the Benedictine plan, but Sir William Hope noted that most canons' churches were originally cruciform and aisleless, and that when at a later period it was deemed advisable to enlarge their churches by

[1] *Derbyshire Archæol. Soc. Journal*, VI, pp. 87–9.
[2] *Sussex Archæol. Collections*, XLIX, pp. 67, 68.
[3] *Archæol. Journal*, XLI, p. 17.

the addition of aisles, it was only possible, owing to the cloister and conventual buildings abutting against the nave, to add to it one aisle on the side remote from the cloister. With regard to the choir no such obstacles intervened, and there was nothing to prevent two aisles being built as was done at Kirkham.[1]

The Cistercian Plan.

'The buildings that opened out of the cloister of a Cistercian abbey are enumerated in proper order in the direction in the *Consuetudines* for the Sunday procession, as follows: *capitulum* or chapter-house, *auditorium* or parlour, *dormitorium* or dorter, and *dormitorii necessaria*, or rere-dorter, *calefactorium* or warming-house, *refectorium* or frater, *coquina* or kitchen, *cellarium* or cellarer's building.'[2]

'The frater, instead of standing east and west against the cloister, as in Benedictine, Cluniac and Canons' houses, in the Cistercian abbeys, stands north and south with its end only against the cloister. The reason of this is difficult to see. It has been suggested that it was the desire to bring the kitchen into direct communication with the cloister (from which in houses of other Orders it was almost always detached), because, amongst the Cistercians, the monks themselves acted as cooks by turns. This may be so, but it should be noted that among the Cluniacs, where the same rule was followed, the frater always stands east and west with the kitchen away from the cloister.'[3]

'During the detailed examination of the abbey buildings [of Kirkstall] . . . a curious fact came to light in connection with those forming the southern range, viz.: that the warming-house, frater, and kitchen, as at first planned, were arranged quite differently from those that eventually occupied their sites. . . . That the Cistercians occasionally built fraters standing east and west, after the Benedictine fashion, had already been noticed by Sir William Hope in the case of Sibton Abbey, in Suffolk. The Kirkstall example, therefore, does not form a solitary English one. Sir Harold Brakspear has, however, since suggested that at first it was general for the Cistercians to build their fraters east and west like other Orders, and that it was not until about 1150 that the change was made of placing them north and south. . . . No doubt all the abbeys that were originally affiliated to Savigny also had east and west fraters, as at Furness.'[4]

---

[1] *Archæol. Cantiana*, XV, p. 62.
[2] *Kirkstall*, p. 28.
[3] W. H. St. J. Hope, *Fountains*, p. 93.
[4] *Kirkstall*, pp. 52, 53.

In recent years Mr. E. W. Lovegrove has given a different explanation of the position of the Cistercian fraters. He has observed that as the whole western range of Cistercian houses was occupied by the numerous lay brothers, less space was available for buildings on the south side of the cloister than was the case in houses of other Orders, and therefore to find room for the kitchen it was essential to build the frater north and south.[1]

'In the *Consuetudines* the cellarer's building is called the *cellarium*, a name which, except as showing that it formed part of the cellarer's department, does not give any clue to its actual use. As a matter of fact this building was for the accommodation of the *conversi* or lay brothers: their frater and various offices forming the ground floor, while the upper story was their dorter. The division of the abbey buildings into two great groups, for the use of the monks (*monachi*) and for the lay brothers (*conversi*) respectively, is a feature peculiar to the Cistercians. . . .' The nave of the church was the choir of the lay brothers, and the buildings for their accommodation, which included a dorter, frater, infirmary, etc., were in immediate connexion therewith, just as the monks' buildings adjoining their part of the church.'[2]

'According to the [Cistercian] Customs in force down to 1240, it was directed that within the monastery let no one eat flesh or anything fat, except the sick and workmen, and by an institution of the general chapter between 1240 and 1256, this rule, which seems to have been originally adopted in 1157, was re-enacted in more precise terms. But within a hundred years later circumstances had so far changed that by a constitution of Pope Benedict XII in 1335 the monks were allowed, under certain conditions, to eat meat in the infirmary, and, by invitation, with the abbot in his lodging. By the end of the fifteenth century it had become the general custom for the monks to eat meat three days a week; on Sundays, Tuesdays, and Thursdays, except in Advent, Septuagesima, Lent, and other seasons of fasting; while on the other days they were restricted to the vegetarian diet prescribed by the older rules. But the relaxation in favour of meat did not permit it to be eaten in the frater, nor to be cooked in the common kitchen. It became necessary, therefore, to provide a special hall, or "misericord," as it was called, for the purpose. As the first indulgence was at first permitted only in the infirmary, the new chamber actually formed part of that establishment, as at Waverley and Fountains, the meat being cooked in the infirmary kitchen. . . . But at Kirkstall the case was met in another way, by dividing the frater into two stories, and using the lower as

[1] *Archæologia Cambrensis*, 1921, p. 403.
[2] *Kirkstall*, p. 54.

the misericord and the upper as the frater. A new meat kitchen was also built on the south-east to serve the misericord.'[1]

The Gilbertine Plan.

The only plan of a Gilbertine house which has been excavated is that of the double monastery of Watton, eight miles north of Beverley.

'The south-western quarter of the site is practically cut off from the rest by ditches on all four sides, as if to form a precinct in itself. In the centre of this stood what was no doubt the house and court of the nuns. It consisted of a cloister with the church on the south, the chapter-house and warming-house, etc., on the east, the frater on the north, and a western range with buildings extending from it westwards. . . . The church . . . consisted of a presbytery, central tower, and nave, a north transept with two eastern chapels, and a broad south aisle extending the length of the church, with a south transept, a south chapel, and another adjunct opening out of it. The arcade dividing the main part from the aisle seems to have stood upon a wall of some height . . . and thus formed a barrier between one half of the church and the other . . . The main or northern division served as the nuns' church, and had their choir under the crossing, with probably the choir of the sisters in the nave. The aisle or southern division served as the choir of the canons, probably with the choir of the *conversi* on its western half. Between the two presbyteries was (1) an archway for the passage of processions, etc., and (2) a turn through which the nuns could take holy water and receive the pax, and be communicated. . . . From a doorway in the middle of the east wall of the dorter subvault, a covered passage, about five feet wide, with thin walls, led eastwards for about eighty feet to a small building of doubtful dimensions of which only some scanty fragments remained. . . . As the building stood midway between the two cloisters, it probably also communicated with the eastern or canons' cloister by another passage leading directly to it, but this had been utterly destroyed. . . . It is likely that the building formed the *domus fenestre*, or window-house. This seems to have contained a very small window (*fenestrœ parvula*) at which conversation was carried on between the nuns and canons, and a great turning window *magna fenestra versatilis*) through which food and other things could be passed. . . . The buildings of the canons' court, so far as they have been traced, consisted of a cloister . . . surrounded by vaulted alleys . . . having on the east the dorter above an undercroft containing the chapter-house, warming-house, etc., on the south the

[1] *Kirkstall*, pp. 47, 48.

chapel, on the west the hall, and on the north the frater. . . . Attached to the south-west angle of the cloister was the prior's lodging.'[1]

The Premonstratensian Plan

'The architecture of the Premonstratensians with special reference to their buildings in England' is the subject of a study by Mr. A. W. Clapham.[2] Their thirty-one houses for canons in England were founded on sites remote from cities. The type of their churches approximates very closely to that of the Cistercians; all had square-ended aisleless presbyteries and most of the early houses had the solid walls dividing the chapels in the transepts from one another, though in the thirteenth century, as in the Cistercian churches, these walls became open arches with screens between them. The chief difference between the Cistercian and the Premonstratensian church is the aisleless nave which the English Premonstratensians kept in most cases until the dissolution because they needed no choir for the lay brothers; in a few churches there is a single aisle on the side opposite the cloister, an afterthought as at Shap in Westmoreland. One characteristic of the Benedictine and Augustinian church is commonly absent: Lady Chapels do not exceed in size and importance chapels of other dedications. In many of the early churches there was no masonry tower and it is a later addition. The domestic buildings follow closely the arrangements of the Augustinian Canons. The Premonstratensian chapter-houses were like those of the Cistercians, most of them being divided by a row or rows of columns into two or three aisles, two aisles being more usual.

THE DISSOLUTION OF THE MONASTERIES

Students of history and archæology have as much cause to regret the destruction of monastic churches and buildings as the dispersal of their libraries and muniments. In the years immediately following the dissolution of the monasteries, there are among the State Papers an immense number of grants, either for sums of money or in rewards for services to the Crown, of the site, church, steeple and churchyard of one monastery after another. Some were disposed of piecemeal. As a rule only those buildings which could be used for farm purposes were scheduled to stand. At Tewkesbury 'the church with chapels, cloisters, chapter-house, misericord; the two dormitories, the infirmary, with chapels and lodgings within the same; the work-house, with another house adjoining to the same;

[1] *Archæol. Journal*, LVIII, pp. 1–34.
[2] *Archæologia*, LXXIII, pp. 117–46.

the convent kitchen; the library; the old hostery; the chambers' lodgings; the new hall, the old parlour adjoining to the Abbot's lodging; the cellarer's lodging; the poulter house, the gardner; the almary and all other houses and lodgings not otherwise reserved, were deemed to be superfluous.' The nave was used as the parish church of Tewkesbury; but, not content with this, the inhabitants bought the rest of the church, with the exception of the Lady Chapel, from the Crown for the sum of £453, and thus saved it from destruction.

The origin of the parochial use of the nave of some monastic churches of the Benedictines and Augustinian Canons cannot always be clearly traced. Founders of monasteries frequently gave the parish church of the place as part of the endowment, and the religious, as they were called, to distinguish them from the secular clergy, often built on a choir for their own use, as at Wymondham and Boxgrove. If they pulled down the parish church in the course of building their own church, the right of the inhabitants to have a parish church somewhere within the building remained, unless a new church was provided for them outside it. Thus there were virtually two churches under one roof; sometimes they were completely separated by a dividing wall with doors in it, but more usually there was only a high screen, somewhere in the nave, against which the people's altar was set. This arrangement not infrequently led to quarrels. Some of the townsfolk of Rochester complained that the parochial altar of St. Nicholas in the nave of the cathedral had been moved to a new place against their wishes.[1] After an appeal to the archbishop an award was given, in 1312, to the effect that neither the vicar nor his substitutes should without notice celebrate Mass at that altar except on Sundays, and the festivals of All Saints, St. Nicholas, Christmas Day, and the Purification, and even on those days Mass should be at an hour which would least clash with the services of the monks in their choir. The vicar might preach a sermon immediately after Mass, but not before it. The parishioners also promised that if a suitable church should be built for them, they would give up their claim to the altar of St. Nicholas. After many years a church was begun, but further difficulties arose. The question was finally settled by Bishop Yong in 1421. He decreed that the parishioners of St. Nicholas should have power, by leave of the convent, to finish the church begun on the north side of the burial ground of the priory, but not to enlarge it without permission, except by the addition of a tower. 'The church must be finished in three years: walls, windows and roofs, fit for the due celebration of divine service. It is to have a font, and a vestry for keeping books,

[1] A. I. Pearman, *Rochester*, pp. 210–13.

robes and ornaments. The tower is to stand at the north-west end and may contain bells, to be rung at proper hours, not before five in the morning nor after eight in the evening, except for, by chance, an early Mass, when only one bell shall be used. As soon as the new church is ready the vicar and parishioners shall renounce their rights in the cathedral, but shall be entitled to bury in the church, in Greenchurch Haw, or in the other cemetery to the west of the cathedral.' The church was finished, and in the nave of the cathedral, between five and seven in the evening of December 18th, 1423, the vicar of St. Nicholas and two representatives of the parishioners renounced their rights in the cathedral in the presence of the prior, the Bishop of Dromore and others.

At Sherborne quarrels between the monks and the townsfolk led to a riot in 1437.[1] The nave was used as a parish church, but probably owing to disagreements, the townsfolk built the church of All Hallows against the west end of the nave for their own use. Technically All Hallows was not a parish church but a chapel, and all children were taken into the nave to be baptized. The monks moved the font to another place in the nave, and made the door into it from All Hallows much narrower. Some of the parishioners then set up a font in All Hallows, and the monks appealed to the bishop against the usurpation of their rights. Robert Neville, then Bishop of Salisbury, came to Sherborne to hold an inquiry, and gave his award on January 8th, 1437. He ordered that the font in All Hallows should be removed forthwith, that before Christmas the font in the nave should be replaced in its old position, and that all children born in Sherborne should be baptized therein. Before Christmas, also, the monks should enlarge the door by which the parishioners entered the nave. The monks should set up at their own expense a partition between their choir and the nave, so that there should be a distinct separation between the monks and the parishioners. Whether there were delays or evasions is not clear, but the monks never altered the doorway. When Leland visited Sherborne he wrote down the story of the riot: 'Whereupon one Walter Gallor, a stoute Bocher dwelling yn Shirburn, defacid clene the Fontstone, and after the Variaunce growing to a playne sedition and the Townes-Menne by the Mene of an Earl of Huntendune lying yn those Quarters and taking the Townes-Mennes Part, and the Bisshop of Saresbyrie the Monkes Part, a Preste of Al-Halowis shot a shaft with fier into the Toppe of that part of St. Marye Chirch that devided the Est Part that the Monkes usid from that the Townes-Men usid: and this Partition chauncing at that Tyme to be thakkid yn, the Rofe was sette a fier, and consequently all the hole Chirch,

[1] *Archæol. Journal*, XXII, pp. 179–98.

the Lede and Belles meltid, was defacid.' Mr. W. B. Wildman has pointed out that the 'partition' which was thatched must have been the central tower which was being raised, and was covered with a temporary roof to keep out the rain. The walls of the choir are to this day reddened by the fire. After the dissolution Sir John Horsey bought Sherborne from the King. He sold the abbey church to the vicar and parishioners for 100 marks, and afterwards All Hallows became ruinous. At Great Malvern and Selby also the townsfolk bought the monastic church to use instead of their parish church. At Romsey, St. Albans, Christchurch, and a few other places where the nave or a part of it was parochial, they showed the same public spirit as at Tewkesbury, and bought the rest of the church. At Dorchester in Oxfordshire Leland noted that a great rich man dwelling in the town bought the east part of the abbey church for £140 and gave it to augment the parish church in the nave. At Malmesbury a rich clothier, Stumpe by name, took the leading part in the purchase of the nave of the abbey church for use instead of the old parish church. At Leominster, Bridlington, Thorney, Wymondham and Binham, only the parochial nave has survived. Where the townsfolk had fine parish churches, they had no reason to pledge themselves and future generations to the far greater cost of maintaining the fabric of a larger church, and therefore the abbey churches of Bury St. Edmunds, Evesham, Cirencester, Winchcombe, Abingdon and Glastonbury, were destroyed. Of the Cluniac Order only four churches of small priories with parochial naves are in use as parish churches, Church Preen in Shropshire, Little Horkesley in Essex, Malpas in Monmouthshire, St. Clears in Carmarthenshire. Of the churches of Augustinian Canons it is probable that only 37 out of over 200 had parochial naves. Possibly two or three churches of the Gilbertine Canons had parochial naves, but the Premonstratensian Canons and the Cistercians had none. The Premonstratensian church of Blanchland in Northumberland was rescued from ruin in 1752 when the thirteenth-century choir, north transept and tower were restored for use as a parish church. Of the Cistercian churches the choir and transepts of Dore in Herefordshire were restored for a parish church by Viscount Scudamore a hundred years after the dissolution and reopened in 1634. Holme Cultram abbey church in Cumberland was granted for a parish church at the dissolution, but gradually became so ruinous through neglect that only a portion of the nave without its aisles is now in use. The nave of Margam Abbey in Glamorganshire, and the refectory of Beaulieu Abbey in Hampshire also serve as parish churches.

A document in the handwriting of Henry VIII sets forth his opinion 'that it is thought therefore unto the king's highness most expedient and necessary that more bishoprics, collegiate and cathedral churches should be established, instead of these aforesaid religious houses within the foundation whereof other titles before rehearsed shall be established.'[1] On a second sheet of paper there is another document written by the King, but apparently incomplete, listing the 'Bishoprics to be New Made.' Out of these only six were created, Westminster, Oxford, Chester, Gloucester, Bristol and Peterborough. The bishopric of Westminster was suppressed in 1550 when Thirlby was translated to Norwich. It was not until the nineteenth century that bishoprics were created for Hertfordshire, Cornwall, Lancashire, Nottinghamshire and Derbyshire; bishoprics for Suffolk and Surrey are more recent and Shropshire still lacks a bishopric.

Cardinal Gasquet has described the process of realizing the value of monastic buildings in a very interesting chapter of his book, *Henry VIII and the English Monasteries*: 'The chief source of profit was the lead with which the monasteries were mostly covered. It was stripped from the roof of the finest church without hesitation and melted at a fire made, probably, with the wood of the stalls, screenwork or rood. . . . Bands of workmen went from place to place throughout the country, lit their fires in the naves or chancels of abbey churches, and occupied themselves for days, and even in some cases, weeks, in melting the coverings of roofs, and the gutters, spouts and pipes from the building into pigs and fodders, the sale of which might add a few pounds to the royal plunder. . . . For eleven weeks, as an example, the Commissioners wandered about Somerset, "defacing, destroying and prostrating the churches, cloisters, belfreys and other buildings of the late monasteries." ' They had orders to spare only those buildings which could be used for farms or other purposes. There were few to buy up the materials of the numerous monasteries of Lincolnshire, and one of the Commissioners there recommended that the walls should be left standing as a quarry for future sales of stone to builders.

The policy of long neglect has been changed at last, and in the twentieth century, through the generosity of noble owners, an increasing number of ruined monasteries have been given to the nation. The Commissioners of Works are their guardians to preserve them for future generations.

[1] F. A. Gasquet, *Henry VIII and the English Monasteries*, pp. 430, 431, ed. 1899.

SHORT BIBLIOGRAPHY

(a) *General Works*

Cambridge Medieval History, Vol. I, chap. xviii, 'Monasticism,' by Cuthbert Butler; Vol. V, chap. xx, 'The Monastic Orders,' by A. Hamilton Thompson.

Medieval England, ed. H. W. C. Davis, chap. x, 'Monasticism', by R. Graham.

U. Berlière, *L'Ordre Monastique* (Maredsous).

Dictionnaire d' Histoire et Géographie Ecclésiastique, ed. Baudrier, Vol. VII, Ordre, Bénédictin by Dom P. Schmitz, O.S.B.

F. A. Gasquet, *English Monastic Life*.

R. Graham, *English Ecclesiastical Studies*.

A. Hamilton Thompson, *English Monasteries* (Cambridge Manuals).

M. R. James, *Abbeys*, (Great Western Railway, 1925.)

D. M. Knowles, *The Monastic Order in England*. 1940.

D. M. Knowles, *The Religious Orders in England*, Vols. I and II. 1948, 1955.

F. H. Crossley, *The English Abbey*. 1935.

(b) *Original Sources and Records*

The following Chronicles chiefly concerning internal affairs are published in the Rolls Series with prefaces: *Gesta abbatum monasterii S. Albani. Chronicon Abbatiæ de Evesham. Chronicles and Memorials of the Reign of Richard I*, Vol. II: *Epistolæ Cantuarienses. Annales Monastici. Chronica monasterii de Melsa. Memorials of St. Edmund's Abbey.*

Dugdale, *Monasticon Anglicanum*.

Sir Ernest Clarke, *A Translation of the Chronicle of Jocelin of Brakelond*.

J. M. Wilson, *The Worcester Liber Albus:* glimpses of life in a great Benedictine monastery in the fourteenth century.

Durham Account Rolls, ed. J. T. Fowler. (Surtees Society.)

W. A. Pantin, 'The General and Provincial Chapters of the English Black Monks,' *R. Hist. Soc. Trans.* Fourth Series, X, pp. 195–263; *Chapters of the English Black Monks* (Camden Third Series, R. Hist. Soc.).

G. F. Duckett, *Visitations of English Cluniac Foundations*.

Statuta Capitulorum Generalium Ordinis Cisterciensis, ed. J.-Mia Canivez (Bibliothèque de la Revue d'Histoire Ecclésiastique).

J. Willis Clark, *The Observances in use at the Augustinian Priory at Barnwell*.

E. A. Webb, *Records of St. Bartholomew's, Smithfield*.

H. E. Salter, *Chapters of the Augustinian Canons* (Canterbury and York Society).

D. M. Knowles and R. N. Hadcock, *Medieval Religious Houses in England and Wales*. 1955.

D. M. Knowles, *The Monastic Constitutions of Lanfranc*. 1951.

C. R. C. Davies, *Medieval Cartularies*. 1958.

(c) *Special Studies*

Millénaire de Cluny (Académie de Mâcon, 1910).

W. A. P. Mason, 'The beginnings of the Cistercian Order,' *R. Hist. Soc. Trans.* New Series, XIX, pp. 169–207.

A. M. Cooke, 'The Settlement of the Cistercians in England,' *Eng. Hist. Rev.*, VIII, pp. 625–76.

E. Speakman, 'The Rule of St. Augustine,' *Owens College Essays*, ed. Tout and Tait.

W. H. Frere, 'The Early History of Canons Regular,' printed in *Fasciculus J. W. Clark dicatus*, pp. 186–216.

F. A. Gasquet, 'The English Premonstratensians,' *R. Hist. Soc. Trans.* New Series, XVII, pp. 1–22, *Collectanea Anglo-Premonstratensia* (Camden Third Series, R. Hist. Soc.).

R. Graham, *St. Gilbert of Sempringham and the Gilbertines.*

A. Hamilton Thompson, 'Double Monasteries and the Male Element in Nunneries,' *Appendix VIII to the Archbishops' Report on the Ministry of Women.*

E. M. Thompson, *The Carthusian Order in England.*

R. Graham, 'Four Alien Priories of Monmouthshire,' *Journal of the British Archæological Association*, New Series, Vol. XXXV.

R. Graham and A. W. Clapham, 'The Monastery of Cluny, 910–1155,' *Archæologia*, Vol. LXXX.

M. Morgan, *The English Lands of the Abbey of Bec.* 1946.

J. C. Dickinson, *The Origins of the Austin Canons.* 1950.

H. M. Colvin, *The White Canons in England.* 1951.

G. Baskerville, *English Monks and the Suppression of the Monasteries.* 1937.

R. H. Snape, *English Monastic Finances in the later Middle Ages*, 1926.

(d) *Books, Illuminations, History and Monastic Art.*

C. Jenkins, *The Monastic Chronicler and the Early School of St. Albans.*

J. Wickham Legg and W. H. St. John Hope, *Inventories of Christchurch, Canterbury.*

E. G. Millar, *English Illuminated Manuscripts from the Tenth to the Thirteenth Century.*

J. D. Le Couteur, *English Medieval Painted Glass.*

W. R. Lethaby, 'The Romance Tiles of Chertsey Abbey,' *Walpole Society*, Vol. II.

P. B. Clayton, 'The Inlaid Tiles of Westminster Abbey,' *Archæological Journal*, Vol. LXIX.

R. Vaughan, *Matthew Paris.* 1958.

(e) *Monastic Architecture and Descriptions of Particular Houses.*

A. W. Clapham, 'The Architecture of the Premonstratensians with special reference to their buildings in England.' *Archæologia*, Vol. LXXIII.

Numerous plans and architectural descriptions are included in the *Victoria County Histories*, e.g., *Peterborough* by Sir Charles Peers, Northampton, Vol. II, and in the volumes of the *Royal Commission on Historical Monuments*; cf. also the guide-books issued by the Office of Works.

AN ESSAY ON ENGLISH MONASTERIES

A. Hamilton Thompson, *The Premonstratensian Abbey of Welbeck.*

R. C. Fowler and A. W. Clapham, *Beeleigh Abbey.*

A. W. Clapham, *Romanesque Architecture in Western Europe; English Romanesque Architecture after the Conquest.*

W. H. St. John Hope and J. Bilson, *Architectural Description of Kirkstall Abbey.* Thoresby Society, 1907.

A. Hamilton Thompson, *History and Architectural Description of the Priory of St. Mary, Bolton-in-Wharfdale, with some Account of the Canons Regular of the Order of St. Augustine and their Houses in Yorkshire.* Thoresby Society, 1928.

T. D. Atkinson, *Ely Cathedral Priory* (with nineteen small plans of Benedictine houses).

Westminster Abbey, *Royal Commission on Historical Monuments.*

W. H. Godfrey, *The Priory of St. Pancras at Lewes.*

A. W. Clapham, *Lesnes Abbey.*

Sir H. Brakspear, 'Beaulieu Abbey,' *Archæological Journal,* Vol. LVIII.

Sir H. Brakspear, *Waverley Abbey* (Surrey Archæological Society, 1905).

W. H. St. John Hope and H. Brakspear, 'The Gilbertine Priory of Watton,' *Archæological Journal,* LVIII.

W. H. St. John Hope, 'The Architectural History of Mount Grace Charterhouse,' *Yorkshire Archæological Journal,* Vol. XVIII.

R. Graham, 'The History of the Alien Priory of Wenlock.' *Journal of the British Archæological Association,* Third Series, Vol. IV. 1939.

R. Graham and H. S. Braun, 'Excavations on the Site of Sempringham Priory.' *Journal of the British Archæological Association,* Third Series, Vol. V. 1940.

R. Graham, 'A History of the Buildings of the English Province of the Order of Cluny after the Dissolution of the Monasteries.' *Journal of the British Archæological Association,* Third Series, Vol. XV. 1952.

D. M. Knowles & J. K. St. Joseph. *English Monastic Sites from the Air.* 1952.

SIR FRANK STENTON

The Development of the Castle
in England and Wales

In 1910, when this essay was originally published, any account of
the development of the art of castle-building in England was bound,
at the outset, to take a tentative form. The question whether the
origins of the English castle were to be sought in the private fortifications of Anglo-Saxon thegns, or in the defensive works of
Norman knights or barons, had not yet reached a final settlement; it
was still impossible to speak with certainty about the relation which
the fortresses raised in the days of the first two Norman kings bear
to the earthworks which have descended to the present time from
the period which lies beyond 1066.[1] At the present time there is no
serious opposition to the view that the art of castle-building, in the
usual acceptation of the phrase, was introduced into England as a
result of the Norman influence which became predominant in the
eleventh century. The remarks in regard to this point of Ordericus
Vitalis, who finds a main reason for the rapidity of the Norman
Conquest of England in the fact that the English had possessed
very few of those fortresses which the Normans knew as castles,[2]
are supported both by the recorded progress of castle-building in
the country during the reign of William I, and by the resemblance
in general plan between the earliest Norman castles in England and
the remains of contemporary fortifications in Normandy, and it is

[1] *See* references in Bibliographical Note, below p. 122.
[2] *Historia Ecclesiastica*, ed. Le Prévost, II, 184.

very significant that the first work of the Conqueror as he passed over his new kingdom was the establishment of castles in all the greater towns of the country, and along all the more important lines of road. Little as we know about the internal history of England during the Conqueror's reign, we can at once compile a list of from fifty to sixty castles built during the twenty years which followed 1066. It is at least evident that William I felt that his hold upon England would never be secure until the land was planted everywhere with castles in the hands of persons whom he could trust, and that it is from his activity in this matter that the great majority of the castles existing at the close of his reign derive their origin.

THE EARLIEST ENGLISH CASTLES

The Norman origin of the English castle is only rendered the more evident by the existence of a small but remarkable group of such fortresses known to have been built before the coming of the Conqueror. In Herefordshire, a considerable number of Norman settlers had been established before the year 1050, and three of the castles which they founded before 1066 to the disgust of the countryside can be identified at the present day. The castle which they built at Hereford itself is likely to have been the strongest of the group; but a portion of its bailey is all that now remains of its defences, and its fame in history is less than that which attaches to the fortress raised by Richard, the son of Scrob, in the north-eastern angle of the county. Owing in part to the exaggerated respect formerly paid to the forcible language in which the compiler of the Laud manuscript of the Anglo-Saxon Chronicle expresses his disapproval of the Herefordshire castle-men, in part to the erroneous view which assigned to these early fortresses much greater solidity of structure than ever belonged to them in fact,[1] Richard's Castle has acquired a sinister reputation which is not borne out by the actual evidence relating to the history of this elementary earthwork. The third castle of the series, Ewias Harold, at the southern entrance of the Golden Valley, is chiefly interesting in that its name perpetuates the memory of the son of the Norman Earl of Hereford, Ralf of Mantes, the Confessor's nephew. At the other end of the country there is a distinct probability that Clavering Castle, in Essex, was the work

---

[1] The section in Professor Freeman's *Norman Conquest* (II, 136–8), headed, in the Contents, 'Outrages of the Normans in Herefordshire', is largely responsible for these ideas. In 1868, the erection of stone castles of the keep and base-court type, was greatly antedated; and Professor Freeman's remarks on 'the tall, square, massive, donjon of the Normans' are highly anachronistic when applied to the English fortresses of 1051.

97

of Swegen, the native sheriff of that shire; and if we may trust the contemporary accounts of the negotiations which passed between William of Normandy and Harold, son of Godwin, at the time of the latter's famous oath, the castle had already been built at Dover which was in being when the Norman army marched to that town after the capture of Romney in 1066. All the castles which have just been named were built after the pattern subsequently adopted by the first generation of Norman settlers—a pattern which will shortly be described—and were regarded as unwelcome innovations by the native chroniclers of the period, in this respect no doubt reflecting the general opinion of the country. But it may be remarked in passing that if the instinctive conservatism of the average Anglo-Saxon thegn had only permitted his imitation of these foreign models of defensive work, the permanent reduction of England would certainly not have been accomplished within five years of the battle of Hastings.

ANGLO-SAXON FORTIFICATIONS

The existence of this little group of fortresses hardly affects the general accuracy of the statement that the first phase of the art of castellation in England belongs to the years which immediately followed 1066. But it must at once be admitted that from a remote period of their history the Anglo-Saxons had recognised the necessity of founding fortified posts in the land. Their practice in this respect has left abundant traces on the surface of English local nomenclature among the numerous place-names which end in the familiar terminals borough or bury.[1] It is even possible, though all the evidence makes in the opposite direction, that here and there, on the eve of the Conquest, a wealthy thegn may have raised for himself a fortress after the Norman plan;[2] that, for example, the remarkable earthworks at Laxton in Nottinghamshire may possibly have been thrown up by Tochi the son of Outi, lord of the manor in 1066, rather than by Geoffrey Alselin, its Domesday owner or his successors. But the number of cases in which this may conceivably have happened is exceedingly small; and the private defences of the Anglo-Saxon period, in so far as we know them, were but rudi-

[1] It may be noted that 'borough' commonly represents the nominative, and 'bury' the dative—byrig—of the O.E. burh, a fort or stronghold. The primitive character of these works may be gathered from the famous interpolation in the Old English Chronicle under the year 547, to the effect that Ida of Northumbria 'built Bamburgh (Bebban burh), it was first enclosed with a hedge, and afterwards with a stone wall.'

[2] The sentence from Ordericus Vitalis to which reference has already been made points in this direction. Its tenor suggests that its author was referring to castles in native hands, not to Norman fortresses such as those in Herefordshire.

mentary affairs. Eddlesborough or Bucklebury can hardly have been more than a line of hedge or palisading drawn round the farm-steadings of Eadwulf or Burghild; and even those fortresses which were intended to protect the country at large against an invader were elementary in design and simple in construction. The normal plan of an Anglo-Saxon borough, an imitation of the defences with which the Romans had surrounded the more important settlements, civil and military, which they founded in Britain, merely implied the enclosure of an area generally approaching the rectangular with a rampart and external ditch, such as may be seen in perfection at Wallingford and Wareham; and the strongest towns of the period were those in which, as in the cases of Lincoln, Chester, and York, the remains of Roman masonry composed, or had been incorporated into, the borough wall. The weakness of this arrangement lay in the fact that when the town was attacked, its defenders were in general too few to man the entire round of the ramparts. It is one of the vexed questions of later Anglo-Saxon history whether, in the early tenth century, when the attempt was made to provide the country at large with a series of defensible posts, recognition of this danger led to the erection of fortresses comparable in area with the castles of the Norman period. The evidence in relation to this point is conflicting; for the contemporary section of the Anglo-Saxon chronicle, in recording the activities of Edward the Elder and Æthelflaed of Mercia in the building of *burhs*, says little as to the nature of these works, which can only be inferred, at best, from the dubious evidence supplied by their existing remains. At Stamford and Bedford it seems certain that Edward's work consisted in the foundation and enclosure of new boroughs to the south of the rivers upon which those places respectively stand; at Worcester he appears to have fortified an ancient borough with a stone wall; at Maldon and Witham, the remains of wide, rectangular enclosures, sur-rounded with earthen ramparts, suggests that he followed the plan and scale of the boroughs of an earlier age even when his work was not determined by any relation to an existing town. On the other hand, it seems probable that the two *burhs* at Nottingham were merely forts commanding the bridge between them which spanned the Trent at this point; and at Towcester and Bakewell, existing mounds of earth with no obvious indications of external works have been thought to represent the results of Edward's fortifications at these places. But whatever may have been the exact nature of his works, and they probably varied between place and place, they rapidly lost their significance as factors in a general scheme of national defence. When William the Conqueror landed, the walled town was the only type of fortress with which he had to deal; and except in the solitary case of Exeter, its reduction seems to have given him but little difficulty.

THE MOTTE AND BAILEY

If we may form conclusions from the existing remains of such defensive works as may be referred to the eleventh century, a remarkable uniformity of plan underlies the great majority of the earliest Norman castles in England. The type to which they conform— a type now commonly known from its distinctive features as that of the motte and bailey—is of frequent occurrence among the castles of Normandy; and it was reproduced on an extensive scale both during the Norman occupation of South Wales in the early years of the twelfth century, in Scotland under David I, and his successors, and in the course of the conquest of Ireland a generation later.[1] The main features of the type may here, for the sake of brevity, be reduced to two: in the first place, a mound of earth, with a ditch surrounding it and a wooden palisade crowning it; in the second place, and below the mound, a base-court or bailey, encircled with its own ditch, rampart and stockade, and separated from the mound by the former. At the summit of the mound there would be a dwelling-place of some kind—in most cases apparently a wooden tower—to which the garrison could retire in case of need. Within the bailey would stand the stables, domestic buildings and hall. Of these buildings, for obvious reasons, only the scantiest of traces are discernible at the present day, but that wood and not stone was the material commonly employed in the castles of the Conqueror's reign is proved by abundant evidence. The almost universal absence of any masonry which can reasonably be referred to the eleventh century is of itself highly significant, and the literary evidence points in the same direction. The real strength of the castle lay in the height of its mound and the depth of its ditch; the nature of the buildings contained within it was a matter of quite inferior importance.

Earthworks of this type are distributed over the whole of England and Wales, although the number contained within a given county bears no obvious relation either to its area or to its geographical position. It is natural enough that the shires along the Welsh border should be thickly planted with such earthworks, of which Hereford-shire contains thirty-two, but it is more remarkable that the type should be illustrated by numerous and highly developed examples in central England, where the necessity for frontier defence did not

[1] See Orpen in *Eng. Hist., Rev.* XXI., 417. A detailed investigation of the mottes of South Wales is much to be desired.

arise. Warwickshire contains at least ten such fortresses, while Leicestershire contains four certain examples, Nottinghamshire five. One is on safer ground in asserting that an earthwork of the motte and bailey pattern will often be found in a place which was the *caput* of a feudal honour, and that the seats of the more important mesne tenants of the eleventh century will not infrequently be distinguished in the same way. At Tutbury, Pontefract, Eye, Dunster, Cainhoe (Bedfordshire), Wigmore, Dudley, Tickhill, Belvoir, Tamworth, Berkhamstead, Laxton (Notts), the *capita* of the Domesday fiefs of Henry de Ferrers, Ilbert de Lacy, Robert Malet, William de Moion, Nigel de Albini, Ralf de Mortimer, William the son of Ansculf, Roger de Bulli, Robert de Todeni, Robert 'Dispensator', Robert Count of Mortain, and Geoffrey Alselin, a motte and bailey in each case marks the site of the lord's residence. Sometimes, as at Tutbury and Belvoir, the building of the castle was followed, in accordance with continental ideas, by the development of a new borough in front of its walls, and by the foundation of a religious house in its neighbourhood; but in many cases, the centre of the honour was fixed in one of the ancient shire towns of the land, and William Peverel, Hugh de Grentemaisnil, and Henry de Beaumont seem each to have fixed their chief residence in the castles which they respectively held for the king in the boroughs of Nottingham, Leicester, and Warwick.

Among the hundreds of such fortifications which survive in a reasonable state of preservation a rigid uniformity of design could not be expected to prevail, although the main features of the type are in fact reproduced with general consistency, amid the most diverse of local conditions. It is in regard to the number and disposition of the baileys, and in their relation to the castle mound, that variations were commonly made upon the simple type. Where more than one bailey occurs in a single castle, the second bailey will generally extend beyond the first on the face remote from the mound, as at Ongar, Essex; less frequently, both baileys, with a ditch between them, will abut upon the mound as at Newtown, Montgomery, and in a small group of castles, to which Nottingham, Arundel, and Windsor belong, the mound occupies the centre of the whole fortification.[1] In the latter case, however, it is a reasonable inference that one or more of the baileys represents later addition to the original fortress since the normal position of the mound on the outer edge of the defences was undoubtedly felt to be of value in giving to its defenders, in the last resort, a means of egress to the open country. In regard to the more important English

---

[1] *See* plans of Windsor in Vict. Hist. Berkshire I., and of Nottingham in Clark, *Mediæval Military Architecture*.

castles, it is generally possible to establish a rough correspondence between the several parts of the fortress as they have descended to the present day and the statements in chronicles or records relating to the progress of building operations on the site; and the result,

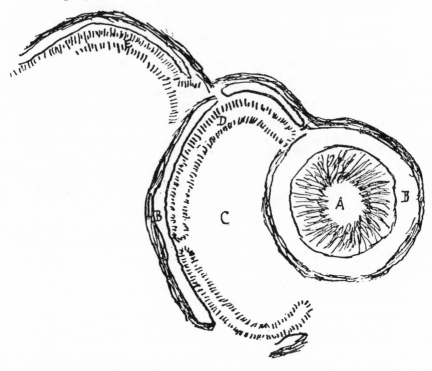

A. Motte.
B. Moat.
C. Inner Bailey.
D. Rampart to carry Stockade.
E. Rampart of Outer Bailey.

ONGAR, ESSEX
Founded on V.C.H., Essex I, 297

save in the rarest instances, is to leave the mound with its external bailey as the nucleus around which defensive works of greater elaboration have been grouped by later designers.

The nature of the sites on which these early castles were planted varied indefinitely in different cases. Many a site which would be recommended by its inaccessibility would be held unsuitable for lack of water, while, on the other hand, in the days before gunpowder, it was immaterial that a castle should be overlooked by higher ground near it so long as that ground lay beyond missile shot. In general, there is a strong tendency for an early castle to stand immediately against some river or stream, one side of the defences thus being impregnable from the outset. When a castle was built in order to command a town, it will nearly always be found to stand on the borough walls, or just outside them; and as most towns are built on rivers, the castle will commonly stand at the point where the wall and river defences of the town coincide. This is the case at Oxford, Cambridge, Wallingford, Bedford, Chester, York, Warwick, Stamford, Hereford, Leicester, and Shrewsbury, to name a few examples. Stafford and Lincoln are exceptions; resulting, in the latter case, from the fact that the town wall itself was drawn along the face of the hill at a considerable distance from the river below, in the former case, apparently, from the wish to command the important road which led from Shrewsbury to the Midlands. The motive which planted the castle on the edge of the borough defences was evidently the wish to facilitate communication, in case of siege, with a relieving army, combined with a recognition of the danger which would follow from the firing of adjacent houses by an enemy. No single principle determined the sites of the more numerous castles which arose in the open country—it can only be said that the advantage of obtaining a view over as extensive a tract of country as possible was undoubtedly felt and acted upon in numerous instances. Belvoir castle, overlooking the lowlands of south Nottinghamshire; Rockingham Castle, dominating the Welland valley; Richard's Castle near Ludlow, commanding the whole north-eastern corner of Herefordshire, are cases in point. The castle-builders of the eleventh century were keenly alive to the facts of local geography.

It is not difficult to understand the reasons which caused this type of fortress to be so widely adopted by the conquerors of England. It was cheap in the building, and when built it could be defended adequately by a very small body of men. The Norman baron who wished to erect a castle had only to capture a sufficient number of rustics and make them dig. Then, too, the speed with which these primitive castles could be thrown up was an important consideration. In 1068, in the course of a campaign which only lasted a month or two, William the Conqueror founded the castles of Warwick, Nottingham, York, Lincoln, Huntingdon, and Cambridge, with, probably, those of Leicester and Stamford as well. In 1069, a second castle was built in York, the mound of which, known as the Baile Hill, still survives, and the building of which took eight days. Even at this early date, on bare hill-sides where stone was more plentiful than earth or timber, stone towers may have been built at the outset, but the possible examples are few and uncertain. The rectangular towers of Peak Castle and Clitheroe stand upon sites of this character which were already fortified in 1086; but neither of these towers is as early as the Conqueror's reign, and that of Peak Castle is a representative example of the square keeps of the twelfth century. A stone keep might well take a year or more in the building, it was very expensive, and it demanded labour of a more highly skilled sort than was at the service of the average baron under ordinary circumstances. Then, too, it was highly important that the castle should only present a very small frontage to an attack. When we remember that in 1086 the total number of knights in England probably amounted to something under 5,000 and that trained and efficient men-at-arms were relatively few, it will appear that the average castle could not have been constructed so as to require a large force for its defence. We certainly must not endow the conquerors of England with anything approaching the resources of men and money possessed by their sons and grandsons.

THE SHELL KEEP

It was quite certain, however, that as the Norman baronage became more firmly settled in the country, and times became quieter, the consequent leisure would permit improvements in the art of fortification; and the most obvious of these developments was clearly the substitution of stone for wood in the buildings of the castle. The stockade which had originally surrounded the crest of the mound would be replaced by a stone wall, and stone buildings would gradually arise upon its inner face. To a structure of this kind archæologists have given the name of a shell keep; a ring of wall, polygonal or circular, enclosing an open space. As it is highly unsafe to erect heavy stone buildings on made ground, such as the crest of an earthen *motte*, some considerable time had commonly to pass before this improvement was brought about; but by the end of the twelfth century it had already been reached in numerous instances. Among surviving castles, Lincoln, Carisbrooke, and Totnes had already developed shell keeps before 1154; Arundel, Berkeley, and Windsor reached this stage before the close of the century, and similar defences were added to other castles of the motte and bailey type until at least the reign of Edward III., to which period the shells of Durham and Lewes have been referred. In the meantime, a stone wall was generally substituted for the original palisade which ran along the scarp of the bailey; and domestic buildings, of which a fine, though late, series exists, for example, at Dudley, were erected within its limits. The course of the latter development is illustrated by payments for work on the 'King's houses' in many of his castles, recorded in the Pipe Rolls of the late twelfth century. The entrance to the castle, which always gave immediate access to the bailey or ward rather than to the motte, was commonly fortified with stone at an early date; and stone bridges and stairways came to replace the planks and ladders which had formerly crossed the moats, and led from the bailey to the summit of the mound. On the other hand, it should be noted that the appearance of stonework on the line of the bailey may well, in any given case, be antecedent to the erection of masonry on the motte ; at Bedford there was a stone tower on the bailey before the shell keep was planted on the motte, and while there are now no traces of any building upon the ill-compacted soil of the motte at Stamford, the remains of a chapel of the thirteenth century exist upon the inner face of the castle wall. This reservation does not affect the general course of development followed by the mound and court castle, but it is remarkable that in many instances no signs of masonry are now to be discovered anywhere within the precincts of fortresses which remained positions of military importance for an extended period. There is hardly a parallel elsewhere in England to the twelfth century hall which still stands on the line of the original bailey at Christchurch, Hampshire. Full allowance must be made in this connection for processes of destruction in modern times; processes which, for example, have denuded the motte and bailey of Fotheringhay of every trace of the buildings within which the tragedy of 1587 was enacted, but it cannot be doubted that wooden erections frequently sufficed for the accommodation of the lord of the castle so long as he continued to fix his residence there.

RECTANGULAR KEEPS

Such was, in outline, the later development of many of the earthen defences raised in haste by the first generation of the Norman settlers in England, the castles of the period 1066–1100. But from the death of William II. onwards through the twelfth century, rapidity of construction was no longer a matter of supreme importance in the building of a castle. The native English were becoming reconciled to the Norman rule, and save for the years of anarchy under Stephen the central government was, in general, strong enough to keep the peace of the realm. Accordingly Anglo-Norman barons of the twelfth century, in founding their castles, will generally build them of stone from the beginning;[1] and the plan which they adopted was that which has come to be regarded as the typical form of a Norman castle in England—the square tower with a walled enclosure appended to it. The square tower had been employed in French fortifications at least twenty years before the Norman Conquest; but its introduction into England was slowly accomplished, and the 'White Tower' of London and the keep of Colchester are the only examples certainly anterior to the death of William I. Now the component parts of such a typical castle, the tower and the enclosure, though almost universally found in combination, represent distinct stages in the art of fortification. The enclosure corresponding to the bailey of the older type of castle—the *castellum*, strictly so called—derives in the last resort from the rectangular *castra* of Roman times; it represents a reproduction, on a smaller scale, of the normal defences which surrounded the towns of the Anglo-Saxon period. The tower or 'keep' is a device of medieval invention, appropriate to the new conditions of society which rose with the development of the feudal system. Accordingly, it will not infrequently be found that within a single fortress the tower and enclosure beneath it came into being at different dates. Sometimes, as at London, and probably at Bristol, the original fortress consisted of the tower; more frequently, as at Rochester and Newcastle, the tower was added to a pre-existing ward. At Ludlow, recent excavations show the existing rectangular keep to have been developed from the gate-house of the original enclosure. But by the second quarter of the twelfth century the normal castle had come to include both features, and the original distinction between them was already by way of being forgotten.[2]

In connection with castles of this type, the main feature is the fact that their strength depended almost entirely upon the facilities which they afforded for an extended period of passive defence. Their walls are, in general, enormously thick; a feature due in great part to the inferior quality of the mortar used by their builders, but allowing the passages required for internal communication to run within the wall itself; and the structure is in most cases further strengthened by flat buttresses. A series of rectangular slits in the thickness of the wall would commonly suffice for windows, though at an early date round-headed openings, such as are found in ecclesiastical buildings of the eleventh century, were occasionally introduced

[1] At Lincoln, Porchester, and Pevensey, adjacent remains of Roman masonry were turned to account in the original construction of the castles in question. The first and last of these belong to the *motte and bailey* type; Pevensey was founded in 1066, Lincoln in 1068. At Porchester and Pevensey the whole *enciente* is composed of Roman walling.

[2] *See* Round, *Geoffrey de Mandeville*, Appendix: 'Tower and Castle', pp. 328–46.

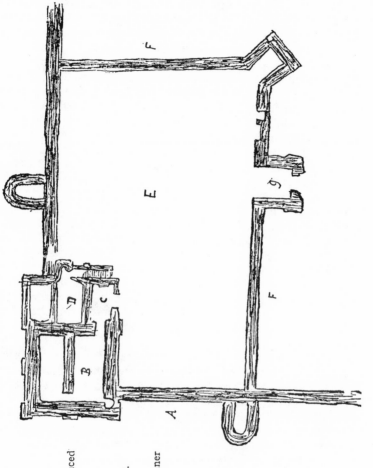

PORCHESTER CASTLE, HAMPSHIRE, after V.C.H. Hants III. 156.

(Buildings later than Twelfth Century ignored).

A. Line of Roman Wall—produced to include Outer Ward.
B. Keep on Mound.
C. Chapel.
D. Forebuilding and Stairway.
E. Inner Ward.
F. Twelfth Century wall of Inner Ward.
G. Gatehouse.

107

into the upper stories of the keep. The only entrance to the keep was usually fixed on the first floor, access being given to it at first by a ladder or open staircase as at Guildford, but in later times by a fore-building, such as is well seen, for example, in the tower of Newcastle. A well was commonly sunk through the foundations of the keep, though at times, as at Ludlow, the well-head appears within the fortifications of the inner ward; the roof of the tower was usually crowned with battlements. With regard to the disposition of the several rooms comprised within the keep there is the greatest variety between different castles. A store room, a hall, a private chamber for the lord of the castle, are fairly constant features; not infrequently, as at London, Guildford, Colchester and Newcastle, a chapel or oratory also is included; but in the course of years there was a tendency to erect chapel, hall, guard rooms, domestic offices, and other buildings required for the life of the castle in time of peace, within the limits of the adjacent ward rather than in the keep itself. In time of war, the garrison would concentrate their efforts upon the defence of the keep, and for so long as their provisions held out the chances of the event were wholly in their favour. It was always difficult, and frequently impossible, for a besieging host to undermine an opposing fortress; mine could be met by countermine, and a tower which stood upon rock was invulnerable from beneath. A stone wall twelve feet thick, such as composed the keep of many castles of the twelfth century, was fairly proof against the rudimentary siege engines of the time, and a direct assault was in general out of the question. Reduction by famine was the only certain means which could be employed against such a fortress, and the patience of a feudal host was commonly too small for an effective blockade to be sustained for a sufficient period. In relation to contemporary methods of attack, and for purposes of a purely passive defence, the perfected Norman keep was a structure most admirably adapted to the ends which it was designed to serve.

The obvious advantages of a solid keep led in a number of cases to its addition to the defensive works of castles originally built after the pattern of the motte and bailey. At Gloucester, the keep, now vanished, seems to have stood in the middle of the bailey, probably enlarged for the purpose; at Newcastle, it certainly occupied a site distinct from the original motte. At Guildford, and at Clun in Shropshire, a rectangular keep was placed upon the motte itself; a retaining wall at Guildford converting the remainder of the summit of the motte into a middle ward, while at Clun there exist the remains of a shell keep upon the motte in addition to the rectangular tower. At Nottingham, there is evidence to show that a square tower of the early thirteenth century was placed upon the motte; but in general this plan was rarely adopted, owing, no doubt, to the fact that the artificial mound afforded an insecure foundation for the tremendous weight of a rectangular keep. In the two great royal castles of Kent, at Canterbury and Rochester, a new site, apparently outside the limits of the original bailey, was chosen for the square towers built there in the twelfth century. At Oxford, the place of a keep seems to have been supplied by the remarkable tower, of early Norman date, which dominates the river face of the bailey wall. But at Shrewsbury and York, until the thirteenth century, the king was content with wooden towers upon the crest of the respective mottes, when the tower of Shrewsbury appears to have collapsed of its own accord, and that of York was blown down by the wind.

The general difficulty of determining the exact date at which rectangular keeps were erected in English castles gives especial importance to the case of Bridgnorth on the Severn, in regard to which we possess the necessary information. In 1102 Robert of Bellême, Earl of Shrewsbury, in preparation for his revolt against Henry I., abandoned the fortress of the motte and bailey pattern which he possessed at Quatford on the left bank of the river, and proceeded to build a new castle of stone upon the strong peninsular site where the town of Bridgnorth now stands. The work was done in haste, but the keep of the new fortress has survived in the massive rectangular tower which, severely damaged at the time of the Civil War, may with accuracy be assigned to the year 1102. It was probably in consequence of the intrinsic strength of the new work that Robert of Bellême, when war broke out, entrusted its defence to three of his knights in command of a force of eighty mercenaries, choosing himself to defend the weaker castle of Shrewsbury in person. Upon the king's advance the castle was cut off from external support, a counter-work was erected against it, and it was assaulted with siege engines. The besiegers possessed an overwhelming superiority in numbers, but even so, the siege lasted for a month, and the castle was only surrendered at last against the will of the mercenary portion of the garrison, through the defection of the knights in command, who were intimidated by the king's threats and by a sense of their own numerical inferiority. It is significant that Robert of Bellême declined to stand a siege in the motte and bailey earthwork of Shrewsbury.

In view of the defensive strength of the new rectangular keeps it was always a matter of policy for a strong king to insist that his licence should be obtained before any one of his barons raised a private fortress. Under a weak ruler, the work of castle-building invariably passed beyond the royal control. And so, during the eighteen years in which King Stephen contested his crown with the Empress Matilda, the number of castles built was greater than in any previous period of equal length. The ease with which great numbers of them were dismantled in a few months when Henry II. had restored order suggests that for the most part they were rudimentary structures; few of them can have shown the elaboration of a well-developed motte and bailey castle, and we know on unexceptionable authority that they were largely built by forced, and therefore presumably unskilled, labour. For the most part they would seem to have been demolished before written record had been made of their existence; and if any traces of them survive to the present day, they must be sought among the many scattered earthworks of defensible purpose for which no definite origin can be assigned. So far as our knowledge goes, the 'adulterine' castles of Stephen's day mark a relapse from the methods of fortification practised in the time of Henry I, and have no place in the general development of the art of castle-building in England.

In the mid-twelfth century, the most highly developed form of castle in the country consisted of a square, solid keep, commanding a walled enclosure. The keep was the cardinal point of the whole fortress; the enclosure might well fall into an enemy's hands without materially endangering the security of the defenders of the tower. The strength of such a fortress was, as we have seen, wholly passive; it could not be taken without the expenditure of a wholly disproportionate amount of time and labour,[1] but its defenders could do but little actively towards the discomfiture of their besiegers. It was consequently impossible for a garrison to do anything of itself to force the abandonment of a siege. It was this fact which was the essential weakness of the Norman castle; it was a valuable precaution against an English rising or a Scotch raid, but its garrison could inflict little harm on an enemy. The development of the castle into something effective as a base for an offensive strategy was inevitable; but in England its accomplishment was late in comparison with the similar process occurring on the Continent.

It would be an error to regard the remarkable change which came over the methods of English fortification in the early thirteenth century as a sudden revolution, unconnected with what had gone

---

[1] A besieging general, at this period, would commonly begin operations by entrenching his troops in a series of counterworks, placed so as to command the means of egress from the castle before him. This method was already adopted by William I, when Duke of Normandy in the sieges of Domfront (1048), and Arques (1054), it was followed by William II at Bamburgh (1095), by Henry I at Arundel and Bridgnorth (1101), by Stephen at Castle Cary and Harptree (1138), Ludlow (1139), and Wallingford (1139–40), and by Richard de Lacy at Huntingdon (1174). The introduction of the rectangular keep does not seem to have produced any immediate effect upon the methods of siegecraft.

before. Despite the general conservatism of English castle builders, there are not wanting signs to show that some time before the close of the twelfth century they were gradually working their way towards fortifications of greater elaboration than had sufficed in the times of Henry I or Stephen. Already before 1175, Henry II. had built the highly abnormal tower of Orford (Suffolk), polygonal without, cylindrical within, strengthened with large turrets and entered through a fore-building. A twelfth century castle of the type of Conisboro', in which the outline of the defensive works was defined with accuracy according to the lie of the land, shows that a change in the type of the English castle was already imminent. Architects were ceasing to rely for strength upon mere solidity of structure, and were endeavouring by greater intricacy of ground-plan to make compensation for the abandonment of the impregnable defences of the keep. Fortification, in fact, was becoming somewhat of a science, replacing the empirical methods which had prevailed in the past.

THE CYLINDRICAL KEEP

To this time of transition may probably be assigned the introduction into English castles of a new type of defensive work, the cylindrical tower, sometimes known as the juliet or donjon. Rarely attaining in England the development which it reached, for example, in such a French fortress as Coucy, the cylindrical tower was recommended to builders on account of its combination of solidity with economy in material, and remains a remarkable feature of thirteenth century fortification. Skenfrith Castle in Monmouthshire consists of a single ward, in shape an irregular quadrilateral, enclosing such a tower, 40 feet high, 36 feet in diameter, and with walls 7 feet in thickness. More remarkable as an illustration of the type is the donjon of Pembroke, 75 feet high, its unbuttressed walls, pierced with narrow loopholes, resembling in thickness the square keeps of an earlier age, its roof formed by a solid cone of masonry. But the greatest work of the kind in England is the keep of Conisboro', which probably dates from the very close of the twelfth century. Upon the line of the curtain wall there rises a cylindrical tower, 90 feet high, its walls, 14 feet thick, supported by six deep buttresses, its entrance, on the level of the first floor, reached by an external stairway. The basement is vaulted; and the tower contains a chapel or oratory ornamented with the architectural details characteristic of the period. The passive strength of such a tower was at least as great as that possessed by any of the rectangular keeps built earlier in the century; like them it formed a base, if need arose, for the final stand of the

111

garrison. But the donjon, its strength notwithstanding, was rarely introduced into an English or Welsh castle of the first class.

THIRTEENTH CENTURY CHANGES

The characteristic features of thirteenth century fortification receive, in this country, their fullest expression in the great castles built to command the Snowdon range by Edward I. In Normandy, a century earlier, they had been carried into effect by Richard I, in his great work of Château Gaillard. The essential principles which underlie the construction of these new fortresses may, with some sacrifice of detail, be reduced to two. In the first place, the plan of the castle follows, and is determined by, the contour of the ground on which it is placed. Instead of reproducing the type of the motte and bailey, or of the keep and base-court, with little regard to the details of the local situation, the builders of the thirteenth century planned their castles with the utmost care so as to make the fullest use of whatever advantage the ground might present. As a result, the ground-plans of these new fortifications are hardly ever identical in any two instances, and it is therefore impossible to do more than indicate the prevailing types to which the individual castles approximate in greater or less degree.

THE CONCENTRIC IDEA

But when due allowance has been made on the score of these variations of plan, the second principle active in thirteenth century fortification still remains evident—the idea of opposing a series of defences to an attack, expressed in the adoption, where expedient, of a concentric disposition of the several wards of the castle. The sketch which is annexed here is intended to indicate the rough outline of an ideal concentric castle; it may serve to show the nature of the change from the rudimentary structures of the keep and base-court type, although in actual fact the concentric outline was only attained through many intermediate stages, and in England at least, is rarely carried out in perfection. We have here a series of three enclosures, or three wards, no two of which are bounded at any point by the same line of wall. As in practice the walls increased in height as one passed from the outer to the inner ward, each ward in turn was commanded by the one which lay within it, and the defenders of the castle had by no means a hopeless task before them, even when the outer and middle wards had been stormed. The gates of each ward were narrow openings, each commanded by its own pair of towers; and the gates themselves were so arranged that even when one of them had been carried by assault, the enemy were compelled to pass under the fire of the garrison for some distance before they could attack the entrance to the next ward. Such a fortress was, in fact, equal to three castles in one, and its capture became almost impossible so long as the garrison were adequately supported by an army in the field outside. The failure of provisions, or treachery among the garrison, were the most frequent reasons for the rare collapse of the defensive.

The 'Concentric' Outline.

In matters of detail, the most notable advance marked by the new castles of the thirteenth century was made in relation to the structure of the castle walls. In the older castles, the garrison could not command the ground immediately at the foot of the castle wall except by dropping missiles upon it. In the new type of castle, long stretches of bare wall, and angles pointing to the interior of the structure were alike avoided; and the wall of each ward was set with towers placed so as to afford a lateral fire upon the men who were attacking it at any single point. It was deliberately attempted to prevent any portion of the wall of any ward from exposure to an attack which could not be met by transverse fire, and in every castle built after the period we have reached, whether it conforms to the concentric type or not, we shall find the mural tower a prominent feature.

To the same period also belongs the introduction into England of those mural defences upon which the names of bractices and machicolations have been conferred, devices already adopted in France in the previous century. A soldier leaning over the top of a wall to discharge missiles at an enemy underneath became an

113

obvious target for the enemies' arrows and slings. Accordingly a plan was introduced by which the defenders of a castle, while still able to annoy the enemy, would be sheltered from the latter's weapons. A series of stones was removed from a line near the summit of the wall, wooden posts were built into the resulting holes, and a line of planks was laid upon them, this line being perforated at intervals so as to admit of missiles being sent through the floor upon the enemy beneath. A roof was erected over the whole structure, or *bractice*, of which the most serious defects were the inflammable nature of its materials and its liability to gradual decay under exposure to the weather. The *machicolation* results from the bractice by the simple substitution of stone for wood in its construction; and mural defences of this kind were commonly erected in stone from the outset in castles built after the middle of the thirteenth century.

EDWARDIAN CASTLES

The three castles in the British Isles which are most strictly built on concentric lines are the Tower of London, Beaumaris in Anglesea, and Caerphilly in Glamorganshire. The concentric outline of the Tower of London results from the addition of later enclosing wards to an eleventh-century rectangular keep; it is a remarkable illustration of the manner in which an early Norman fortress might be developed into a perfect example of the thirteenth-century type. Beaumaris consists of two wards only: the outer wall, an almost regular octagon, with towers at each angle, and in the centre of each face, except in the quarter fronting the main entrance; the inner ward, a square, enclosed with a wall of great height, strengthened with towers of extreme solidity and crowned with battlements. Caerphilly, erected by Gilbert de Clare, Earl of Gloucester, about 1270, from the standpoint of general design, is perhaps the strongest fortress in the country—it occupied an island in the middle of an artificial lake, and is accessible only by a narrow causeway starting from its eastern and western shores. Whitecastle (Mon.) is an early example of approximation to the concentric model. But perhaps a more fully typical example of thirteenth-century methods of castle-building occurs at Kidwelly, on the shores of Carmarthen bay. Kidwelly Castle, which was founded by Payn de Chaworth within a few years of 1250, stands on the right bank of the river Gwendraeth, at this point a wide stream affording valuable protection to the eastern face of the defences. The whole plan of the castle was determined by the security of its river front, which is composed of a single line of wall, of no remarkable height or strength. This line of wall, in relation to the outline of the whole castle, forms the chord

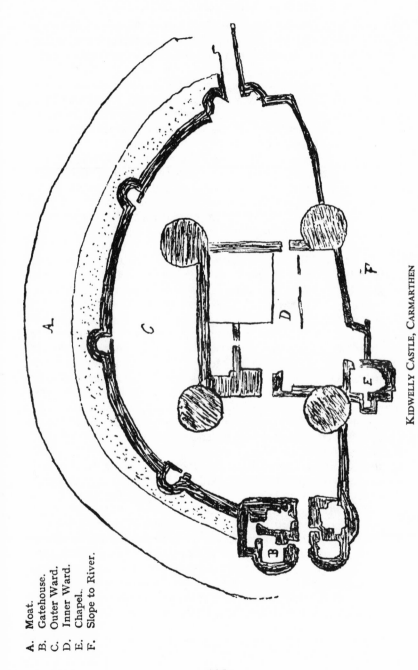

A. Moat.
B. Gatehouse.
C. Outer Ward.
D. Inner Ward.
E. Chapel.
F. Slope to River.

KIDWELLY CASTLE, CARMARTHEN

115

of a semicircle, of which the bounding wall, on the side remote from the river, is set with mural towers and is protected by a deep moat. The entrance to the castle, situated near to its south-eastern angle, is formed by a massive gateway, three stories high, strengthened with towers at each corner, and containing guard-rooms and store-houses, built of excellent masonry. This gateway gives immediate access to the outer ward of the castle, which surrounds on three sides the rectangular inner ward, the central point of the whole fortifica-tion. The fourth side of the latter coincides throughout its entire length with the central portion of the river face of the outer ward; a departure from the strictly concentric form of ground plan which is evidently occasioned by the natural strength of the eastern front of the castle. Each angle of the inner ward, within which lay hall, chapel, and domestic buildings, was protected with the large circular towers characteristic of the period, and the whole castle is an early and successful example of the fortresses of the thirteenth-century type.

It will be evident that a castle of the concentric type is most likely to be found in the middle of a stretch of open country, where all sides of the castle are equally exposed to attack. A castle built on the edge of a precipice will only need a single line of wall on the side which overlooks the precipice.[1] A good illustration of this fact, and incidentally an interesting comparison between the methods of fortification practised in the eleventh and thirteenth centuries, is afforded by the two castles of Montgomery. The fortress which is commonly known as Montgomery Castle stands on a narrow tongue of land, protected by a steep descent on three sides. Along this tongue of land are arranged four wards, each one separated from the next by a broad ditch cut in the solid rock. The first ward, looking towards the only point from which an attack could possibly be made, and the second ward, stand on virtually the same level; the third ward is distinctly lower than the others, and could hardly have been defended when the second ward had fallen. On the other hand, the fourth ward is no less distinctly the highest of the whole series; it stands on the very edge of the cliff, and the position of an enemy in the low third ward would have been tenable only with great difficulty under the missiles of the garrison in the fourth. Mont-gomery Castle then is obviously planned with a careful eye to the nature of the ground, but this is hardly its main interest. In Domes-day Book we are told of a castle built at this place by Roger de Montgomery the first earl of Shrewsbury. It used to be supposed that this was identical with the fortress which we have been con-

[1] Carreg Cennen castle on the edge of a precipitous cliff in south Carmarthen-shire, built in the thirteenth century by Rhys of Wales, illustrates this arrange-ment.

sidering—'the second seat of the power of Earl Roger,' says Professor Freeman, 'was, no less than the fortress of William Peverel in the Peakland, a simple vulture's nest upon a crag.' But we can now see that a fortress of this type, so admirably suited to the ground on which it is built, and so costly in the building, is quite unlike the elementary castles run up by the companions of the Conqueror. And in the immediate neighbourhood of Montgomery, more than a mile from the castle on the hill, and in the low land on the bank of the Severn, there stands a simple earthwork of the motte and bailey pattern,[1] which is undoubtedly the humble fortress of the Conqueror's friend; the castle which was demolished by the Welsh in the rising of 1095. The Earl of Shrewsbury chose a site where a castle could be raised with the least possible expenditure of time and labour; long before he had cut the first ward out of the rock on the top of Montgomery hill, the Welsh would have been upon him. He wished for temporary security and nothing more.[2] And so, just as at Wallingford we can compare the fortresses of the time of Alfred with those erected by William I., at Montgomery we can measure the advance in the art of fortification between the time of the Conqueror and that of Henry III.[3]

The conquest of Gwynedd by Edward I. was rendered permanent by the establishment of a ring of castles at the base of the group of mountains of which Snowdon is the chief. Aberconway and Carnarvon, on sites previously unfortified, Criccieth, and Harlech, replacing earlier Welsh strongholds, are the most famous of these fortresses, and it is in them that the art of castle-building reaches its highest point in this country. The skill with which they are designed in connection with the ground on which they stand, the excellence of their masonry, and the strategical sense which planted each castle at exactly the points which enabled it to command the widest possible area, are beyond all praise. But although the Edwardian fortresses of Wales, as regards the purpose and circumstances of their erection, form by themselves a well-defined group, there is little in common between the several ground plans on which they are respectively based. Beaumaris is purely concentric, Harlech and Rhuddlan approximate to the concentric outline as demanded by the contour of the ground: and it is no doubt significant that these three castles were each the work of the same builder, James of St.

[1] The significance of this earthwork, known locally as the Hen Domen, was pointed out by Mr. Davies Pryce, *Eng. Hist. Rev.* XX, 709, 710.
[2] The converse process, by which a hill fortress became abandoned for a valley site, is illustrated by the rise of Conway at the expense of Deganwy.
[3] At Rhuddlan a motte, undoubtedly representing the castle held in 1086 by Robert of Rhuddlan of the Earl of Chester, stands a short distance to the south of the Edwardian fortress.

George. It may well be in conscious opposition to his ideas of castellation that Aberconway and Carnarvon were founded upon a different plan. The former consists of an irregular oblong area, divided into two wards by a line of wall drawn across its narrowest portion; the whole of Carnarvon Castle forms but a single ward, built, in accordance with the lie of the land, in a form resembling an hour-glass, but in each case the defences of the town, being continuous with those of the castle, made of the former a kind of outer ward. The peculiar strength of Carnarvon Castle lay in the structure of its walls; within which, upon the face most exposed to an attack, a double gallery was constructed, commanding through loopholes the ground in front of the castle, and surmounted by a rampart, the whole defence admitting of a simultaneous triple fire upon an enemy advancing from this quarter. At Carnarvon, as in every other of the group to which it belongs, the walls were thickly set with mural towers; for the security of the Edwardian castle depended upon the strength and disposition of its walls, and in none of the great fortresses of North Wales was any keep ever constructed. Adopting the language of the twelfth century, we may say that the *castellum*, the enclosure, had come to supplant the *turris*, the keep, as the essential factor in castellation.

The activities of the age of Edward I. in the matter of castle-building were not confined to North Wales. At Corfe, Chepstow and Pevensey, there remain additions made during his reign to the defensive works of the eleventh century. At Builth, a twelfth-century motte and bailey have been converted into a castle of the concentric type by the addition of a circular rampart enclosing the whole of the earlier fortification and by the erection of further defences upon the motte. Elsewhere in this quarter, there is evidence of a desire to modify fortresses of the older type in accordance with the ideas of the thirteenth century. At Bronllys, near Talgarth, the motte has been crowned with a cylindrical tower of the type which has already been described. At the castle of Tretower, near Crickhowell, a tower of this kind was inserted within the remains of an older rectangular keep, and it would seem that at Builth a donjon was placed upon the motte within the shell keep of the thirteenth century. But these Edwardian additions are only brought forward here in illustration of the last phase of the art of castellation in this country.

DECLINE OF THE CASTLE

For from the end of the thirteenth century onwards, the castle steadily tends to become a less important factor in the military organisation of the country. Except in the extreme north where the constant imminence of border raids produced, in the peel towers of this district, a form of defensive work resembling the rectangular keeps of an earlier age, few new castles were built, and those that existed tended to fall into neglect. In 1337 Edward III. ordered his castellans of North and South Wales to put all their fortresses into a defensible condition; in 1341 the king was told that the doors of Criccieth Castle were so feeble that they could scarcely hold up against the wind. It is this neglect, rather than any improvement in methods of siegecraft, which accounts for the remarkable contrast between the course of events in the Barons' War, which largely turned upon the defence of such fortresses as Kenilworth and Rochester, and the details of the revolt of 1322, when the castles of Tutbury, Leeds (Kent) and Tickhill severally fell without any protracted resistance in the course of a brief campaign. The changed significance of the castle is one of the main facts which distinguish the history of the fourteenth century from that of its predecessors.

The suppression of militant feudalism represents one aspect of the process by which this change was effected. As a menace to the integrity of the realm and the authority of the crown, the baronial castle was already an anachronism when Edward I. died. The establishment of the universal jurisdiction of the king's courts, the strict inquisition into feudal franchises, the legislative activities, which distinguish the reign of Edward I., are only the more obvious signs of a permanent order, a general obedience to law, incompatible with the maintenance of strongholds in which a subject could resist the sovereign. On the other hand, it is evident that this result was greatly furthered by the changes which were coming over the art of war at this time, changes which everywhere tended to give the military advantage to the side which could put into the field, and handle effectively, the largest masses of men-at-arms. The development, under Edward I., of an infantry combining supreme efficiency in missile tactics with complete independence from the system of the feudal levy, gave to the king, the best paymaster, an advantage hardly shared by any of his individual barons.

The final passing of the medieval castle as a dominant fact in war, is generally ascribed to the introduction of gunpowder and the rise of an effective artillery. If the period between 1450 and 1650 be regarded as a whole, such a view is no doubt correct; otherwise it requires qualification. The decay of the castle had already gone far by 1450. The country south of the border shires had long enjoyed immunity from civil war, and when in Wales a national rising unexpectedly broke out under Owen Glyndwr, it found the castles of the central valleys and the south ill-prepared for extended resistance. To this, in great part, is due the rapidity with which Owen was enabled to reduce fortresses planned for the domination of extensive tracts of land. On the other hand, when at last in the Wars of the Roses artillery is found employed against the walls of an ancient castle, its efficiency is seen to be dependent upon somewhat stringent conditions. The reduction of Bamburgh and Dunstanburgh by the aid of artillery in 1465 merely shows that where cannon could be posted within short range of a fortress unsupported by an army in the field, its capture would thereby be facilitated. It had no bearing upon the defensive power of a castle under circumstances where these conditions did not prevail. The protracted resistance of Harlech in the campaign of 1474 may be set against the fall of Bamburgh. And in the early stages of the great Civil War, when once again the ancient castles of England became the centres of military operations, their capacity for resistance was still very considerable. The first phase of the war was materially affected by the fact that the defences of Nottingham Castle, though weakened by a century of neglect, closed to the royal armies the western line of the road to York; and in 1648 the walls of Pembroke Castle proved too strong for the light cannon originally at the disposal of Cromwell. The general advantage of the defensive at this time is well shown by the determined resistance made by many fortified posts of no particular strength, such as the isolated manor houses garrisoned in large numbers in the first months of the war. Despite the artillery, such as it was, at the disposal of the Parliamentary commanders, their reduction on an extended scale proved impossible so long as there existed royalist forces in the field capable of making a diversion. The bad roads of the seventeenth century seriously impaired the mobility of heavy artillery, and the earthen outworks of a castle admitted of reshaping in accordance with models derived from continental examples, as in the case of the motte of Cambridge. If it be true to say that artillery killed the medieval castle, we must add the qualification that it took some two centuries in the process.

THE LAST ENGLISH CASTLES

Last among the reasons which made for the decay of the castle, though perhaps of higher importance than any other, were the social forces which played their part in this matter. It was certain that the extreme discomfort of life within the walls of a medieval fortress would no longer be endured when the fortress itself was ceasing to fulfil its original purpose; and in the south and east of England the older castles were rapidly altered to give opportunity for the amenities of life, at a considerable sacrifice of their defensive security. The greater castles of the Midlands, such as Warwick and Kenilworth, play no part in the military business of the Wars of the Roses; they were the residences of their lords in intervals of peace, but they were not garrisoned in time of war. And in the few English castles which were built towards the close of the Middle Ages, the evident desire to combine effective defensive works with residences of reasonable comfort leads to results of some incongruity. The Lincolnshire castle of Tattershall, on the Witham, overlooking the fens of Kesteven and Holland, which was built by Ralf Lord Cromwell at the middle of the fifteenth century, is a good illustration of these tendencies. Of this castle, the building of which cost more than 4,000 marks, the great tower, now only a shell, and the rectangular ward beneath it, remain. The tower and the walls of the ward are composed of brickwork, excellent brickwork it is true, but hardly possessing the intrinsic strength of the stone and rubble employed in the keeps and curtains of an earlier age. The tower is four stories high, provided with large traceried windows, reproduced on a smaller scale in the four turrets which strengthen the angles of the building; the several floors of the interior were supported on massive timber balks, and the large and ornate fireplaces show that the structure was designed as the permanent dwelling of its lord. Considered, on the other hand, as a defensive work, the tower contains a feature of exceptional interest in the singularly complete system of machicolation with which its roof is provided. Along the crest of the tower there runs an overhanging gallery, commanding the ground beneath through openings in its floor, provided with square-headed windows, admitting of a fire over a wider field, and surmounted by battlements. Against cannon, indeed, the tower would be defenceless, for its position, surrounded by level ground on every side, gave to an attacking commander the power of placing a battery at any point which might suit his convenience, but the power of artillery had not been demonstrated against English fortresses when Lord Cromwell died at the beginning of 1456.

With Tattershall Castle this sketch of the development of the English medieval fortress may fittingly close. It remains an exceptional work for the period at which it was constructed, for when in the fifteenth century we find a baron or knight building anew, he commonly builds a hall, a manor house, rather than a castle. Social convenience was steadily triumphing over military necessity; the typical building of the fifteenth century is a fortified dwelling such as Oxburgh Hall in Norfolk, or such as Lord Cromwell's other work at Wingfield, in Derbyshire, itself one of the many manor-houses which stood a siege in the Civil War. For we may say, with substantial truth, that it was the decay of the castle, and of the habits of life and methods of thought which the castle implies, which gradually gave scope for the parallel development of English domestic architecture.

BIBLIOGRAPHICAL NOTE

The literature which relates to the art of castle-building in England is of vast volume, and of many varying degrees of value. As a comprehensive survey of the whole subject, *Military Architecture in England*, by A. Hamilton Thompson (1912) supersedes earlier studies of the kind. Nevertheless the *Mediæval Military Architecture* of G. T. Clark (2 vols., London, 1884) is still worth study, although large portions of the work are now obsolete. The main value of the book lies in the numerous plans with which it is illustrated; the author's views on the castles of the early Norman period show a tendency to antedate the practice of erecting fortifications in stone, and his identification of earthworks of the mound and base-court pattern with the *burhs* of pre-Conquest times can no longer be upheld. For French castles, C. Enlart's *Manuel d'Archéologie française, Architecture*, Vol. II, may be studied. The modern study of this subject is particularly associated with the names of J. H. Round and Mrs. E. Armitage. The former in his *Geoffrey de Mandeville* (London, 1892) was the first to suggest the distinction marked in early Norman times between the keep (*turris*) and the adjacent ward (*castellum*); a distinction which has had the effect of referring many rectangular keeps to a date considerably later than had previously been assigned to them. In his paper on 'The Castles of the Conquest' (*Archæologia*, LVIII) Round argued against the widely accepted equation of *burh* and *motte*, and assigned a number of the earliest Norman castles in England to the motte and bailey pattern. In this last matter Mrs. Armitage ('Early Norman Castles of England,' *Eng. Hist. Rev.*, XIX), by investigating in detail the several castles recorded in Domesday Book, placed the universality of the motte and bailey plan at this date beyond the range of doubt. Her later work, *The Early Norman Castles of the British Isles* (1912), carries these studies further; it is illustrated with plans, and forms an indispensable introduction to the subject. A similar service was performed in regard to the earliest castles of Ireland by G. H. Orpen ('Mote and Bretasch Building in Ireland,' *Eng. Hist. Rev.*, XXI). For Welsh castles in general, compare J. E. Lloyd, *History of Wales* (1911). The development of Scottish castle-building is described by W. M. Mackenzie, *The Mediæval Castle in Scotland* (1927). For individual castles, reference should be made to the relevant sections of the *Victoria History of the Counties of England*. In the articles dealing with ancient earthworks, a full and well illustrated account is given of all earthworks of the motte and bailey pattern contained within each county, and descriptions of castles are included in the topographical portions of the *History*. Castles naturally fall within the sphere of the *Royal Commission on Historical Monuments*, and the descriptions of buildings and earthworks in the volumes issued by the Commission are of the first importance. For a concise survey of the development of military architecture in the Middle Ages reference should be made to Professor Hamilton Thompson's chapter in the *Cambridge Mediæval History*, Volume V, to which a bibliography of the subject is appended. On the place of the castle in early feudal society I may refer to my *First Century of English Feudalism* (1932). A list of castles for the period 1154–1216, with annotations, was published by R. A. Brown in the *Eng. Hist. Review*, LXXIV (1959).

C. J. FFOULKES

European Arms
and Armour

Fʀᴏᴍ the earliest prehistoric days of the present era, man has exercised all his ingenuity in devising weapons by which to attack his enemy at a distance. The long sapling and wooden club were superseded by the flint-headed spear and axe, and these in turn were followed by bronze or iron weapons, with the addition of the sword. Next in order of progression came the sling, the throwing stick, and the bow, and these in course of time were discarded in favour of firearms.

It is only when we come to those periods of which we have some historic record that we find man endeavouring to defend himself while he is attacking, the early leather shield and helmet being the best protection that he could devise. As late as the Norman period the craft of the metal-worker was crude and inexpert. Although he could fashion comparatively small articles in iron, his experience and his appliances were such that he could only use metal in small plates applied to fabric or leather. The thick leather coat and the padded or quilted fabric were fairly adequate protection against the badly-tempered weapons in use, but by the sixth century these defences had been reinforced by plates of metal, sewn or riveted on, while the shield was often a practical defence of wood or toughened leather covered with metal.

The shaping of the helmet presented great difficulties. The typical Norman helmet, conical in shape, was made of two or four pieces

124

connected with vertical bands of metal, and provided with a long nasal piece which protected the nose and part of the face. (*Fig. 1*).

Figure 1
DUKE WILLIAM: BAYEUX TAPESTRY

Our most useful record of this period is the famous Bayeux Tapestry, but we are faced with some difficulty as to details of equipment shown thereon. The Norman and Saxon soldiers are depicted wearing armour formed apparently of rings, or trellis-like material; but whether this represents interlaced chainmail, which was such an outstanding feature of the thirteenth century, or whether the armour was composed of quilted fabrics with plates of metal superimposed, there is a diversity of expert opinion. The contemporary chronicles of the twelfth century certainly mention armour, for man and horse, as being of iron, possibly of mail. If this was the case it could have only been great leaders

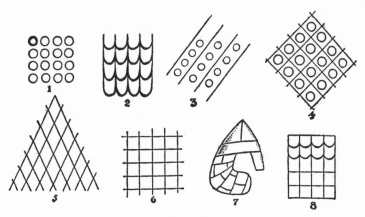

Figure 2
DETAILS OF ARMOUR: BAYEUX TAPESTRY

who could have afforded this complicated defence, which was certainly introduced from the East. (*Fig. 3.*)

The weapons of this period were those which had persisted for several centuries. The heavy and unpractical cutting sword, the lance, the axe and the club, were all in use. The bow was certainly actively employed at the Battle of Hastings, for it was by an arrow that Harold met his death, and archers are shown on the Bayeux Tapestry. It need hardly be said that little if any of the armour of this period survives, as the cost of manufacturing iron was so great that armour and weapons were continually being remade to suit new military fashions and needs, and iron, if not protected from rust, perished quickly.

The periods of which we have the most detailed records are the thirteenth and fourteenth centuries, and from illuminated manuscripts, sculptured monuments and incised brasses, we get such wealth of detailed record that it is quite possible to reconstruct the military panoply of the period with great accuracy.

One of the most important axioms of the craft of the armourer was to provide not only material impervious to sword and lance, but also to

Figure 3
HORSE ARMOUR
From a painting formerly in the Painted
Chamber, Westminster, Thirteenth Century

offer a glancing surface which would deflect the full force of the weapon. The Norman helmet was extremely practical in this respect, for the blow of the sword would be deflected off the pointed surface, and would fall with reduced force upon the body defences. But for some inexplicable reason we find that the helm in universal use during the thirteenth century was a metal cylinder with slits for the eyes and a flat top. This was, of course, worn over a heavily padded cap, but there was no attachment by which the helm could be kept rigid, and the full force of a blow on the head was retained by the flat top. (*Fig. 4.*)

The armour at this period, for the mounted man at any rate, was

126

almost universally 'Chain Mail', and this, of necessity, was invariably worn over thick padded underclothes; otherwise the mail would have been driven by a blow into the flesh of the wearer, with disastrous results. Mail is composed of small rings interlaced with each other, the ends of each ring being either welded by heat or flattened, drilled and closed by minute rivets. Here we have one of the mysteries of the craft of the armourer, for there must have been vast quantities of this mail used not only in Europe, but also in the East; and yet we have no accurate knowledge as to how it was manufactured. Students of arms and armourers, in the early nineteenth

Figure 4
GREAT SEAL OF EDWARD I, 1272

century, neglected to obtain first-hand information when mail was still being made by Oriental nations, but at the present day, so far as we have been able to discover, nobody is left who is practising this craft. Mail covered the head under the helm, the body, the arms and the legs. The weight, including the padded undergarments, must have been well-nigh insupportable, for a shirt of mail alone will weigh between twenty and thirty pounds.

It was the barrel-shaped helm which, by concealing completely the face of the wearer, introduced the complicated 'science'—if it may be so called—of Heraldry, for it was of vital importance that the fighting man should distinguish friend from foe. These heraldic bearings were worn as crests on the helm, emblazoned on the shield or embroidered on the long surcoat which covered the body armour. The surcoat served another purpose, for it protected the wearer from sun and rain, both most unpleasant and injurious to armour.

The horse, though occasionally protected with mail, was generally furnished with a long padded 'Trapper' which reached down to the hocks, thereby impeding its movements considerably, though giving it very serviceable protection. The shield which, at the time of the Norman Conquest, was a long kite-shaped affair, must have

127

been extremely cumbersome when used by mounted men, and by the thirteenth century it was reduced considerably in size.

By the fourteenth century the armourer had become more expert, and he was able to fashion a pointed top to the helm. This is known popularly as the 'Sugar Loaf' helm, which rested on the shoulders, and provided an excellent glancing surface to opposing weapons. It is with the advent of this helm, which required skill in forging, that we find the craft of the armourer progressing almost year by year, till it culminates in the complete defences of the sixteenth century. At the same period a lighter headpiece, called the basinet, was introduced. This only covered the crown and back of the head, the face being exposed or protected by a movable visor. The neck, throat and chin were covered with the camail or hood of mail laced to the helmet with leather faces and studs.

The military man is ever a staunch conservative, and in spite of its unpractical nature mail lingered for long in the nations of Europe. But at the end of the fourteenth century small additions of plate were made; first on the knees and shins, for these were the most vulnerable parts of the mounted man, who, while engaged with his mounted adversary, could easily be attacked by a foot soldier. Then the arms, elbows and armpits were protected by small plates of metal; all these pieces at first being attached to the mail with leather thongs, which, it should be pointed out, would be often cut in battle. (*Fig. 5.*)

By the middle of the fourteenth century the armourer became a highly skilled craftsman. Piece by piece articulated plates of metal were added, which allowed comparatively easy movement of the feet, knees, elbows and hands. This skilled craft-work culminated in the complete suit of plate about the year 1400, when the body was protected by a heavy cuirass, and all the limbs covered by articulated plates; mail alone surviving as a protection to the neck and for the arm-pits, which would be exposed in raising the arm in using the sword or axe. (*Fig. 6.*)

Before proceeding to the description of plate armour, it is of some interest to note the requirements of the fighting man, and the rules which govern the craft of the armourer, and indeed all crafts of a utilitarian nature. The rules are :

1. that the work should fulfil its object in the best possible manner.
2. that it should be simple and convenient in use.
3. that it should proclaim its material.
4. that any added decoration should be subservient to its purpose.

With regard to the first, the rule is obvious, for the object of the armourer was to protect his patron as far as possible. This was achieved by tempering the metal, by making it thick in front where

the blows would more frequently fall, and above all by providing on every part of the body a glancing surface from which the weapon would slip. The second rule—convenience in use—is of equal if not of greater importance, for it was essential that the fighting man should be able, at any rate, to use his arms with comparative freedom. The legs were not of so great importance, as the fully armed man was invariably mounted. In discussing the making of armour with his chief armourer the Emperor Maximilian I negatived certain suggestions made to him, and remarked:

'Arm me as I wish, for it is I and not you who will take part in this tournament.'

Figure 5
BRASS OF SIR JOHN EFFIGY OF THE BLACK
D'ABERNON, 1327 PRINCE, CANTERBURY
CATHEDRAL, 1376

Figure 6

The third rule would appear to be superfluous, and yet armourers in the sixteenth century simulated puffed and slashed fabrics, even reproducing seams and stitching in metal, and yet in no way improving the use or beauty of the production. The observance of the fourth rule—subservience of decoration—was exemplified in the fine engraving and very shallow embossing of the armourers of the fifteenth century; but later on when the master metalworker, Benvenuto Cellini, and his school flooded Europe with masterpieces of incoherence and yet of extraordinary skill, defensive armour suffered by being embossed in such high relief that not only the glancing surface entirely disappeared, but the actual strength of the material was seriously jeopardised.

One of the earliest records that we have of a complete suit of armour with no covering of surcoat is the brass of Sir Robert Suckling at Barsham, Suffolk, about 1415, and here the man is completely covered with plate with no mail in evidence. The armpits are protected by bound plates known as 'Pallets' or 'Motons'. At the lower edge of the cuirass are horizontal hoops of 'taces' joined with slotted rivets so as to give some freedom of movement. (*Fig. 7*). It is this type of armour which was in fashion when Joan of Arc

129

took command of the French troops in 1429, and it persisted, with certain improvements and alterations, up to the middle of the fifteenth century, when the Italian armourers introduced what is now known as 'Gothic Armour'. The outstanding feature of this armour is its fine constructive and graceful lines, the larger pieces being fashioned with shallow flutings which not only provide additional glancing surfaces to the opposing lance, but also, as is the case with modern corrugated iron, strengthen the material without adding to its weight. (*Fig. 8*). At this period the horizontal strips over the thighs have attached to their lower edges plates of metal known as 'Tassets'.

The breast-plate, which up to this period had been a heavy rigid defence, was now made in two parts pivoted at the sides so that there was a certain ease of movement of the body backwards and forwards. The finest example in the world of this armour is the bronze effigy of Richard Beauchamp, Earl of Warwick, in St. Mary's Church, Warwick, made in 1454. Every minute detail, including straps and buckles, are shown on this effigy back and front, so that it is possible for modern craftsmen to reproduce the suit exactly. The typical helmet of this period is the 'Sallade', similar to the modern sou'wester hat, which covered the upper part of the head and nose, the chin being protected by a separate defence. This, like so many other details of armour, must have been most unpractical, for it was very easy to displace.

Figure 7
BRASS OF
SIR R. SUCKLING,
1415

Figure 8
'GOTHIC' ARMOUR,
LATE FIFTEENTH
CENTURY

At the end of the fifteenth century we find the details of civilian dress reproduced in armour and the extravagantly long shoes of the courtier are reproduced in the 'Solerets' or foot coverings of the fighting man. To such an absurd extent was this fashion popular that the long toe-pieces were attached to the rider's foot after he was mounted, as walking in them would have been well-nigh impossible

By the sixteenth century the armourer and his patrons had

evidently realized the drawbacks to the Sallade, and a close helmet, or 'Armet', was evolved, with movable visor and chin-piece, or 'Beavor'. This protected the head and neck, and at the same time allowed comparative freedom of movement. (*Fig. 9*).

The shield of the mounted man had been gradually getting smaller from the fourteenth century, and when the full suit of articulated plate had become a practical proposition, the shield was entirely dispensed with. As the armour of the man was perfected, so the horse was covered with plate defences, lined with padded leather. The front of the head was protected with a 'Chanfrin' of plate, the neck with a 'Crinet' of articulated 'lames', or strips of metal—the breast and crupper with large plates riveted together. At the same time it is worthy of note that although both rider and horse were covered with weapon-proof armour the legs of the horse were entirely undefended, and it was therefore a matter of little difficulty for the foot-soldier, with a knife or axe, to place both rider and horse out of action; and, when unhorsed, a completely armed man was almost invariably at the mercy of his enemy — for his armour weighed anything from forty to sixty pounds.

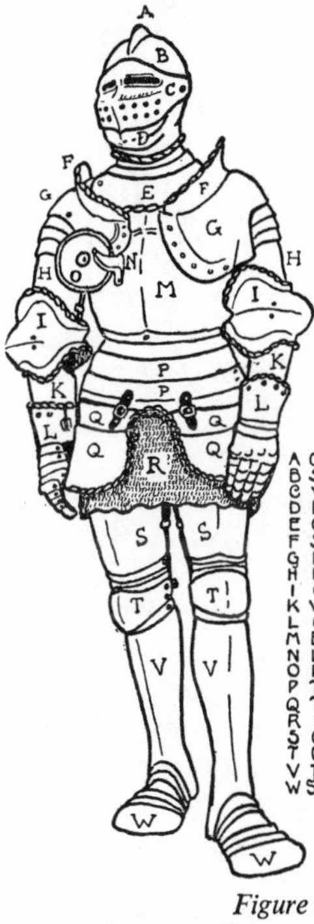

During all the period from the fourteenth century onwards the foot-soldier was, from force of circumstances, obliged to content himself with any odd pieces of armour which might be spared from his master. He generally wore a helmet of simple form, and, as regards his body-armour, was equipped in leather or padded fabric. (*Fig. 10.*) From the fourteenth century, the latter was reinforced by plates of metal on the arms and knees, and here it should be pointed out that the full plate-armour for the leg was always a most serious inconvenience for the mounted man when fighting on foot, and we have frequent records of men discarding their leg armour in order to move with greater ease.

A Crest
B Skull
C Visor
D Beavor
E Gorget
F Shoulder-Guard
G Pauldron
H Rerebrace
I Coude or Elbow-cop
K Vambrace
L Gauntlet
M Breast
N Lance-rest
O Palette or Rondel
P Taces
Q Tassets
R Breech
S Cuisse
T Genouillère or Knee-cop
V Jamb
W Soleret

Figure 9

ARMOUR, SIXTEENTH CENTURY

131

In the fifteenth century a very definite form of body defence appears. This was of two types—the 'Jack', and the 'Brigandine'. The 'Jack' was composed of several thicknesses of canvas, between which were inserted small square plates of metal, with a hole in the centre. Through these holes passed a complicated system of lacing which kept canvas and metal together, the canvas being often soaked in vinegar, as a preventative of vermin—in all centuries one of the most unpleasant enemies of the fighting man. For personal use in peace-time rather than for strenuous war, the Brigandine was

Figure 10
ARCHERS
From MS. British Museum, 1480

greatly in favour with the higher classes. This was composed of a canvas or linen lining and cover, between which were small oblong plates of metal, overlapping each other upwards, and over these was a covering, generally of crimson velvet, the whole being riveted together with the gilt heads of the rivets on the outside. (*Fig. 11.*)

The weapons of the period are, in the main, the same as in former ages. The sword, from the fifteenth century onwards, was lighter and better balanced, with sharp point for thrusting. The dagger, almost invariably worn on the sword-belt, was for close combat, and for finding the joint in the armour of the fallen man. The lance was still a comparatively light weapon for the horseman, but for the foot-soldier a multitude of strangely designed weapons were gradually introduced. Some of them, such as the 'Gisarme', with its long upwards pointing back hook, and the 'Hal-

Figure 11
BRIGANDINE
From MS. British Museum, 1485

132

berd', a long-shafted combination of axe and spear, must have frequently caused great confusion when wielded by troops in close order.

Figure 12
CROSS-BOWMEN
From MS. British Museum, 1485

As early as the period of the Crusades, the cross bow is found, obviously introduced from the East, but it is not until the fifteenth century that we find the complicated arrangements for winding-up and discharging the bow. (*Fig. 12.*) In spite of the fact that fire-arms of a very primitive nature had made their appearance, the long-bow was still in many cases the deciding factor in a battle.

With the sixteenth century we have the golden age of the armourer. He had formed guilds and trade associations to protect his craft, and these trade guilds had produced master-armourers who, as workers in metal, have never been surpassed. The different schools in Italy and Germany vied with each other in the making of armour more protective and more convenient in use, and by the middle of the sixteenth century the craft had reached its high-water mark. Italy, possibly on account of her climate, favoured a lighter and more graceful style, while Germany inclined to a heavier type of design. The most popular armour of this period was known as 'Maximilian', because its invention is attributed to Emperor Maximilian I. (*Fig. 13.*) The whole surface of this armour is covered with vertical flutings, so designed that the point of the opposing lance would be deflected away from the vital parts of the body. And here it should be noted that the military commander of the sixteenth century relied largely upon shock tactics—that is, large bodies of troops very heavily armed and mounted on large and sturdy types of

K 133

war-horses. For this form of attack, a much stronger and thicker lance was needed, and as an additional protection the lance was furnished with a circular steel hand-shield, or 'Vam-plate'. The mace and horseman's hammer were introduced for breaking up and opening various parts of the armour at close quarters.

Cannon, which had been used experimentally from the fourteenth century, now became part of the regular outfit or equipment of the army, but, owing to the uncertain composition of gunpowder, they could only be used at close quarters. Probably they were more useful as creating a moral effect on the enemy, than as causing serious casualties.

With the sixteenth century we find the tournament had taken root in all the courts of Europe as a very definite military exercise. In the fourteenth and fifteenth centuries these jousts, as they were called, were generally practised by knights wearing their war equipment, and the contests of necessity frequently ended in the death or disabling of one or other of the combatants. With the increased popularity of this sport among Kings and Princes of Europe, it was essential that the participants should be very heavily protected. The scores were made by breaking lances, or by throwing the opponent. The combatants passed left arm to left arm, bringing the lance across the horse's neck, thereby giving the whole weight of man and horse on the thrust. In armour for tournament, therefore, the left side of the helmet, arm and body defences, were very much more heavily armed than the right, and the reinforcing pieces are invariably smooth and curved, so as to deflect the lance. The average suit or armour weighed about fifty pounds, but some of the tournament armours scale one hundred pounds or even more. (*Fig. 14.*) When to this is added saddle, clothing and the heavy armour for the horse, it will be seen that the furious charge of 'knights in the list' is a poetic fancy! As a matter of fact, the tournament must have been a rather dull entertainment.

At the same time, the productions of the armourer for the tourna-

Figure 13
MAXIMILIAN I, 1508

ment are examples of the finest possible skill in metal-work. The armour made for Henry VIII to fight in the lists on foot weighs nearly ninety pounds, and is composed of two-hundred and fifty-three pieces, which cover every part of the wearer, back and front, the articulated 'lames' giving perfect freedom of movement to all the limbs, and at the same time there is no opening for the opposing weapon.

At the end of the sixteenth century the craft of the armourer was on the downward grade. Craftsmen in England, such as Jacob Halder and John Pickering, still kept up their fine traditions of technique, and their work will compare favourably with any of the

Figure 14
Tournament Armour, German, 1557

foreign craftsmen, but in Europe the armourer, finding that there was nothing more to be done in the technical forging of metal, had recourse to misplaced decoration for advertising his dexterity. The surfaces were covered with heavy embossing, and the constructional details often were omitted, and, what is perhaps worse, were simulated; that is, where several plates of the earlier armourer were joined by easy working sliding rivets, in the later examples the defence was made of one rigid plate set with imitation rivet heads. The gilded armour in the Tower Armouries, made for Charles I, but never worn by him, is so constructed that the armour for the thighs could only be worn when the rider was mounted, and was quite useless when he was standing upright. The foot armour is so carelessly devised that it is impossible to bend the foot.

The armour of the mounted man of the late sixteenth and early seventeenth centuries was greatly reduced, and consisted of a comparatively light helmet, arm pieces often reaching only to the elbow, a cuirass and thigh pieces of small articulated 'lames', the lower leg being only protected by thick leather boots.

By the end of the sixteenth century we find that the fire-arm, though extremely clumsy and unreliable, was in general use in the armies of Europe, and the object of the armourer was to provide an adequate defence. This he did by increasing the weight of the

Figure 15	Figure 16
PIKEMAN, SEVENTEENTH CENTURY	MUSKETEER, SEVENTEENTH CENTURY

breast-plate and the helmet to such an extent that, although both were bullet proof, the weight was insupportable.

By the end of the sixteenth century horse armour had entirely disappeared. Owing to more extended military operations and tactics, the defences of the foot soldier were gradually lessened, the pikemen and musketeers wearing only a light helmet, breast-plate and tassets. (*Figs. 15 and 16.*) At the Restoration of Charles II, armour was gradually discarded and was replaced by the buff coat.

Towards the end of the sixteenth century weapons were simpler in design, the complicated staff weapons were given up, and the infantry relied more especially upon the pike, which was sometimes as long as ten or fifteen feet. The English long-bow died hard;

for the fire-arm, though universally used, was very uncertain and unreliable. Even as late as the Civil War Charles I enrolled a regiment of archers at Oxford.

The fire-arms of the earliest days were simply tubes of iron with touch-hole, fired with a match. Then the cross-bow lock was adapted so that the match held in a clip could be brought on to the touch-hole by pulling the trigger. This rough and ready form of fire-arm had, however, great disadvantages in wet weather when

the match cord would fail to ignite and in dry weather the sparks glowing on the matches gave away the position of troops; also if infantry were posted anywhere near ammunition stores there was always the danger of accidental explosions. (*Fig. 17.*)

Figure 17
MATCH-LOCK, SIXTEENTH-SEVENTEENTH CENTURY. Tower Armouries

In the middle of the sixteenth century we find the 'Wheel-lock'. (*Fig. 18.*) This was a wheel with roughened edges, similar to modern cigar lighters, worked on a spring. The clip which had held the match in the match-lock was provided with a piece of iron pyrites, which was depressed on to the wheel, and the pulling of the trigger

Figure 18
WHEEL-LOCK, LATE SIXTEENTH CENTURY
Tower Armouries

released the spring and revolved the wheel, causing sparks to shower on to the touch pan. According to Sir Samuel Meyrick—the great authority on armour—this still had its adherents in 1827. It was, however, costly in manufacture, and was seldom used in war. The match-lock was displaced by the flint-lock, which consisted of a cock with a piece of flint screwed into its jaws. This on pulling the trigger struck against the steel hammer and sent sparks on to the

137

touch-hole. (*Fig. 19.*) This was far cheaper to manufacture than the wheel-lock, but was not so reliable, as it often mis-fired.

Up to the middle of the eighteenth century commanders had relied on the pikemen for repelling cavalry, but about the year 1680 the bayonet was introduced. This was in design a short dagger with a wooden handle which was inserted into the musket barrel, but it is needless to say the musket could not be fired when the bayonet was fixed. About the year 1690 the French evolved a

Figure 19
FLINT-LOCK PISTOL (SNAPHAUNCE)
MIDDLE OF SEVENTEENTH CENTURY

bayonet with rings which could be passed over the muzzle of a musket, making it possible, therefore, to fire with a fixed bayonet. This was very soon followed by the socket bayonet, which persisted in every army in Europe up to the end of the nineteenth century. And so, piece by piece, armour was discarded, till at last the only remaining detail was the small gilt gorget worn by officers in the eighteenth century, and it was only at the Coronation of George IV that the cuirasses and helmets of the Life Guards were reintroduced.

SHORT BIBLIOGRAPHY

J. Hewitt, *Ancient Armour and Weapons in Europe*. 3 vols. 1855–60 (out of print).

C. H. Ashdown, *British and Foreign Arms and Armour*, 1909 (Jack).

C. J. Ffoulkes, *Armour and Weapons*, 1909 (Clarendon Press).

A. Demmin, *Weapons of War*, 1870 (out of print) (Bohn's Artist's Library).

A. HAMILTON THOMPSON

The English House

In a well-known line of the *Nun's Priest's Tale* Chaucer refers to the two component parts of the ordinary dwelling-house of his day. Of the dairywoman's cottage he says, 'Ful sooty was hir boure and eek hire hall'. The simple cottage of which he was writing was the traditional English house, familiar in examples great and small, with its two rooms. The larger room was the hall, the smaller the bower or chamber, the first the main room of the building entered directly from outside, the second an inner and private room to which access was obtained from the hall. Such a house as Chaucer describes was probably little more than a hut of wood or of wattles daubed over with clay, and there is playful irony in his application of the terms 'bower' and 'hall' to such a building at a period when they were commonly used of far more important structures. Nevertheless the essential elements of the manor-house and of the domestic buildings which rose within the precincts of castles were present in the smallest cottage. The requirements of human nature at either extreme sought expression upon a different scale, but in the same way, and, when civilisation began to emerge from the simplicity of the nomad tent and the beehive hut, its earliest effort was to combine the publicity of daily life carried on in the main living-room with some degree of privacy supplied by the inner room. Primitive as the arrangement may seem, it was only by slow degrees that the dwelling-house, from its nucleus of hall and bower, attained its ultimate complexity and variety of plan; and recent excavations on the site of the royal palace of Clarendon show how closely a building on whose adornment by artists and craftsmen Henry III lavished money, adhered to the traditional house-plan without large extension.

The hall (*aula*), the common living-room and meeting-place of the household, large or small, was the original centre from which the house developed. Literary references to it occur in the earliest sources and in heroic surroundings, as, for example, to the great timber hall of Heorot in *Beowulf* where Hygelac's warriors feasted, played, slept and fought. Such a hall we may picture in the famous parable uttered by one of Edwin's wise men, as related by Bede, at the council which in 627 debated the acceptance of Christianity by the Northumbrian Kingdom; the hall through whose light and warmth the bird flew from the outer darkness into the night beyond. Large wooden halls of this kind, divided into a number of bays by arched trusses known as crucks, were still being built in this country in the twelfth century and later. In districts where building-stone was scarce, this method of timber construction long survived; it remained a normal method of constructing barns and cattle-sheds, and it is often possible that an old barn may contain traces of its original purpose as a dwelling-house. Of the arrangements of the hall we shall speak presently. Here, however, it may be noted that the hall was intended for general use, and in the larger houses it was the scene of a large amount of business which was not purely domestic. To the present day the principal house in an English village constantly retains its time-honoured name 'the Hall'; for the hall of the medieval manor-house was the central point of village life, where the lord or his steward or bailiff held their courts and from which the activities of the estate were directed. It played a part in the public life of a self-contained community which can hardly be realised in our own day, supplying its chief means of contact with the life of the world outside. Just as the hall of the royal palace of Westminster became the centre of English national life, so on a smaller scale the manorial hall was of similar importance to the district which depended on its lord.

Thus the word 'hall,' though it might be applied to the whole house of which the hall was the principal room, acquired a special public significance. Guildhalls, town-halls, halls of colleges and other institutions, usually forming part of groups of buildings whose plan was derived from that of the private house, associated it with the life of corporations and larger communities. On the other hand, the private house of the individual owner received a special name which, though it has long been obsolete and was always more familiar in its Latin that in its English form, was derived from the inner and private apartment. It was the *camera* or chamber of its owner, his bower, like the royal manor-house which gave to an Essex village the name Havering-atte-Bower, or the *bur* mentioned in the tale of the murder of Cynewulf of Wessex in the Anglo-Saxon Chronicle for 755. While the Latin word *domus* and its English equivalent house were used for any kind of building, and while *aula* came to signify a house of official and public importance, *camera* was the name for a private dwelling. Thus the abbot's house in a monastery was *camera abbatis*, including his hall and his chapel in addition to his private chamber. In one direction the word underwent an expansion, characteristic of medieval usage. In the private chamber were kept the valuables and treasure of its master, as the story of Edward the Confessor and the thief reminds us, under the charge of his *camerarius* or chamberlain. For this reason his private treasure was known as his *camera*. The Londoners boasted that their city was *camera Regis*, the source of wealth which the king was invited to regard as his own. The Chamber was the name of one of the departments of state which administered the royal revenues, like the papal *Camera* at Rome. But, whether the word refers to a house or a treasure, it implies this individual, private meaning.

The private house had another common name, which, however, it shared with houses of a different kind. It was often called *hospitium* or inn, like the New Inn in Thames Street which was the town house of Richard II's half-brother, the Earl of Huntingdon, or those numerous houses in Essex and Hertfordshire with names like Audley End, in which the word has been generally corrupted. In this case, however, the private significance of the word has now disappeared. Just as in Latin countries to-day, the private dwelling is the *appartement*, the single word for the whole, so the *camera* was the private house of the middle ages; and it is the story of the *camera* and its subsequent development that we are about to tell.

II

IT is occasionally stated that the English house-plan derives its origin from the arrangements of the keep or great tower which was the dominating feature of a castle. We shall see that domestic buildings within the precincts of castles played an important part in the development of the house, and that tower-houses, of which the castle-keep is the earliest pattern, were at certain periods a favourite type of dwelling. Any attempt, however, to give them the first place in the history of the dwelling-house overlooks the facts, first, that the keep was primarily intended for military purposes; secondly, that the castle, the symbol of feudal dominion, did not appear in England before the middle of the eleventh century and then under Norman influence; and thirdly, that even when after the Norman Conquest castles were built in considerable numbers, they formed a special and exceptional type of structure to which it is highly unlikely that the ordinary person who wished to build himself a house would look for his model.[1]

That model, as a matter of fact, was ready to hand in the dwelling which at the time of the Conquest was, and long had been, the principal house in the English village settlement, the house of the land owner upon whom the community was in economic dependence. When, as an immediate result of the Conquest, society was completely feudalised, this type of house acquired a new political significance, but in its outward characteristics remained unchanged. Indeed, the manor which was the unit of feudal jurisdiction derived its name from the *manerium* or *mansum*, the dwelling-house inhabited by the lord or his representative. Such a house was not necessarily of imposing size; but it was larger than its neighbours and its characteristics were theirs on an extended scale. In the manor-house, whether built of timber or of stone, the hall and bower had room for development, and the house-plan assumed the settled form which controlled its history until the seventeenth century.

The Bayeux Tapestry gives us a picture of Harold's mansion at Bosham in Sussex which may be regarded as typical of the larger houses of the eleventh century. Like the pictures of castles and churches in the same work of art, it is a purely conventional representation of the sort of building with which the makers of the tapestry were thoroughly familiar. Above a vaulted substructure of stone carried by piers there is an upper story, apparently of timber with a shingled roof rising to a central apex crowned by a dragon-like figure which does duty for a weathercock. The house is shown in section, the upper story forming a large undivided room in which Harold and his company are feasting, entered at one end by an outside stair. The messenger who has come from Duke William stands upon the stair and appears to be supporting one end of the roof with his head, as the artist no doubt found it difficult to give his figure sufficient prominence without suppressing at this end the roof-post whose counterpart is shown at the other side of the hall.

In this picture the artist's object was to tell a story clearly, and just so much of the house is shown as was necessary for the purpose. It is not therefore entirely accurate, and the cross-section reveals only the principal room in the upper stage. We cannot point to any existing English house which is of so early a date, but a considerable number of houses remain from the middle of the twelfth century

[1] Cf. above, pp. 97 sqq.

in which we can still see the characteristics of the house of the Bayeux Tapestry. There is no more complete example of the type than the old manor-house preserved in the grounds of the Hall at Boothby Pagnell in Lincolnshire. Though it was built at least a century after the Norman Conquest, it shows no appreciable advance upon Harold's mansion. The dwelling-rooms are on the upper floor, entered by an outer stair set against the wall. Two-thirds of the space are occupied by the hall: the remaining third is the private chamber, divided from the hall by a thick partition-wall in which there is a doorway. The ground-floor rooms, which have their own outer doorway, correspond to those above. The room beneath the hall is ceiled with ribbed vaulting in two bays, while that beneath the chamber has a barrel-vault. There is a fireplace in one of the side walls of the hall, the smoke from which escaped through a tall cylindrical chimney which is still perfect.

The 'Norman House' at Christchurch in Hampshire is a well-known example of the same type. Here, however, the house was built within the precincts of a castle. Castles, indeed, offered good opportunities for the development of domestic buildings within their areas. While the timber keep upon the earthen mound in the earliest form of castle was often used as a residence, its purpose was mainly defensive. It was moreover limited in size and difficult of access. The great tower-keeps, such as those at London and Colchester and those which were built in large numbers during the reign of Henry II, gave ample house-room; but there again military considerations were more important than domestic comfort. The provision of a separate dwelling-house in the inner ward or bailey of the castle was probably not general before the thirteenth century; but timber buildings may often have existed which have since been destroyed, and occasionally, as at Christchurch, stone houses were erected. At Richmond in Yorkshire, where there was originally no keep and a large walled enclosure, entered by a gate-house, formed the castle, a spacious hall, built above a cellar on the further side of the area, was part of the earliest arrangements. When, between 1174 and 1177, the keep was built on the site of the original gatehouse, part of which was retained in its structure, no attention was paid to its use as a dwelling-house, sufficient accommodation for which existed in the hall and its adjoining buildings. By the end of the twelfth century permanent stone dwelling-houses were becoming an important adjunct to castles, and the great three-storied building, consisting of cellars and lower and upper halls, which Bishop Hugh Puiset erected in Durham Castle about 1175, is an example of the size and splendour which they sometimes achieved. As time went on, the dwelling-house nowhere assumed such ample proportions as within the shelter of castle walls, and nowhere else can the growth of comfort and privacy be traced so easily.

Throughout this development, however, the hall above the cellar remains the characteristic nucleus of the plan. It is the essential feature of the large dwelling-houses in Ludlow, Warwick, Kenilworth, Portchester and many other castles. In these, blocks of building, not contemplated in the simple houses of the twelfth century, have been added at either end, but the hall, enlarged and beautified, is the centre of the composition, and the steep outer stair has become a broad flight of steps with a porch at the head covering the entrance to the 'screens' at one end of the hall.

In early town houses space for building was naturally more constricted than in the country or in the large open spaces of castle wards. Just as in country villages the manor-house and church may often have been the only buildings of stone, so in towns stone houses were the signs of wealth and importance to which the ordinary dwelling-house could not rise. The traditional name, Jews' houses, given to two houses at Lincoln and to the house known as Moyses Hall at Bury St. Edmunds, is probably well warranted by the prominence of Jewish money-lenders in the towns of the twelfth century. In Lincoln no less than four stone houses of this period remain in a fair state of perfection, though much altered internally. In all these and in the house at Bury St. Edmunds the living-rooms were upon the upper floor; but, owing to their situation upon the front of narrow streets, the stair was either internal or a passage was made through the ground-floor to a small courtyard at the back from which the stair mounted.

No definite place can be found for a kitchen in these early plans. Cooking may have been done in the cellar, but the only outlet for smoke was through the doorway, and it is very doubtful whether the ground-floor was generally used for any other purposes than that of cellarage. While, in houses with a first-floor hall, the ground-floor obviously was a convenient place for the kitchen, and examples of this occur at intervals throughout the middle ages, its place in what may be called the first-floor plan was never fully determined. It is probable that cooking in early days was often done at a fire in the open air or in some building separate from the main structure, of the type which, developed on a large scale, produced the great monastic kitchens which survive at Durham and Glastonbury. Even in the fourteenth century at Ludlow Castle the kitchen stood apart from the main block of buildings, while the only fireplace in the hall was the central hearth, carried upon a pier in the ground-floor from which the smoke made its way through an opening in the roof. It may be noted that the picture in the Bayeux Tapestry, in which it is unnecessary to discover any kitchen or fireplace, gives no indication of a chimney; and the wall-fireplace, though not uncommon, was by no means universal until a much later period.

III

THE first-floor plan, however, had its alternatives, and these must be considered. It should be remembered that the type of house which has been described was exceptional. In towns the two-storied house, whether of wood or stone, was eminently convenient for merchants and shop-keepers, for part of the ground-floor, where their goods were stored, could be used as their place of business. But in the ordinary house, whether in town or country, the living-rooms were on the ground-floor. It has already been said that their division into a main room with a smaller 'outshot' was precisely that of hall and bower, and was in fact the primitive form of that division. Similarly, the 'speer' or wooden partition which screened the main room from the draught of the doorway was the prototype of the 'screens', the passage at the lower end of the hall which became an invariable feature of larger houses. The main room was flat-ceiled, and the space between the ceiling and the timbers of the gabled roof was a loft in which stores could be kept, entered by a ladder and trap-door. In such buildings, in fact, the position of hall and cellar was reversed.

While the first-floor plan was doubtless adopted in the larger houses for the sake of ample cellarage and premises which could be entered directly from outside, it became increasingly common as time went on to build halls with their floors on the level of the ground or slightly raised above it. In such cases, as we shall see, the cellarage was transferred elsewhere. The earliest examples of this kind to which we can point are the aisled halls which appear in the course of the twelfth century. These were divided into nave and aisles by columns which were probably in many instances of timber. Until a few years ago it was possible to see at Stansfield, a small village in Suffolk, a barn which, originally the hall of a manor-house, retained timber columns with scalloped capitals of the middle of the twelfth century. It is obvious that the columns of such a hall, if built above a cellar, would need special support from below; and thus the aisled hall was built straight from the foundations without an intervening substructure.

There is a very remarkable example of an aisled hall built of stone in the ruined manor-house of Warnford in Hampshire, not far from Petersfield. Here a hall of moderate size was divided into three bays by very tall and slender circular columns with lofty bases. There are no remains of arches, and it seems that here the cross-beams of a high-pitched roof which covered nave and aisles rested on the capitals of the columns. The date of this hall seems to lie between 1190 and 1200. But by that time the aisled hall had long been familiar in the infirmary buildings of monasteries, as at Canterbury and Ely, and it is possible that this may have had its influence upon its adoption in domestic architecture. The aisles of infirmary halls had a definitely practical use, for they contained the beds of the inmates, while the middle space was left free. In the aisled hall of the house the tables were laid in the middle space, while the aisles were passages which gave free circulation for service.

As a rule, however, aisled halls are seldom found save in houses of considerable importance. The hall of Oakham Castle, built at the close of the twelfth century with a richness of architectural and sculptured detail equal to that of any of the greater churches of the age, is the most beautiful example which remains. Hardly less remarkable is the great hall at Auckland Castle, the chief manor-house of the bishops of Durham, which was repaired after the Restoration and turned into a private chapel. Another conspicuous instance is the hall of Winchester Castle, built in the reign of Henry III. But the normal custom was to build the ground-floor hall, like the first-floor one, without aisles. At the same time, it can hardly be doubted that the aisled hall promoted the employment of a plan which, without wholly superseding that of the first-floor plan, became characteristic of the English manor-house.

The advantage of the first-floor plan had lain in its combination within a compact area of the essential parts of a house: hall, and chamber on the upper level, cellar and possibly kitchen below. Equally compact was the plan in which the chamber formed a third story to a house with a ground-floor cellar and first-floor hall. Purely domestic examples of this are not common, and usually are found where the house stands on a site where its expansion is hindered by neighbouring buildings. It was naturally convenient for town houses closely crowded together, where the only possible method of expansion was by adding one story to another; and in ancient towns there are still many survivals of tall, narrow timber-framed houses of various dates with a series of projecting upper stories. A good example of a stone house of three stories is the abbot's *camera* at Kirkstall, built early in the thirteenth century, where the ground-floor was cellar and service-room, the hall, entered by an outer stair, was on the first floor, and above it was the abbot's private room. There was no need for a kitchen, as meals were served from the kitchen of the infirmary, and there is no fireplace on the ground-floor; but there are fireplaces in both the upper rooms.

This type of plan, of course, approximates closely to that of the residential keep of a castle, a tower divided into three or four stories, with the entrance, approached by a stair contained in a forebuilding, on the first or second floor, and internal stairs in the thickness of the walls and in the angle-turrets. In the later middle ages, especially in the north of England and on both sides of the Scottish border, the arrangements of pele-towers and bastel-houses correspond almost exactly to those of the house just described at Kirkstall. But, as has already been said, the real purpose of these buildings was defensive, and, while the large tower-keeps, from the White Tower which gives its name to the Tower of London onwards, had roomy halls and chambers, yet this was merely a compromise between military and domestic needs. In the fifteenth century, when the keep had ceased to be a necessary portion of the castle, there are many examples in England and on the Continent of large tower-houses in connexion with castles. But the history of the keep and its successor the tower-house touches that of the dwelling-house without exercising noticeable influence upon it. The influence, in fact, was all the other way, and these forms of building simply incorporated and adapted to their own special purposes the elements which the dwelling-house had shown to be necessary to domestic life.

IV

WE have thus arrived at three types of dwelling-house, the house with hall and bower adjoining each other on the upper floor, the house whose nucleus is the hall which occupies the ground-floor and corresponds in height to the two stories of the first type, and the three-storied house in which the bower is above the hall. In all these the hall, the common room of the house, is the essential feature: in the first and third types hall, bower and cellar are combined in one block. In the second type the importance given to the hall relegates bower, cellar, and kitchen, as we shall see presently, to adjacent blocks. It was in this second plan that the future of the English house lay, and the ultimate expansion of the house into the quadrangular and the single-block plans was upon the lines which it developed.

Those lines, however, showed signs of development where the hall was still upon the first floor. We may take as an example the moated manor-house of Markenfield near Ripon, still partly occupied with very little disturbance of its original arrangements. Markenfield Hall was built in the early years of the fourteenth century for John of Markenfield, a wealthy landowner who was in holy orders, a clerk in the king's service and a canon of York. The house stands on the north side of the area, at once forecourt and farmyard, enclosed by the moat and entered by a bridge and a small gatehouse. It consists of a principal block running east and west in two stories, of which the east part is projected southward as a three-storied wing. The first floor of the main block is a lofty hall which still keeps its original two-light windows and was entered near its west end by a stair built against the face of the wall. This has now gone, and the doorway at its head has been blocked, but the roof-line of the porch which covered the landing remains. Beneath the hall was the kitchen, with its own outer doorway and with cellars to the east beneath the end of the hall.

There are now no traces of the usual screen which here may have covered the west end of the hall and so shut off the doorway. At the east end of the hall, behind the site of the dais and the high table, a wall divides the hall from the bower or great chamber. The way to this is through a doorway on the south side of the dais, which is also the way into the first floor of the wing. It leads into a room, the east half of which was screened off as a private chapel, with an altar against the east wall and a piscina, which still remains, in the south wall. North of this, entered from the ante-chapel, is the great chamber, with a fireplace in the east wall, and a doorway to a small garderobe which projects near the north-east corner and the shoot of which had an outlet to the moat. The rooms in the wing south of the chapel, which, as has been said, was of three stories, were probably used as household offices and guest-chambers, and were provided with a turret stair, projecting into the forecourt and communicating with each floor on its way to the roof.

Markenfield is an early example of a house planned with a number of rooms in addition to those intended for the accommodation of its master. In a medieval house such privacy as there was was confined to the great chamber, the withdrawing-room and bedroom of the lord of the house and at any rate some of his family, to say nothing of occasional guests. Members of the household who were in constant attendance, the gentlemen, yeomen, and grooms who were attached to every establishment of any size, slept in the hall, making their beds on the benches and tables. Complete privacy for individuals was not achieved until a much later date; but throughout the fourteenth and fifteenth centuries the number of separate rooms was greatly increased.

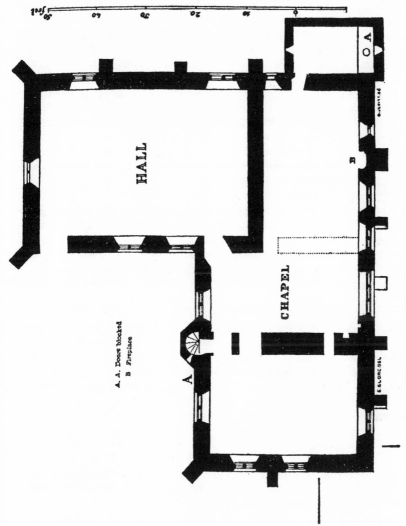

HALL

CHAPEL

A. A. Doors blocked
B Fireplace

MARKENFIELD HALL, YORKSHIRE. First-floor plan

At Markenfield also, where the kitchen was beneath the hall, the great chamber and chapel were above cellars. This was no novelty, for it simply repeats the disposition of bower and cellar in such twelfth-century houses as those at Boothby Pagnell and Christchurch. But at Markenfield the bower and chapel are actually part of the wing-block at the end of the hall. In houses where the hall is entered on the ground-floor and there is no kitchen below, there was a two-storied block behind the high table, with the cellar on the ground-floor; and, corresponding to this at the other end of the hall, another block contained the kitchen with the buttery and pantry. These two blocks often projected slightly, leaving the hall recessed; but there was no exact correspondence or uniformity between them. They were the private wing and the servants' wing. Between them stood the hall, and the only way from one to the other lay through it.

This plan was very generally adopted in the later medieval house and survived into the seventeenth century. Examples of it are to be found in every English county, often in large numbers; and, although the original arrangement of the wings has constantly been altered in modern times, the hall usually remains without much change and is frequently intact. The internal arrangements were so uniform that they may be described without reference to any particular house.

The entrance doorway was always at one end of the hall and was sometimes covered by a porch with a room above. It led into a passage formed by a wooden screen, in which there were usually two doors, set across the hall. Above the ceiling of this passage, which was called the screens, was a gallery for the minstrels who played at feasts, and at the further end of it a doorway opened into a yard or base-court. In the wall opposite the wooden screen, there were usually three doorways. The middle one opened into a passage leading to the kitchen: those on either side were the doorways of the buttery and pantry, and in the buttery door there was a hatch through which drink was served. A fourth doorway, near the far end of the screens, opened on the stair to the minstrels' gallery and to the upper rooms of the porch and kitchen wing, the use of which probably varied.

The hall, entered through the screen-doors, was a large oblong apartment open to the roof. It was the centre of the whole life of the household, the place for their common meals and indoor recreation; the hall of a manor house was the nucleus of the activities of the community dependent upon its master, the place where his courts were held and to which his tenants resorted for direction in their work. At the end opposite the screens the high table was set across the hall upon a platform or dais, a step above the floor-level. The tables for the inferior members of the household were in the body of the hall, set lengthways. The windows in the side-walls as a rule were well above the floor: the walls below them were wainscoted, and their upper parts plastered and painted with designs of various kinds. The floor was strewn with rushes, which seem very often to have been changed only at long intervals, between which they became matted together with mud and filth of all sorts. In the middle of the hall, as may still be seen at Penshurst Place in Kent, was the hearth, and above it a hole in the roof covered by a louvre with openings for the smoke. Wall-fireplaces, however, were from quite early days an alternative for the central hearth, and became general in the fourteenth and fifteenth centuries. Their mantels and chimney-breasts afforded good opportunities for carving and painting, while externally their chimneys, from the tall cylinders of the twelfth to the elaborately moulded brick chimneys of the sixteenth century, exhibit a remarkable variety of design.

In the fifteenth century it became a common practice to throw out a bay-window in one of the side-walls close to the high table, in which a sideboard was set. Sometimes, as may often be seen in the manor-houses of Somerset and the adjoining counties, the bay was a deep rectangle, almost a room in itself, and was divided into two floors. The chamber on the upper floor sometimes had a window opening into the hall, the place of which, at Great Chalfield in Wiltshire and some other contemporary houses, was taken by a grotesque head, the eyes, nostrils and mouth of which were pierced with peep-holes. More usually the bay was a half-octagon, carried up the whole height of the wall without division into floors.

The timber roof of the hall was high-pitched, though in the fifteenth century, in accordance with general practice, the pitch was considerably flattened. In construction and detail it followed the ordinary lines of development, often attaining a high degree of beauty, enhanced by the painting and gilding of the beams and flat surfaces. In the painting and decoration of roofs and walls the royal palaces, from the reign of Henry III onwards, set a high standard. The most magnificent timber roof in England is that of Westminster Hall, constructed in the reign of Richard II, while the hall-roofs of Eltham Palace and at a later date of Hampton Court were designed with an artistic and technical skill in the display of which smaller houses often did not fall far behind them.

We have already mentioned the minstrels' gallery which was at the lower end of the hall above the screens. This was not an invariable feature, and sometimes the space above the screens was boarded off from the hall by a high wooden partition in which there were one or more small windows. Other features which may be noted in connexion with the hall are the provision of cupboards and sometimes of recesses for sideboards in the walls, and of stone washing-troughs in the screens. The wall sideboards and lavatories, like the fireplaces, were treated with much variety of decoration.

Beautiful examples of the first kind can be seen in Harewood Castle and the ruins of the Old Palace at Lincoln, while, among lavatories which remain, those in the house of John Flore at Oakham, the so-called Knight's House at Lincoln, and Northburgh Hall near Peterborough, deserve special mention.

Near the back of the high table a doorway opened into a lobby from which the cellar was entered and a stair led to the great chamber above. The position of the doorway followed convenience or necessity, but, where a bay-window was built, it was customary to place it in the space between the bay and the end wall, so that the door opened into a stair-turret adjoining the bay. The cellar was vaulted, and what windows it had were small and narrow. The great chamber, on the other hand, was well lighted, and a common name for it was the solar (*solarium*), which originally meant a sunny apartment, but in process of time was applied to any upper room or loft, such as the room above a church-porch or the loft on the top of a rood-screen. It was a spacious room, in early times of the same breadth as the adjoining hall: at a later date, however, its size was increased, so that, as may be seen at Haddon Hall, the block formed by cellar and solar was built out to form a projecting wing. Its walls were plastered and painted or hung with 'painted cloths' of arras or tapestry. There was a fireplace, either in the wall next the hall or in the wall opposite. The wooden roof followed the longer axis of the room, which was at right angles to that of the hall. The window recesses were habitually continued downwards to the floor, with stone benches on either side. The windows themselves, until the close of the fourteenth century, were seldom entirely glazed: the upper parts only were grooved for glass and were divided by a transom from the lower lights, which were closed with shutters. This applies also to the windows of the hall: the transom, introduced for purely practical reasons, was retained after windows were glazed throughout and became a normal feature in large windows of the later Gothic period. For the furniture of the great chamber no general rules can be laid down; but much of it must have consisted of couches which were seats by day and beds by night. It should be remembered that the numerous bequests of 'beds' in medieval and later wills refer to bedding which served this double purpose, and regular bedsteads were exceptional until the sixteenth century.

Occasionally the solar, as in the early fourteenth-century example at Stokesay in Shropshire, had an outer stair of its own, but the turret-stair from the hall was the normal arrangement. Now and then variations may be found in the position of the solar block, and two conspicuous examples may be noted in which it was placed between the hall and the kitchen. The first of these is the Bishop's Palace at Lincoln, where the aisled hall, built early in the thirteenth century, occupies a ledge of the hill which descends steeply to the south. The kitchen was built above a cellar at a much lower level and formed a separate tower connected with the hall by a bridge and a passage on either side of which were the buttery and pantry, with the great chamber on the floor above. In modern times this two-storied block, which had long been in ruins, was converted into the chapel of the house adjoining the site. The stone benches of the windows in the great chamber, now high above the floor, remain, and the passage over the kitchen bridge was made into a vestry.

The other instance is in the fine ruined manor-house at South Wingfield in Derbyshire, begun by Ralph, Lord Cromwell, towards the middle of the fifteenth century. This house and its offices cover a large area, divided into two courtyards, on the summit of a hill which descends abruptly on three sides. The hall is entered by a porch from the inner court, but was built above a large vaulted cellar on the slope beneath the edge of the hill. This cellar, a splendidly conceived piece of architectural design, is thus lighted on one side and communicates with the hall and the adjoining buildings by four stairs, one at each angle. It was probably in order to gain more room for the cellar before the slope became too steep that the great chamber was built above the passage to the kitchen and the rooms on each side, beyond which the passage was continued between the buttery and pantry to the kitchen, a large and lofty room with three great fireplaces. Few medieval houses will be found without some individual feature of plan due to exigencies of site, but few which show so radical a departure from common form. The medieval builder, however, knew well how to adapt his traditions to practical demands, and these two buildings are outstanding illustrations of his skill.

The chapel, which we have noticed at Markenfield, was by no means an invariable feature of a private house, and a special licence was required for it from the diocesan bishop in order to safeguard the rights of the parish church. There is therefore no fixed place for it in the plan. At the manor-house of Little Wenham in Suffolk, a remarkable example of thirteenth-century brickwork, it adjoins the first-floor hall, and is divided from it by a screen with traceried openings on each side of the doorway, and there are numerous

153

other instances in which, as at Broughton Castle in Oxfordshire, it formed part of the house, so arranged that it ran east and west. But it was sometimes a separate building, and the chapel at Haddon Hall is actually a parochial chapel which was included within the precincts of the house when they were first enclosed by a wall. One characteristic feature of the private chapel, common in the later middle ages, was the division of the west end into two floors, of which the upper was on the level of the great chamber and formed a gallery used by the master of the house, his family and guests, while the servants worshipped on the lower floor. A well-known instance is at Berkeley Castle, and many others might be cited: the custom survived into modern times and was preserved in such rebuildings as those at Belvoir Castle and Alnwick Castle. In episcopal palaces the chapel was often of some size and beauty, as at Wells, Chichester and Hartlebury, the chief manor-house of the bishops of Worcester; and it has already been said that at Auckland the great hall of the castle was transformed into a chapel soon after the Restoration.

V

WE have seen how at Markenfield Hall, early in the fourteenth century, definite provision was made in the house-plan for a number of additional rooms. This was not usual at so early a date, when privacy was not even thought of and the entertainment of guests, even in the largest and, for their day, most luxurious houses, was of a rough-and-ready character. The guest-houses of monasteries, which followed the ordinary domestic arrangement of hall and great chamber or solar, must at certain festivals have been filled by pilgrims : the arrival of a guest simply meant the provision of a shake-down in one or other of these rooms. In the fourteenth century, however, the need for more privacy was being felt. It was about this time that the practice of dividing monastic dormitories into cubicles came into use by degrees and spread to the construction of private cells in infirmary halls for the old and ailing. But it was not until the later part of the century that considerable additions for the sake of extra accommodation were made to dwelling-houses, and the most noticeable examples of enlargement which remain belong for the most part to a still later period.

During the fourteenth century, indeed, the rebuilding of halls upon a larger scale was a more important consideration than the addition of new lodgings. This is well illustrated in the domestic buildings of certain castles which have been mentioned above. At Ludlow, for example, the great hall was rebuilt in the fourteenth

154

century with the usual blocks or wings at either end; but no great advance in private accommodation was made here until, in the later fifteenth and early sixtenth centuries, the solar wing was extended to contain a number of additional private rooms. These extensions were made by prolonging the range of domestic buildings along the north side of the inner ward of the castle, and, where the area of such a ward, as at Warwick, was large, the dwelling-house could be confined to one side of it. Where space was more limited, the buildings occupied two or more sides, and by successive additions, as may be well seen at Portchester Castle, the inner ward became a quadrangle surrounded by a dwelling-house.

The metamorphosis of the castle into a fortified mansion need not concern us here save in so far as the process illustrates the demand for increased accommodation which became prevalent in the later middle ages. Moreover, while in the older castles the growth of the dwelling-house took place at irregular intervals and the opportunities for its expansion were casual and limited, in the later structures in which dwelling-house was combined with stronghold in a single plan, domestic convenience was still modified by military exigency. The result can be well studied in the Welsh castles of the reign of Edward I, in which the character and position of the domestic buildings, in themselves most interesting and plentiful in their variety, were entirely subordinate to plans in which the art of defence reached its summit, or in the quadrangular castles with massive angle-towers of the north of England, designed with less art but with defence as their foremost object.

Haddon Hall, however, the most famous and perhaps the most beautiful of ancient English houses, grew to its present state by a series of enlargements very similar to the process by which the development of the house within the castle was achieved. In the beginning it was probably no more than a tower or small manor-house with an open courtyard attached and fenced with timber. Late in the twelfth century a defensive wall of which a portion remains was built round this courtyard, which was considerably enlarged so as to include at its south-west corner the chapel of the neighbouring hamlet. In the first half of the fourteenth century the hall, with a solar block at its south and a kitchen block at its north end, was built across the courtyard, dividing it into two quadrangles, a front court and base-court. The front court was entered by a gatehouse at its north-west corner, and the base-court was reached through the screens of the hall, to which a porch was added later in the same century. Towards the close of the fifteenth century a suite of first-floor rooms entered from the great chamber, was built on the south side of the front court, with cellars beneath which enclose part of the original boundary wall. This wing stopped short of the east end of the chapel, close to which an outer stair descended into the court. Subsequently, early in the sixteenth century, the west and north sides of the court were enclosed by buildings containing a large number of separate rooms and incorporating a new gatehouse; and about the same time a similar range was built along the north side of the base-court. Here at the north-east angle of the buildings, there is a massive tower pierced by a gateway which appears to be partly of an earlier date and may mark the site of the original tower or house. Finally, in the reign of Elizabeth, the enclosure of the base-court was completed upon the east side, and the south side was covered by the range the first floor of which was occupied by the long gallery. Through communication was established between the first floors of all these buildings, broken only by the chapel at the south-west angle, and the whole effect of a plan which actually developed piecemeal is singularly uniform, as though it had been intentional from the beginning.

The quadrangular plan thus attained by a series of efforts was frequently adopted as a consistent plan of new houses in the fifteenth century, long before it reached completion at Haddon. We have seen, for instance, how at South Wingfield there were two quadrangles surrounded by buildings, with the house itself on the far side of the second court. The development of the plan was notably assisted by, and indeed found its normal pattern in the collegiate buildings which were erected in considerable numbers in the fourteenth century. Here communities of secular clergy, bound to the services of particular churches, were housed in separate lodgings with a common hall as the centre of their life. The hall of course was very like the refectory of a monastery; on the other hand the monastic refectory was in its general appearance and arrangements, with its high table, its screens and its buttery and pantry, similar to the hall of a dwelling-house. In no other respect did the collegiate and monastic plans coincide: the collegiate building was simply a dwelling-house, a collection of separate lodgings under one roof with the hall as its principal feature. The great chamber above the cellar at one end of the hall was the lodging of the master or warden; at the other end of the hall was the kitchen. The lodgings of the fellows were in wings, with separate doorways to each pair, upper and lower. The earliest colleges of this type probably followed no very consistent arrangement, and even at the end of the fourteenth century there are examples, as at Irthlingborough in Northamptonshire, of lodgings which seem to have stood apart from the common hall. Even the colleges of Oxford and Cambridge, of which it is natural to think in this connexion, did not possess this plan

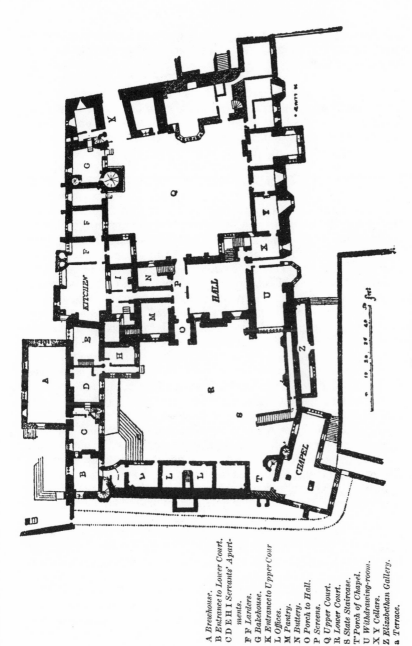

A. Brewhouse.
B Entrance to Lower Court.
C D E H I Servants' Apart-
  ments.
F F Larders.
G Bakehouse.
K Entrance to Upper Cour
L Offices.
M Pantry.
N Buttery.
O Porch to Hall.
P Screens.
Q Upper Court.
R Lower Court.
S State Staircase.
T Porch of Chapel.
U Withdrawing-room.
X Y Cellars.
Z Elizabethan Gallery.
a Terrace.

HADDON HALL

157

from the beginning. But there is an early example of a small collegiate quadrangle at Merton College, Oxford, founded in 1274, and the buildings of Corpus Christi College, Cambridge, founded in 1352, exhibit a complete quadrangular plan. The quadrangle, now the Old Court, was entered through a gateway near its north-west corner: on the south side was the hall, between the kitchen and the master's lodging. The rest of the buildings were divided into rooms, where the fellows and their pupils lived and slept, the pupils being accommodated in bunks round the walls.

The resemblance between the plans of Queens' College at Cambridge, founded in the middle of the fifteenth century, and Haddon Hall has often been remarked. Here the first court is a complete closed quadrangle with a tower-gateway in the middle of the east side. Opposite it, on the west, is the hall, with the kitchen buildings to the south and on the north the president's chamber above the fellows' common (or, according to Cambridge usage, combination) room. On the north side of the court was the library, upon a first floor, with the chapel, occupying the full height of the range, to the east. The hall-screens give access to a second court, built a few years later between the hall and the river, and surrounded by a cloister walk; and along the north side of this in the sixteenth century the president's lodge was extended from his original chamber, with a long gallery on the first floor. Almost everything to be found at Haddon is in its corresponding place here: the main differences are that the gateway at Queens' is in the middle, not at the corner of the entrance range, and the chapel (now no longer a chapel) is not a separate building, but is an integral portion of the first court. While Haddon is the result of gradual growth, the first court of Queens' is a considered design of a single period, embracing all the constituent parts of a college. But the college is nothing more nor less than a quadrangular dwelling-house.

Neither at Oxford nor at Cambridge was education the sole end of a college. Fellows and scholars, as part of the duties

> Gan for the soules bisily to praye
> Of those that yaf hem wher-with to scoleye

and, though in the first instance their daily services were often held in neighbouring or adjoining parish churches, the chapel became a necessary part of the plan. The importance given to chapels in the plans of the medieval colleges at Oxford, was greater than at Cambridge, where the noble chapel of King's was begun on a site to the south of the original quadrangle. In three Oxford colleges, New College, All Souls and Magdalen, hall and chapel stand back to back on one side of a quadrangle, and the emphasis given to the chapel here and in later buildings where it is in the same range as the hall introduced variations in the positions of the apartments which at Cambridge and in the ordinary house formed part of the hall-range.

The quadrangular plan by the close of the middle ages had become the favourite form of the large English house, as at Penshurst Place and Hurstmonceux Castle, the latter a great fifteenth-century manor-house whose fortifications are more apparent than real. It gave opportunity for the introduction at the entrance of the quadrangle of gatehouse towers of which magnificent examples remain, for instance, at Oxburgh Hall in Norfolk, of the fifteenth, and Layer Marney in Essex, of the sixteenth century. Its most perfect development on a moderate scale may be seen at Compton Winyates in Warwickshire, a house with a single quadrangle; at its highest splendour in Hampton Court Palace. It was used also, though less commonly, in small houses such as the manor-house at Little Hempston in Devon, where the hall occupies one side of the court, and the main entrance is through its screens.

It should be remarked that, while the house-plan developed on these lines, there are instances in the later middle ages of houses built in the form of a tower. In these we come back to the defensive aspect of medieval domestic architecture, and we have already alluded to the northern pele-towers. Many of these were built as residences with courtyards attached into which the local villagers and their cattle could take refuge during Scottish forays. At more than one place in Northumberland the rectory or vicarage house took the shape of a pele-tower. Occasionally, as in the prior's lodging, now the Deanery, at Carlisle, Yanwath Hall, near Penrith, and Mortham Tower near Barnard Castle, the pele-tower, at one end of the hall, contained the great chamber on the first floor. Here and there towers of unusually large size, like the early fifteenth-century towers at Belsay and Chipchase, were built with some attention to comfort: at Belsay the tower was provided with a projecting wing containing several small rooms, each with its own fireplace. But the crowning example of a tower-house in England is the great brick tower of Tattershall Castle in Lincolnshire, built for Ralph, Lord Cromwell in the second quarter of the fifteenth century. It has lately been pointed out that he was probably influenced by the splendid donjon towers which at this period were being built in castle-palaces abroad. His tower, though it strongly recalled the keeps of earlier days whose memory had been kept alive in France more continuously than in England, and though it formed part of a castle, was nevertheless in itself a private palace with large state apartments on each floor, carved fireplaces and vaulted wall-passages of remarkable beauty, and covered battlement-walks and turret-chambers whose warlike appearance was largely a matter of artistic effect. Although the late medieval tower-house is a by-path of the subject, it will be remembered that at an earlier date there are examples of kindred dwelling-houses with three stories. At Warkworth Castle in the fifteenth century a tower-house was built upon the earthen mound, square in shape with a projecting bay in the middle of each face. The ingenuity exercised in a very contracted space is remarkable: hall, chapel, great chamber, kitchen, with other rooms and abundant cellarage, all find their place in the design without undue crowding, and the whole work must be regarded as one of the greatest achievements of medieval planning.

VI

WITH the accession of the Tudors, English domestic architecture came under new influences. It cannot be repeated too often that in the mind of the medieval builder distinctions between ecclesiastical and domestic architecture did not exist. A church needed one kind of plan, a house another. It is true that the effect of a great cathedral or abbey church, with funds continually enriched by bequests and contributions great and small, was far more elaborate and splendid than that of a house built for the workaday uses of a private owner: the church afforded a wider field for the exhibition of structural skill and ornament. Nevertheless, the art which produced both was one and indivisible: it was guided by practical considerations of material and form, and, when an ordinary medieval village church is compared with a neighbouring manor-house of the same period, it is easy to see that the builders of both were applying the same vernacular to two different ends. The mouldings of doorways, the tracery of windows, the form of buttresses are the same in church and house; and the implications of this fact are unconsciously admitted by persons who, at the sight of a traceried window in the wall of some ancient house, assume that it must have been built for an ecclesiastical purpose, or by the legendary attribution of the title abbey or priory to some medieval dwelling-house.

With the end of the Wars of the Roses and the rise of a new nobility and gentry, anxious to display their recently acquired importance and growing wealth, houses increased in size and architectural splendour. Although the age produced great masterpieces of church-building like Henry VII's chapel at Westminster, the opportunities of the church-builder grew less with the approach of the Reformation. If they did not altogether cease after the suppression of the monasteries, they were for the most part confined to works of repair in existing buildings. Monasteries, where they did not fall into ruin, were often transformed by their new owners into dwelling-houses. Sir William Paulet made a great quadrangular mansion out of the church and cloisters of Netley Abbey. At Titchfield Sir Thomas Wriothesley built a great gatehouse tower in the middle of the nave of the abbey church, turned the refectory into a hall and made the rest of the buildings into lodgings and offices. At Lacock, in Wiltshire, Sir Edward Sharington destroyed the church of the nunnery and built a new range in its place, adding new upper stories to the cloister buildings which he fortunately preserved. The monastic quadrangle presented obvious advantages to an age in which the quadrangular house was in fashion.

By this time also the influence of Renaissance art had reached England. The employment of Italian artists at the court of Henry VIII had its effect upon architectural detail: foreign craftsmen, Italian and French, took part in the decoration of houses and in the design of monuments. The work of planning and construction, however, seldom went out of the hands of English masons, and the attribution of existing houses to architects such as the alleged John of Bologna and John of Padua may be dismissed as mythical. That type of English architecture which is styled Early Renaissance was fundamentally English Gothic with an overlay of Renaissance detail. Nor was the influence of Italy and France lasting. After the Reformation had broken the religious bond which united us to the Latin nations, our artists turned for inspiration to Germany and the Netherlands and to patterns of so-called classical design which, with much vigour of invention, were fantastic and clumsy and bore a very distant relation to the delicate and imaginative classicism of Italy and the rich play of fancy with which it was used by its French imitators. The dignity and picturesque effect of Elizabethan and Jacobean house architecture are never more conspicuous than when it is free from the heavy and expensive trappings imposed upon it by models taken from Teutonic albums and illustrated treatises.

The later influence, however, did not take hold of English architecture until the reign of Elizabeth, and during the earlier half of the sixteenth century the characteristic style of the English house is the natural development of the 'Perpendicular' Gothic which had ruled English architecture for so long. Decorative elements were used sparingly, the four-centred and flat-headed arches of doorways and fireplaces were moulded and carved with devices in which heraldic motives played a great part, the square-headed window with uncusped lights began to supersede the arched window-opening. At the same time, the domestic Gothic of the reign of Henry VIII produces a remarkably ornate general effect, sometimes by the emphasis laid upon some particular feature like the great bow-window at Thornbury Castle in Gloucestershire with its multiplied curves, sometimes, as at Barrington Manor in Somerset, by the prominence given to the carved finials of the gables and to the twisted and spiral surfaces of the chimneys. The decorative value of the chimney-stack was highly appreciated, especially in the brick architecture of East Anglia, where the variety of chimney design, as in the manor-house of East Barsham in Norfolk, imparts a singular beauty to structures which are otherwise plain and eminently practical. The custom of diversifying a red-brick surface with patterns formed by courses of blue brick was a method of decoration which had been prevalent since the later years of the fifteenth century. Italian influence was responsible for the occasional introduction of terracotta ornament, as may be seen in the gatehouse at Layer Marney and the rectory house at Great Snoring in Norfolk, and in the circular plaques inserted in the brickwork at Hampton Court. Such influence may sometimes be seen in structures accessory to houses: thus in the garden of the prebendal manor-house at Horton in Gloucestershire there is a summer-house in the form of an open loggia, the back wall of which is decorated with large medallions representing classical and semi-legendary worthies. But foreign influence is exceptional, and nothing could be more thoroughly English than the porch of the gateway at Compton Winyates, with its combination of brick with freestone dressings and heraldic carving.

Throughout this period the quadrangle maintained its popularity. Some houses, Barrington Manor for instance, adopted the block plan with a cross-wing at either end. But the quadrangular plan was all the fashion. Nowhere can it be seen to greater advantage than in the great house of Cowdray in Sussex, ruined by fire in 1793, where, however, the place of the ordinary kitchen block is taken, as in many medieval castles, by a kitchen tower. The gatehouse tower remained an important feature of the entrance front, so important that at Holcombe Rogus, on the borders of Devon and Somerset, it dwarfs the rest of the buildings.

After the accession of Elizabeth the number of houses built round quadrangles became somewhat less frequent. Burghley and Longleat are examples of large quadrangular houses: Burghley has two quadrangles, with a gateway tower in the entrance front and the hall, the earliest portion of the house, at the far end of the second court. Audley End, built early in the seventeenth century, similarly enclosed two quadrangles, of which the second one has been destroyed: here there was no gateway tower, and the hall is entered through one of a pair of symmetrically arranged two-storied porches in the entrance front. The most beautiful of the greater Elizabethan houses, Kirby Hall in Northamptonshire, now in ruins, was built round a large quadrangle, and close by, at Deene, the old manor-house of the abbots of Westminster was rebuilt in quadrangular form and still shows this type of building to the utmost advantage.

In these houses the gateway tower disappeared, and even at Burghley, it is a survival which has lost its commanding character and is merely a break in a somewhat monotonously designed range of buildings, while it is no longer a direct entrance to the quadrangle, but contains a great entrance hall and staircase. There was also a tendency to dispense with the entrance-range: Dr. Caius, in his remarks upon the planning of his college at Cambridge, had commented upon the advantages of leaving one side of a quadrangle open for the sake of fresh air. Thus houses enclosing only three sides of a quadrangle are sometimes found, like the Jacobean mansion at Temple Newsam near Leeds. But a more compact plan was to treat the lateral ranges as cross-wings at either end of the hall block, thus bringing them into close relationship with the centre of domestic life and avoiding the straggling inconvenience of the quadrangular arrangement. This, from one point of view, was simply a reversion to the old plan of the hall between two blocks. But it is more than that, for the quadrangle had been formed by the extension of these blocks into lateral wings, and the plan just described came into being by the drawing back, as it were, of the wings until they overlapped both ends of the main block.

This is the H-shaped plan, of which Montacute House in Somerset is a striking instance. It has the advantage of compactness in reality as well as in appearance. The drawbacks of the quadrangular plan are obvious at Kirby Hall, where the rooms in the wing used by guests are at a distance from the hall and, though planned *en suite*, must on that very account have been inconvenient and involved the provision of several staircases. Here the hall block was supplemented by a large block of private apartments and state rooms which forms an excrescence at a corner of the plan and is almost a house in itself. The area covered by Montacute is smaller, but here the house is one self-contained block, and what is sacrificed in space is gained in height, for, while Kirby is throughout a two-storied building, Montacute was designed in three stories with a cellar basement which is partly above ground.

The other plan in which the wings project on either side of the main block, and are not carried across it, forms an **m**, the short projection in the middle being formed by the entrance porch. The legend that this E-shape was adopted as a compliment to the queen,

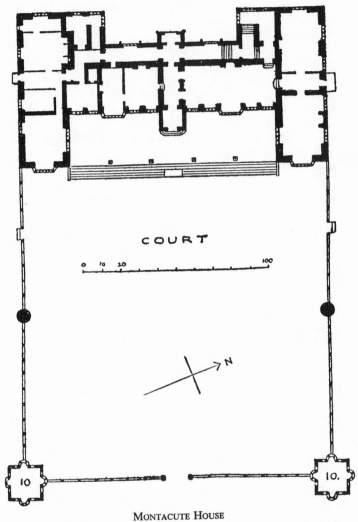

COURT

MONTACUTE HOUSE
From J. A. Gotch: *Early Renaissance Architecture in England*
(B. T. Batsford, Ltd.)

although by no means inconsistent with the tendency of the age to symbolism and allegory, is hardly tenable, for it is the inevitable shape of any building with a hall-porch and two projecting wings, and examples in which the plan exists are found before the reign of Elizabeth.

In each variation of plan the entrance porch is treated as a projection in the middle of the hall-range. This was a new departure, for its normal place in the medieval house was at one end of the hall, where it took its natural place in a composition in which practical needs outweighed any considerations of unity of design or balance of parts. In a medieval house hall-range, solar block and cellar block received architectural treatment, each on its own merits and each expressing the object for which it was built. This is well seen at Haddon, where the hall stands between two blocks designed without any idea of outward correspondence. So entirely were the builders free from a consciously aesthetic purpose that the most prominent feature of the hall-front, before the porch was added, was the large chimney-block which projects between the windows of the hall. But one of the first lessons which English builders learned from the Renaissance architecture which had made such strides upon the continent was symmetry of design. The exterior of the house became an architectural composition in which there was no attempt to express its internal arrangements: the house, in fact, was masked by a façade of which the porch, often with one or more upper stories, was the central point, and on either side, in the main block and in the wings, window corresponded to window and the same ornamental details were repeated.

Examples are abundant, but we may confine ourselves to two illustrations, Kirby Hall and Montacute. At Kirby the hall-range, built between 1572 and 1574, has a porch in the middle with an upper story and a curved gable which is no more than a surface for the display of architectural ornament. The porch is still at one end of the hall, with the result that the hall, with tall oblong mullioned windows, each crossed by three transoms and repeated in a projecting bay at the dais end, is no longer central, but fills one half of the composition. In the other half the windows and the bay are balanced by exactly similar features, but, whereas the hall is the full height of the range, the opposite half was divided into two stories, a fact to which the external elevation affords no guide. Here, too, the solar and kitchen blocks are relegated to wings unseen from the quadrangle, and, as already stated, the solar block becomes a two-storied collection of large living-rooms with cellars half underground.

At Montacute, built about 1580, unity of design is even more striking than at Kirby, a quadrangular house in which the sides of the quadrangle are subordinated to the hall-range, though continuing its characteristic ornament of pilasters and string-courses. The entrance range at Kirby was remodelled between 1638 and 1640 in the correct style which was then beginning to be the vogue. But at Montacute the house, as already shown, is one compact block, and the place of the quadrangle is taken by a raised platform, an open forecourt with small pavilions at the outer angles. The porch, approached by a flight of steps, has no upper floor, and the rows of windows in the two upper stories of the house and the cross-wings are continuous. The hall also is not continued into the second story, so that there was no need, as at Kirby, to introduce tall windows for the sake of symmetry on the other side of the porch. But, as at Kirby, the exterior elevation is no guide to the interior of the house. It is a magnificent and uniform composition, in which the most ample space is given to the long series of mullioned windows on each floor, and in which the importance of the main front, recessed between the wings, is emphasised by the statues in niches between the windows of the first floor.

In both these houses the constructive element is still Gothic, and the Renaissance borrowings, employed in profusion at Kirby and with more reticence at Montacute, are merely superficial decorations of fabrics which make no essential departure from Gothic tradition. If great and costly houses, like Kirby and Burghley, exhibited on their surface forms which, purporting to be classical, showed very little understanding of the principles of classical architecture, there were many houses in which such ornament was entirely confined to doorways and some minor details. Hardwick Hall (1587), which internally shows a remarkable and premature modification of the hall-plan, Chastleton in Oxfordshire, and Fountains Hall in Yorkshire, are three out of many instances; and it is curious to reflect that the last of these, built about 1611, is only eight years older than Inigo Jones' Banqueting House at Whitehall, in which the perfected classicism of the Renaissance stood revealed without a trace of medieval influence.

Meanwhile, the removal of the hall to one side of the entrance front, without altering its importance as the chief living-room of the house, led to certain modifications in the general plan. The great chamber, still on the first floor, became the principal room of a group combined in a wing, and the turret or wall stair which had been sufficient for access from the hall to the solar in earlier times was superseded by the staircase built on a rectangular plan with returned flights. In this arrangement the cellar left its old place on the ground-floor beneath the solar. The transition is well exemplified by the solar block at Haddon, where early in the sixteenth century the cellar was turned into a dining-room or parlour and a large nine-light window was pierced in the wall next the courtyard. This was followed in the Elizabethan period by the removal of the original stair to the solar and the construction of a rectangular staircase which occupies a projection in an angle of the base-court. The parlour and the great chamber were thus enlarged: the great chamber was entirely refitted, a new window was made in its west wall, and from the space gained by the removal of the old stair a bow window was thrown out on both floors. At the head of the new staircase a landing gave access to the great chamber on one side and the long gallery on the other. This was a case of the adaptation of existing material to new circumstances. At Drayton House in Northamptonshire, a singularly complete illustration of the gradual transformation of a medieval dwelling-house by successive re-casings and additions, a three-storied wing with a cellar basement was added about 1580 to a fourteenth-century solar block, and the vaulted cellar at one end of the hall was turned into a vestibule to the new building, with a stair descending from it to the new and larger cellar.

The long gallery, already referred to at Haddon, was an addition which played a very important part in the Elizabethan house-plan. Its use alike as a ballroom and as a promenade in bad weather was employed to the best architectural advantage, and it often occupied the entire length of an upper floor. At Knole, a very large house ranged round a number of courts, space was found for more than one of these long rooms, well lighted by mullioned windows. In quadrangular houses, such as Haddon and Kirby Hall, the upper floor of one of the side-wings, lighted on both sides, was used for this purpose; and at Haddon the space was increased by throwing out rectangular bays at intervals on the outer side. The same feature occurs in the gallery at Hardwick, one of the largest rooms of the kind; but here, in a single-block house, one wall of the gallery divides it from the great chamber and other state rooms, so that the lighting is all from one side. In such houses it was customary, however, to devote the whole of the top floor to the gallery, as in the splendid example at Montacute, where the gallery runs unbroken from wing to wing and is terminated at either end by a bow-window. This gave an opportunity for the provision of fine staircases ascending from the ground-floor to the top of the houses. The long gallery, moreover, gave ample occasion for the display, on a large scale, of those sumptuous fittings in which the fancy of Elizabethan and Jacobean craftsmen found full play.

While these alterations took place at one end of the hall, the transformation at the other end was even more complete. In the new symmetrical designs the old position of the kitchen block, directly adjoining the screens, became inappropriate. At Kirby the kitchen was placed in a short wing at one corner of the building, where room could be made for large fireplaces and chimneys without interference with the design of the principal block, and while the space gained between the hall and kitchen was used for domestic offices on the ground-floor, the upper floor was probably partitioned into bedrooms. In the single-block house, as at Montacute, the kitchen and its offices were relegated to the wing and approached by passages at the back of the living-rooms which now took their place at this end of the hall. In fact, the tendency now was for the kitchen and service-rooms to be planned in a part of the house which was invisible from the entrance-front, while rooms, such as libraries, for which the traditional ground-plan made no accommodation, were introduced into the front part of the building. The ground-floor of the half of the main block corresponding to the hall could be used as a large dining-room or as a parlour, while the range of rooms on the first and the long gallery on the top floor were unbroken from end to end of the house.

There are, of course, many variations to be found in the details of individual houses, but all tend in the direction described. House-plans which depart noticeably from these limits are rare. There are several instances of compact rectangular houses on a tower-like plan, such as Barlborough Hall, near Sheffield and Wootton Lodge in Derbyshire, in which the hall loses its character as the nucleus of the house-plan and is merely a large apartment fitted into the principal floor of the building. One curious and original device may be noted at Wollaton Hall near Nottingham, where the hall is a covered quadrangle in the middle of a house planned round it with tower-like pavilions at the angles. It is lighted by a celestory which rises above the surrounding roofs, and in the seventeenth century it was further heightened by the addition of a many-windowed upper story built for the sake of the extensive view over the vale of Trent.

The great houses of the reigns of Elizabeth and James I are not without faults of design, especially where the architectural merits of a many-gabled house with mullioned windows are abandoned for or concealed by the display of ornament borrowed at second hand from foreign sources. In some houses, as in Kirby Hall, the artlessness with which the designer has lavished would-be classical ornament upon his composition without any knowledge of the laws which govern classical architecture produces a highly picturesque effect; but the profusion of pilasters and characteristically German strap-work patterns which decorate the wall-surfaces at Wollaton is formal and ostentatious, and the general effect of Burghley House, though plainer, is equally formal and, with its strongly marked horizontal string-courses and its roof-lines broken by chimneys imitating classical columns and small cupolas and obelisks inspired by German or Flemish recipes, is extremely heavy. Even where builders confined the fashionable type of ornament to minor parts of the design and concentrated themselves upon the alternation of plain wall-surfaces with large window-openings, their sense of proportion was uncertain. At Hardwick Hall, 'more window than wall,' the exaggerated preponderance of void over solid spaces in the design had the practical disadvantage of rendering the house cold and draughty in winter and shadeless in summer. Here alien ornament is used externally only in the strap-work parapets of the angle-towers, into which the initials E. S., in commemoration of the founder, Elizabeth, countess of Shrewsbury, the famous 'Bess of Hardwick,' are introduced. The custom of employing monograms and mottos in parapets was much in vogue, especially after the beginning of the seventeenth century. It is a sign of the taste of the day for fantastic forms of expression, and the drawings of the Elizabethan surveyor John Thorpe, who was probably the designer of Kirby Hall and other important houses, illustrate the tendency to stray from the serious business of design into by-paths of fancy.

The internal fittings of these houses, although seriously infected by pseudo-classical taste, give them a beauty and charm which compensate for their defects. Roomy and elaborate staircases, panelled walls, great fireplaces adorned with statues in niches, heraldic devices and all manner of fantastic carvings, ceilings and friezes of moulded plaster, wrought with delicate and intricate patterns, windows filled with heraldic glass, combined to produce a rich variety of form and colour, too inviting, even in the most splendid examples, to be overpowering. The builders, in whatever luxuries of design they might indulge, never forgot that these houses were intended to be homes. If here and there, as in the state chamber of Hardwick, with its great plaster frieze picturing Diana and her train amid trees and the beasts of the forest, homeliness was sacrificed to imposing effect, this was rare. Great chambers and long galleries were designed for a spacious and easy life in which large companies could 'fleet their time carelessly, as in the golden world.' Until a few years ago, when most of its fittings except the elaborate plaster ceiling were removed, the great chamber of Gilling Castle in Yorkshire was an unequalled example of the skill with which mason, joiner, glazier and painter united in the work of decoration, and hardly any English county is without houses which illustrate the prodigal talent of craftsmen in this epoch of splendid achievement in so many departments of national life.

Nowhere, however, is the beauty of the house architecture of this period so manifest as in the smaller houses and even in the cottages. Here there was little room for decorative treatment and the forms employed were simple; but country masons displayed to the full that power of using common forms with elasticity and a variety of invention which was an inheritance derived from their medieval ancestors and predecessors. Along the line of that band of oölite limestone which runs from Portland to Lincolnshire, rich in famous quarries, small houses of this date are abundant: in the Cotswolds and Northamptonshire entire villages remain, with their manor-houses, two-storied cottages and barns, which, built of local stone, seem to have risen unbidden from the soil and form part of the natural scenery. The materials and elements of such buildings are of the simplest, dictated by the ordinary daily needs of rural life, but no two houses are quite the same, and almost every one has individual features which elevate it from a mere piece of building to the dignity of a work of architecture. The millstone grit of the West Riding of Yorkshire was fruitful in buildings of a similar character; and, even where the face of the countryside has been changed by modern industrialism, there are many three-storied houses little altered, in which the long row of practically continuous windows beneath the eaves reminds us that the top floor was a long gallery in which, in the days of the domestic system of industry, the weavers employed by the owner worked at their looms. Timber-framed houses, with brick or wattle-and-plaster fillings between the beams, are plentiful in East Anglia and Essex, while the woodlands of the Welsh border gave material for 'black-and-white' houses which is common to large and small houses alike. Such manor-houses as Old Moreton Hall in Cheshire and Pitchford Hall in Shropshire are remarkable instances of the local carpenter's mastery of his art, and enough of this kind of work is left in Chester, Shrewsbury, and Ludlow, and in small country-towns like Ledbury and Weobley, to remind us of the general aspect which such places bore before the current of medieval tradition in architecture had run entirely dry.

VII

In seventeenth-century England medieval tradition was still strong; the builders of the houses of which we have just spoken were using a home-grown art and had learned little from foreign models. Externally their houses showed without disguise the purposes of their various parts, as frankly as any medieval building. On the other hand, the designers of the great houses of the Elizabethan and early Stuart period were strongly affected by foreign influence; the decorative motives which they borrowed were, with all their extravagances, products of the Renaissance spirit; their work, if not in itself scholarly, at any rate shows an appreciation of architectural scholarship. If not directly inspired by the Italian Renaissance, they learned one lesson which Italian classicists, unhampered by Gothic tradition in a country where Gothic at its best was purely an exotic growth, had learned long before, the value of symmetry of design. This does not necessarily mean symmetry of plan; the plan, in fact, may be left to follow its own devices, so long as the symmetry of external elevation is preserved.

In the course of the sixteenth century Italian Renaissance architecture had made great strides. Though classical models were too present and too numerous to allow their imitators to go far astray, yet the architects of the Quattro Cento had gone through a period in which their construction was overlaid with profuse ornament. The architects of the beginning of the sixteenth century, chief among them Bramante, did much to purify their art by their devotion to structural form and the instinctive scholarship with which they handled it. But the reduction of the classical art of the Renaissance to rule was the work of younger men whose leader was Andrea Palladio (1516–80). His observation and measurement of classical buildings led him to compile a treatise which became a standard manual and whose principles he carried out in his work as a practising architect, notably in the brick and stucco buildings executed in his native city, Vicenza. The type of house which he brought into fashion was not his own invention, but it was largely through the influence of his precepts that it permeated architectural practice. In it the hall was merely a vestibule with the doorway in the middle of its entrance wall, approached by steps and covered by a portico or pillared loggia. From the hall a broad stair led to the principal suite of rooms on the first floor, the chief of which was the *sala* or great saloon.

In the application of this plan to the English house, the hall lost its place as the principal living-room of the house. An early example of this may be seen at Hardwick Hall, externally a building remote from any Italian influence. An unpretentious doorway covered by an open loggia leads straight into a hall which for all its size is nothing but an ante-room from which the living-rooms are reached, and from which a broad staircase leads to a gallery on the first floor, giving access to the state rooms. At Aston Hall, close to Birmingham, some thirty years later, the hall, occupying the ground-floor of the main block, is entered by a doorway in the middle of one side. This obviously does away with the screens which were essential to the purposes of a medieval hall; and, although the exterior of Aston Hall preserves all the semblance of an Elizabethan Gothic building, yet the plan of hall and first floor is virtually Palladian. The hands are the hands of Esau, but the voice is the voice of Jacob.

The beginning of Aston Hall is almost contemporary with Inigo Jones' Banqueting Hall at Whitehall and Queen's House at Greenwich, and its designer may very well have been struck by plans from Italy which were entirely different from English tradition. The old type of hall-plan, it is true, died hard; but Inigo Jones and his pupils used their knowledge of Italian architecture so vigorously that, by the time of the Restoration, the new fashions in the plan and elevation of houses were generally accepted. Further, their work was not merely imitative; it had a strong English accent, and such splendid apartments as Jones' double-cube room at Wilton House, and the great first-floor drawing-room which may be his at Ford Abbey, are works of native genius which compare with the best examples in foreign countries.

The assimilation of the new fashion by English builders was gradual, and other influences combined to qualify its immediate acceptance. The ecclesiastical revival of Gothic art in the first half of the seventeenth century helped to prolong the life of conservative elements in house architecture. In addition Palladian influence was strongly modified by the nearer neighbourhood of France, where in *châteaux* and country *manoirs* Renaissance forms had been used with a playful freedom of invention by native architects. Wren's early studies in France were responsible for the lightness of touch and versatility of design which characterised his work at all periods and differentiate it from the more ambitious and pompous efforts of his juniors. But in the period immediately preceding the Civil Wars two closely connected tendencies were making progress in English houses. The conversion of the hall into a vestibule was accompanied by an architectural transformation in which the imposition of quasi-classical ornament upon Gothic construction disappeared. Pilasters and string-courses now became part of the essence of the building; sash windows with pedimented heads, triangular or segmental, took the place of mullioned openings; doorways flanked by classical columns were no longer combined with flat Gothic arches. Pretty and picturesque pieces of display were abandoned, such as the habit of decorating façades with compositions representing the various classical orders in ascending stages, which may be seen at Stonyhurst College and Browsholme Hall, on the borders of Yorkshire and Lancashire, and in a more sophisticated form at Merton College and in the Schools quadrangle at Oxford. The house was considered as a composition governed by recognised laws of proportion in which the orderly and symmetrical disposition of masses, the relation between voids and solids, and the concentration of the design upon an effective point which gave the building cohesion and outward unity, were the objects sought and achieved. In such designs ornament, used with reticence and subtle intelligence, at once relieved monotony and emphasised structural qualities. Anyone who analyses Wren's garden-front at Hampton Court, a long side-wing whose unity in inferior hands might easily have fallen into straggling disorder, will appreciate the unobstrusive skill with which sculptured ornament and window-frames in freestone are used to give complete coherence to the red-brick structure.

The gradual triumph of the style of which Inigo Jones was the pioneer may be seen in such buildings as Raynham Hall in Norfolk, sometimes attributed to Jones, but actually designed and executed by a local surveyor, and in the remodelling of the entrance front at Kirby Hall, also said to be by Jones and probably by one of his pupils. In this second instance much of the old work, including the pilasters between the windows of the inner face, was retained, but a new centre-piece with the 'rusticated' base of which Italian architects had shown the full value was added. But throughout the later half of the seventeenth century the employment of classical orders in private buildings was restricted. It has no place in the fine wings added during this period to the manor-houses of Hinton St. George and Brympton d'Evercy in Somerset, where the effect depends upon the disposition of rows of windows with a varied treatment of the pediments; and in those numerous houses, chiefly of brick, in what is known somewhat too exclusively as the Queen Anne style, the effect is obtained largely by a quiet disposition of well-proportioned parts rather than by any insistence upon classical detail. In certain houses, too, the link which binds the new style to that which it superseded is strongly felt, sometimes in the retention of windows with mullions of stone or wood side by side with the delicate and scholarly detail of the new age, sometimes in the combination of homeliness with spaciousness of which English builders had long learned the secret. Thorpe Hall, near Peterborough, attributed to Inigo Jones' disciple and collaborator John Webb, is a case in point.

It should be remembered that Inigo Jones and Wren, the initiator and the most accomplished master of the English Classical Renaissance, played no great part in the development of the private house. They were employees of the Crown, not architects in general practice: their work lay in palaces like Whitehall, Greenwich and Hampton Court, and was not at the disposal of private employers. A large amount of work has been laid to the credit of both in which

173

neither had a hand, and, as a matter of fact, the smaller type of private house pursued its course quietly, as it had always done, under the supervision of mason-architects who, save where building accounts survive, remain anonymous. On the other hand, the 'high Roman fashion' which had captured public buildings could not fail to extend its influence, not merely by its exhibition of correct proportions and refined detail on a large scale but by its use of stately and imposing forms which appealed to the eye more readily than its subtle qualities of design. Wren's pupils and successors availed themselves with gusto of the Palladian forms which he had used with wise moderation in palaces built for noblemen. William Talman at Chatsworth, Sir John Vanbrugh at Blenheim and Castle Howard, designed houses on the scale of public institutions with monumental porticos, entrance halls of vast size, and long ranges of apartments, the effect of which was enhanced by the planning of approaches through court yards and the formal layout of the grounds. There is no doubt that the production of such spectacular effects was greatly stimulated by the example of Versailles, which, though the palace in itself is more remarkable for its sheer size and weight than for supreme excellence of design, provoked imitation throughout Europe. Occasionally, as at Petworth in Sussex, the work of an unknown architect, French architectural influence is obvious, or again, with the employment of much delicate ornament, in the equally anonymous hall-front added to Drayton House about 1700. The long succession of first-floor rooms and galleries at Hampton Court and at Boughton House in Northamptonshire, with furniture and fittings to scale and ceilings painted with allegorical compositions, emulate in moderation the internal pomp and splendour of Versailles. But the most pervading and permanent influence was that of Palladio and the Italians, obvious in the constant use of classical orders in façades and porticos. Palladio's much admired Villa Capra near Vicenza was imitated, with certain modifications in a design highly unsuited to English climate, at Mereworth in Kent and at Nuttall Temple (recently destroyed) near Nottingham, where the rooms opened from a central hall lighted from the roof.

The love of display characteristic of such houses reaches its highest point in the vast entrance-halls approached by flights of steps and imposing porticos, and adorned by marble columns and statues and busts in niches, at Wentworth Woodhouse in Yorkshire and Sir Robert Walpole's mansion at Houghton in Norfolk. Such entrances were too magnificent for daily use, and the ordinary entrance was through a less ostentatious hall on the ground-floor. Architectural effect on the large scale implied a subordination of ground-plan to elevation, and the emphasis laid upon the splendour of the overpowering main block relegated kitchens and domestic offices to wings which played an insignificant part in the design. Thus at Seaton Delaval in Northumberland and Duncombe Park in Yorkshire, both designed by Vanbrugh, the kitchen in the first instance was in a projecting wing, which, with an exactly similar stable-wing opposite, flanks the approach to the lofty mansion-block, while in the second it was in one of two separate pavilions

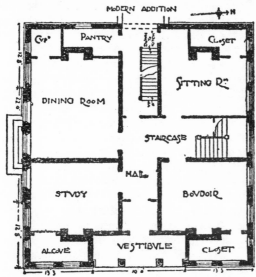

FENTON HOUSE, HAMPSTEAD
Drawn by A. Stratton. From J. A. Gotch: *The Growth of the English House*
(B. T. Batsford, Ltd.)

connected with the house by subways. The sacrifice of convenience to outward magnificence is obvious, and it is to be hoped that in dining-rooms so remote from kitchens the guests consoled themselves by contemplation of the divinities who consumed ambrosia and quaffed nectar without the aid of cooks on the pictured ceilings. But of the beauty and elegance with which the great architects of the eighteenth century invested their main compositions there can only be one opinion, and these qualities increased as the century proceeded. If Vanbrugh's taste for gigantic proportions has given him a not entirely deserved reputation for heaviness of design, English Palladian architecture was capable of lighter effects, and no better example of its complete success can be cited than the beautiful villa, with its rusticated basement and noble Corinthian portico,

175

which the elder Wood designed for Ralph Allen at Prior Park, near Bath.

The earliest and some of the most famous of these great Palladian mansions are contemporary with the prevalence of the 'Queen Anne' style in the small country and town houses. Chatsworth was begun before the end of the reign of Charles II; Castle Howard and Badminton, the last an anonymous house, belong to the earliest years of the eighteenth century. As regards so-called 'Queen Anne' houses, the reign of Anne marks the limit rather than the duration of the epoch to which they belong. The vogue of a style whose characteristics are at once homely and quietly dignified, and in which ornament is used with great reticence and architectural effect is achieved by the use of stone dressings to frame and vary fabrics of red brick, lasted over an indefinite period from the Restoration to the reign of George I. By that time the monumental style affected by the leading architects of the day made its presence felt in the growth of a formal correctness of house design which by the middle of the eighteenth century had become general. The typical Georgian country house of modest proportions is a square building of three stories on a cellar basement and crowned by an attic. The principal front is often provided with a pediment rising in front of the attic: the main entrance is approached by steps, and the hall is a wide passage with reception rooms on either side leading to the inner hall from which the stair ascends to the upper floors. Such a plan, subject of course to numerous variations, gave ample space for dining-room, drawing-room, library and additional sitting-rooms and bedrooms opening from the hall and the landings of the stair-case. The material was very generally red brick, often unadorned and frequently stuccoed, especially in the later part of the century. Houses of this kind are without striking beauty and their general effect is somewhat monotonous; but their builders understood the virtue of correct proportion, and, though their plainness and squareness are often uninteresting, they are seldom merely mean or gaunt. Internally they reflect their owners' taste for spacious and comfortable living: the bareness of large and lofty rooms was relieved by delicately moulded plasterwork and well-designed fire-places, while the walls formed an admirable surface for the exhibition of pictures brought by connoisseur-owners from abroad or of portraits by the contemporary artists whose works are the chief glory of English painting. It must be owned that such houses had their drawbacks. Sanitation as yet was not considered by English architects: the servants were condemned to work by day in twilit basements and sleep in garrets with a borrowed light from the passage-windows of the attics. But such drawbacks were not peculiar to the age, and for more than a century to come there was little improvement in these directions.

The virtues of Georgian house architecture are nowhere more conspicuous than in towns; and nearly every English provincial town contains excellent specimens of Georgian dwelling-houses, still frequently occupied as private residences, which give distinction to street-fronts, forming solid points of interest amid the vagaries of modern commercial architecture. The eighteenth century was a great age of town-planning: abroad such provincial capitals as Nancy and Reims, Mannheim and Carlsruhe, bear witness to the ingenuity with which old cities were embellished and new cities created. It is possible only to mention in passing the splendid achievement of the two Woods, father and son, in Bath. The force of their example is clearly visible, as late as the second quarter of the nineteenth century, in the admirable lay-out and dignified street architecture with which Richard Grainger transformed Newcastle-upon-Tyne.

But with the close of the eighteenth century a change came over the spirit of English domestic architecture. The development of romantic taste turned the channel of art into a backwater where progress was checked and imitation took the place of invention. On the one hand the attraction of the middle ages produced houses like Horace Walpole's Strawberry Hill, in which structural design was hidden beneath superficial detail which professed to be Gothic. On the other hand the Roman tradition to which Jones, Wren and their successors had been faithful was abandoned for an overlay of ornament borrowed from Greek sources, refined and scholarly in itself, but without the life of the past. The nineteenth century began under the influence of archaeological revivals which, combined with the change in economic conditions, produced an architectural chaos. The simple architecture of the countryside, in which local materials had been moulded into forms of beauty by local men, gave place to the cheap and monotonous productions of the building contractor. With many striking and imposing buildings to its record, the nineteenth century succumbed to the craze for imitation, and architects who were also scholars were either content to work in a favourite 'style,' or, in endeavouring to escape from the shackles of one style, fell under the dominion of another. From that chaos, with the growth of new ideals in an age of scientific discovery and experiment, we have not yet wholly emerged, and whether the period of architectural mediocrity whose monuments still surround us has been succeeded by a better age is a question which must be left to the historian of the future.

177

SHORT BIBLIOGRAPHY

R. Blomfield, *A History of Renaissance Architecture in England*, 2 vols. 1897.

Ralph Dutton, *The English Country House*. 1935.

J. A. Gotch, *The Growth of the English House*. 1909. *Early Renaissance Architecture in England*. 1901. *The English Home from Charles I to George IV*. 1918.

T. Hudson Turner (and J. H. Parker), *Domestic Architecture of the Middle Ages*. 3 vols. in 4 pts. (Oxford and London, 1851-9.)

C. H. B. & M. Quennell, *A History of Every-day Things in England*, 4 vols. 1066-1934. 1918-34.

A. E. Richardson, *The Smaller English House from the Restoration to the Victorian Era*. 1926.

A. Stratton, *The English Interior: Decoration of English Homes from Tudor Times to the Nineteenth Century*. 1920.

A recent study of the earlier period of English house-building which may be recommended is *Norman Domestic Architecture*, by Margaret Wood, printed in *Archæol. Journal*, Vol. XCII (1935), pp. 167-242.

No large series of illustrations of English medieval houses has been published; but the successive periods from the Tudor era to the end of the eighteenth century are handsomely illustrated in the following large and costly works:

T. Garner and A. Stratton, *Domestic Architecture in England during the Tudor Period*. 2 vols. 1908.

J. A. Gotch, *Architecture of the Renaissance in England*. 2 vols. 1894.

J. Belcher and M. E. Macartney, *Later Renaissance Architecture in England*. 2 vols. 1901.

SIR FRANK STENTON

Norman London

FOR the study of Norman London there is no lack of material, but it is material of an unusual kind. We must, it would seem, for ever lack that detailed description of the city which should fill the 126th folio of the first volume of Domesday Book. For such a description there is no substitute. We cannot make the vaguest profitable guess at the number of houses in the eleventh century city, still less at the number of its inhabitants, and the considerable body of charter evidence which we possess throws only an uncertain light on the London which resisted the Conqueror. On the other hand, Liebermann rescued from association with other texts a city custumal of Stephen's time, and no other town can show the like. Round established the family relationships of many leading citizens, and traced the dealings of the city with the king. Miss Bateson analysed the fragments of ancient law implied in the liberties which the men of London claimed. Every contemporary historian of the twelfth century was forced to refer to London, and to illustrate, if only incidentally, the importance of the city and the political interests of its citizens. Writers of this kind occasionally supply important facts for which there is no evidence in local records. The materials for the history of Norman London may often be hard to interpret, but they are at least copious.

The city of London stood alone above other English towns in wealth and power, and its citizens were very conscious of the fact. Their remarkable statement in 1135 that to them it belonged of right to choose a king for England[1] was only the most dramatic

[1] *Gesta Stephani*, in *Chronicles of the Reigns of Stephen, Henry II, and Richard I* (ed. R. Howlett, Rolls Series, 1886), III, 5, 6.

assertion of their position. They were known collectively as barons, and this style was allowed them by the clerks who wrote the writs of William II and Henry I.[1] The city was 'refugium et propugnaculum regni';[2] it could be maintained that its liberties were necessary for the well-being of the whole kingdom. London was a political and financial power on which a wise king would keep a careful eye, and its citizens were alert to draw advantage from royal embarrassments. They could extort the legitimation of their Commune from Count John, could play off the empress Matilda against King Stephen. London, to them, was more than a city, it was a commonwealth.

This pre-eminence of London was no new thing. No other town, not Lincoln nor Winchester, included so many moneyers striking pennies for Edward the Confessor or Cnut. But as the history of London is traced backwards beyond 1066, its distinctive significance ceases to be merely that of a great urban centre. London under the successors of Alfred is revealed, sporadically but unmistakably, as in some way the head of a rural district indeterminate but wide. 'This is the decree that the bishops and reeves who belong to London, eorl and ceorl, have published and established with pledges in our peace gild, in addition to the laws that were given at Grateley, Exeter and Thundersfield.'[3] This sentence is enough to prove that external magnates as well as humble folk were regarded for some purpose as subject to an authority established in London. Probably the twelfth-century translator of these laws was right in considering that purpose to be judicial. In any case, it is reasonable to connect this passage with the reference to the lands that 'belonged' to London and Oxford, over which Edward the Elder assumed rule upon the death of earl Ethelred of the Mercians.[4] And so it is easier to understand how in 1097 shires could owe work to London,[5] and

---

[1] For a writ of William II addressed to the barons of London, French and English, see J. Armitage Robinson, *Gilbert Crispin* (1911), p. 137. For the use of the term late in the twelfth century see Hist. MSS. Comm. 14th Report Appendix Part VIII, p. 216, where certain charters are quoted referring to the acquisition of land in London by the bishop of Lichfield, 'with the assent of the mayor and all the barons of the city in the common husting'. The barons of the Cinque Ports are a parallel to the barons of London. On *baro* as a term of social currency see my *First Century of English Feudalism* (1932), 85–90.

[2] Liebermann, *Gesetze der Augelsachsen*, I, 675.

[3] Liebermann, *Gesetze der Augelsachsen*, I, 173; F. L. Attenborough, *The Laws of the Earliest English Kings* (Cambridge, 1922), pp. 156 *seqq.*, where the regulations which follow are translated. The difficult problem of the nature of this peacegild belongs to the history of Saxon, not Norman, London, but the possibility that it may have been this body which gave name to the Guildhall should be noted. On the Guildhall see below, p. 188.

[4] *Anglo-Saxon Chronicle*, under the year 912.

[5] *Ibid*, under 1097. On this entry see Miss E. Jeffries Davis' article *Trimoda Necessitas*, in *History* (1928), XIII, 33–4. In explaining a late eleventh century

how, in the next century, Londoners could enjoy ancient hunting rights in Middlesex, Surrey, the Chiltern Hills,[1] and, according to one informant, Kent, as far as the Cray.[2] This privilege is suggestive; kings may well have enjoined that men should all come for justice from a wide region to some central town, but the right of hunting over more than two whole shires is likely to be a survival. It was certainly a reality: the Conqueror found it necessary to forbid the Londoners to take stags, hinds, or roe deer within archbishop Lanfranc's manor of Harrow.[3] It would be hard to name any period in later Anglo-Saxon history in which the origin of such a right would seem plausible; and where all is speculation, we may perhaps derive this privilege from a time in which the Middle Saxons were still a separate people, and London was their 'metropolis.'

It was inevitable that the Conqueror should attempt to conciliate the men of this ancient and formidable city. Early in his reign, he addressed a writ to William the bishop, Geoffrey the portreeve,[4] and all the burgesses within London, French and English, informing them of his will that they should enjoy the rights which had belonged to them in King Edward's day, and that their property should descend to their children, and that no one should do them injury.[5] The interest of this famous document is political rather than constitutional, for it amounts to little more than a general confirmation of the conditions of 1066 to the men of London. It is the letter of a foreign king who knows that his throne will never be safe while the men of his greatest city are disaffected, and hopes to

---

annal relating to the south of England, it is safe to take 'shire' in the modern sense of the word. In the same volume of *History*, p. 337, Miss Davis showed that land at Alfriston in Sussex needed royal exemption from work on London Bridge. She afterwards called attention to a writ of 1097 (printed in *Essays presented to T. F. Tout*, 1925, p. 50) addressed to the sheriffs of all the counties in which the canons of St. Paul's had lands, exempting those lands 'ab omni opere et castelli Londonie et muri et pontis et balii et carreti.'

[1] Liebermann, *Gesetze*, I, 526.

[2] William fitz Stephen, in *Materials for the History of Thomas Becket*, III, p. 12.

[3] *Monasticon Anglicanum* (edn. 1846), I, 111.

[4] Who can be identified, almost certainly, with Geoffrey de Mandeville, the ancestor of the Norman earls of Essex.

[5] Stubbs, *Select Charters* (Ninth Edition), p. 97; Liebermann, *Gesetze*, I, 486; *Facsimiles of English Royal Writs to A.D. 1100*, ed. T. A. M. Bishop and P. Chaplais, Plate XIV. There is no doubt that the text still preserved in the Guildhall is the original writ issued by William I. Its handwriting and appearance are entirely in its favour. In the language, the only form suggesting a later date is the spelling *portirefan* for *portgerefan*. But the contemporary examples of Old English writing are far too few to justify the statement that the form *portirefan* could not have been used in the early part of the Conqueror's reign. The royal seal, once appendant to it, has recently been described as 'one of the few remaining impressions of the genuine Great Seal of William the Conqueror' (Bishop and Chaplais, *op. cit.*).

secure their good will by assuring them that he will respect their privileges and property and will protect them against aggressors. The most curious feature of the charter is the fact that the king uses the dual number in addressing the men to whom he is confirming their pre-Conquest rights. Translated strictly, the first clause of the charter reads, 'I will that ye both be worthy of all the rights of which ye both were worthy in King Edward's day'. In using this method of expression, the king is clearly distinguishing between the bishop of London on the one hand and the portreeve and citizens on the other. Unusual expressions like this always mean something definite, and the present example can only mean that the Conqueror's charter to London was deliberately phrased so as to cover the bishop as it covered the citizens.[1]

The clearest proof of the insecurity of the king's hold on London at the beginning of his reign lies in the castles which he built, or allowed to be built, there. The city had submitted unwillingly, and the king's first care was to erect fortifications which would keep it in obedience. Immediately after his coronation he moved to Barking, and spent some days there 'while certain strongholds were made in the town against the fickleness of the vast and fierce populace.'[2] There can be no serious doubt that one of these strongholds consisted of elementary defences of moat and bank on the site, just within the south-east angle of the Wall, where the White Tower was afterwards to be built. Historians seem to be agreed in attributing the beginnings of the Tower of London to this time, but they have laid comparatively little stress on the evidence which shows that one if not two fortresses arose under the Norman Kings in the extreme south-west of the city. William fitz Stephen mentions two very strong castles as existing in his time in the west, and two castles in the same quarter are recorded by other authorities. The better known of them was the Baynard's Castle which has left its name to one of the largest wards of the city. The name must have arisen early in the Norman period, for it preserves the surname of Ralf Baignard, a great tenant in chief in eastern England in 1086, and William Baignard, the last English baron of this family, was deprived of his inheritance in 1110.[3] Soon after William Baignard's disinheritance, Henry I gave Baynard's Castle to a member of another family powerful in eastern England, Robert fitz Richard of Clare, and as long as it was defensible it remained in the hands of his descendants, giving much

[1] Liebermann, *Gesetze*, III, 276, choosing an impersonal phrase, represents the dual of the original by 'Bistum und Stadt.'

[2] William of Poitiers, *Gesta Willelmi Ducis* (ed. J. A. Giles, Caxton Soc., 1845), p. 147: 'Dies aliquot . . . morabatur Bercingis dum firmamenta quaedam in urbe contra mobilitatem ingentis ac feri populi perficerentur.' It is clear that more than one castle was raised in London at this time.

[3] Henry of Huntingdon, *Historia Anglorum* (Rolls series, 1879), *sub anno*.

influence in London to the most famous of them, the Robert fitz Walter who led the baronial opposition to King John.[1] The history of the second castle on the west of the city, the Montfichet Castle of later records,[2] is obscure. It probably stood between Baynard's Castle and Ludgate, but its exact site is unknown. It played a much smaller part than Baynard's Castle in the history of the city, and there seems to be only one reference to it as a place of military importance. Jordan Fantosme, the author of a contemporary poem on the rebellion of 1173–4, introduces into his narrative a long passage purporting to be a report on conditions in England brought to Henry II in Normandy by the bishop of Winchester. At the end,[3] the king asks how his barons of London are behaving. The bishop tells him that they are the most loyal people in his realm, and that all of sufficient age are under arms, but that Gilbert de Munfichet has strengthened his castle, and says that the 'Clarreaus' are allied with him. To this the king replies, 'God have mercy, and protect the barons of my city of London'. Gilbert de Munfichet was lord of a large fief in Eastern England, of which the head was Stansted Mountfitchet in Essex. He was a cousin of Walter fitz Robert fitz Richard of Clare, the lord of Baynard's Castle, and it is safe to identify the 'Clarreaus,' whose alliance Gilbert was claiming, with Walter fitz Robert and the great family to which he belonged.[4]

[1] The history of the castles in the west is complicated by a charter of Henry I to Richard (the first), bishop of London, mentioning the *fossatum* of the king's *castellum*, near St. Paul's (*Early Charters of the Cathedral Church of St. Paul, London*, ed. M. Gibbs, No. 28). Its date must fall between 1108 and 1122; it probably belongs to 1114, when the king is known to have sailed from Portsmouth, where it was issued. The passage about the *castellum* reads: 'tantum de fossato mei castelli ex parte Tamesis ad meridiem quantum opus fuerit ad faciendum murum ecclesiæ, et tantum de eodem fossato quantum sufficiat ad faciendum viam extra murum, et ex altera parte ecclesiæ ad aquilonem quantum praedictus episcopus de eodem fossato diruit.' In this context, 'ex parte Tamesis,' clearly means 'on the Thames' side of St. Paul's cathedral'; but the northern boundaries indicated cannot be brought into line with those of Baynard's Castle, and it is probable, as Miss E. Jeffries Davis has suggested, that the *castellum* of this charter really means the walled enclosure of London itself.

[2] There is no direct evidence as to the date when the fortress afterwards known as Montfichet Castle was founded, but on all grounds it is probable that like Baynard's Castle and the Tower it belongs to the Conqueror's reign. It certainly existed before 1136, for its lord was concerned in the plea about the lordship over the water of Thames which cannot be later than that year. It is worth noting that William de Munfichet and Robert fitz Richard of Baynard's Castle attest Henry I's charter to London.

[3] Ed. R. Howlett, in *Chronicles of the Reigns of Stephen, Henry II, and Richard I* (Rolls Series), III, 338.

[4] The significance of this passage in general and the name 'Clarreaux' in particular were first brought out by Round in his article on The Family of Clare, *Archæological Journal*, September, 1899, p. 6. He had previously noted the identification of the Clarreaus with the Clare family in the pedigree of the latter house facing p. 473 of his *Feudal England* (1895).

For the history of London, the especial interest of the passage lies in the importance which it assigns to Gilbert de Munfichet's Castle. It is evident that, at the moment, this obscure fortress, under its hostile lord, was a serious danger to the king's hold upon the city.

From the time of its foundation it is probable that the possession of Baynard's Castle gave to its lord a position of official authority within the city. In 1100 or 1101 Henry I addressed to Hugh of Buckland the sheriff, William Baignard, and the King's ministers of London, a writ confirming to archbishop Anselm's men visiting or resident in London the privileges which archbishop Lanfranc's men had enjoyed.[1] It may be taken as certain that William Baignard was no less responsible than the sheriff and the king's ministers for seeing that the king's writ was carried into effect. But there are few early documents which illustrate the official responsibilities of the lords of Baynard's Castle, and there is a distinct air of antiquarian reconstruction about some of the later evidence. By the reign of Edward I, Baynard's Castle had ceased to be a fortress, and in 1275 Robert fitz Walter II received licence to alienate it for the site of a house of Dominican Friars. But he retained the privileges in the city which had belonged to him before the alienation, and a statement of his case in 1303 brings out the very interesting fact that the earlier lords of Baynard's Castle had been commanders of the host of the citizens of London.[2] A fourteenth century record can only be used with caution for conditions in the Norman period. The case put forward by Robert fitz Walter assumes that the chief magistrate of the city will be a mayor, and states that the horse which the lord of Baynard's Castle receives as part of his fee should be 'saddled with the arms of the said Robert.' Indications like these suggest the thirteenth century rather than the Norman age. But the case includes features which have an ancient air—notably the reservation that Robert should only receive a hundred shillings for each town or castle besieged by the host, even if the siege lasted for a whole year,—and there is direct evidence that the essential part of the fitz Walter claim was recognised in the Norman period. Early in the thirteenth century, a jury reported that none but the owners of certain privileged properties could draw fishing-nets in the Thames between Baynard's Castle and Staines without the licence of the

[1] Printed by Matthew Parker, *De Antiquitate Britannicæ Ecclesiæ*, edn. 1605, p. 118, and Rymer, *Foedera* (Record Commission), I, 1, p. 12. The writ is bilingual, and the *ministri* of the Latin version is represented by *wicnæres* in the English.

[2] The French text of the claim is given in *Munimenta Gildhallæ* II, *Liber Custumarum*, i, 147. There are English translations *ibid.* ii, 554, and in Stow's *Survey of London* (ed. Kingsford) I, 62–5, corrected by Kingsford, II, 278–9. Cf. *Cal. Pat.* 1272–81, p. 98, and *Placita de Quo Warranto* (Record Commission, 1818), p. 472.

lord or constable of Baynard's Castle.[1] The jury based their finding on the result of a plea held in or before 1136 at St. Paul's before the king's council, which gave judgment that the lordship of the water of Thames between these points belonged to the lord of Baynard's Castle as the king's standard-bearer and the keeper—*procurator*—of the city. In view of this definite statement, there is no need to doubt the antiquity of the custom underlying Robert fitz Walter's claim that in time of war he should come to the west door of St. Paul's, mounted, with eleven other knights, and there receive the banner of the city, that he should then direct the choice of a marshall for the city host, order the summoning of the commons, and finally, in the priory of the Holy Trinity, Aldgate, choose two discreet men from each ward to keep the city safely.

It is easy to underestimate the part which must have been played by the army of London in the civil wars of the Norman period, for its activities are rarely mentioned by contemporaries. It is therefore worth noting that on one occasion, in Stephen's reign, it intervened in a campaign with results which affected the general history of the country. In the summer of 1145, Robert, earl of Gloucester, built a castle at Faringdon in Berkshire, which if held would have maintained easy communication between his base in the Severn valley and his important outpost of Wallingford. Its capture was worth a great effort on Stephen's part, and a contemporary historian states explicitly that the king brought for its reduction *Lundonensium terribilem et numerosum exercitum*.[2] The castle was taken, and to the author who has been quoted its fall marked the turning-point in Stephen's fortunes. It is only a single writer who mentions the share which the Londoners had in this success. But it is clear that the 'formidable and large army of the men of London' was something more than a historic survival in Stephen's reign.

The essential link between the military and the civil administration of London was formed by the city wards. In time of war, they formed the basis of the organisation for the defence of the city, and they provided for the keeping of watch within its boundaries in time of peace. We have no direct information about these divisions earlier than the reign of Henry I, when twenty of them are mentioned by name in a survey of the London property belonging to St. Paul's Cathedral.[3] Few of the wards in this early list can be identified with any certainty. Its 'warda fori' and 'warda Alegate' can safely be

---

[1] Addit. MS. 14252, f. 90b, in *Eng. Hist. Rev.* XVII, 486.
[2] Henry of Huntingdon, *Historia Anglorum*, (ed. T. Arnold, Rolls Series, 1897), p. 278.
[3] Liber L. ff, 47–50b: facsimile in *Descriptive Account of the Guildhall* by J. E. Price (1886); printed by the late Professor H. W. C. Davis in *Essays in Mediæval History presented to Thomas Frederick Tout*, p. 55–9.

equated with the later wards of Cheap and Aldgate, and its 'warda Brocesgange' preserves the Old English name of the division now known as Walbrook ward.[1] But each of the other wards in the list is defined by the name of an individual, presumably the alderman who presided over it, and descriptions such as 'warda Haconis' or 'warda Radulfi filii Liuiue' are of little use for purposes of local identification. It is probable that under Henry I as in the thirteenth century the city was divided into twenty-four wards,[2] and it seems certain that each ward had its own court, the wardmoot of later records, which corresponded in function to the court of a rural hundred. The profits of justice done in these assemblies were the king's, though already in the Norman period innumerable properties had passed from the jurisdiction of the ward, its alderman, and his officers, under the authority of privileged private landowners, the lords of sokes. But the rise of the sokes should not obscure the significance of the ward as the fundamental unit of local justice and administration in Norman London.

Among the institutions which covered the whole city the folkmoot is first in dignity,[3] as doubtless it was first in age. If it did not, as one Londoner of the twelfth century liked to think, exist already in the time of Arthur, the most famous king of Britain, many facts point to its antiquity.[4] It was the proper scene for the proclamation of outlawry: in this respect it ranked with the provincial shire court. The burden of suit fell upon all men of London; no individual summons was necessary, it was assumed that everyone would hear the great bell of St. Paul's which rang for the meeting. Three sessions only were held in the year—at Michaelmas, Christmas, and Midsummer. Presumably the sheriff presided, as in the analogous shire court: at any rate, the Michaelmas session met to know who the new sheriff would be, and to hear his command. The Christmas meeting took cognisance of keeping the wards; at Midsummer, the heat of the season led to recurrent provisions against fire. These are ancient provisions, and essential to the life of any town; the complicated business of a great city which was a distributing centre for all

---

[1] The name is interesting as containing the O. E. *gang*, here, presumably, meaning 'watercourse', a word which is very rare in local compounds.

[2] The survey only mentions twenty, but it relates to the lands of St. Paul's alone, and does not necessarily cover the whole city. The marginal numbers in Davis' edition do not correspond to anything in the manuscript.

[3] *Eng. Hist. Rev.* XVII, 502.

[4] Already in King Alfred's time the word *folcgemot* was used to describe the public assembly in which a merchant must produce the men whom he had brought with him. (Liebermann, *Gesetze*, I, 69). This law is of general application, but doubtless referred to London among other places. The word is not infrequently used for a public meeting in later Old English laws, though London seems to be the only place in which it became attached to a particular assembly.

England, in which land changed owners with unusual frequency, was conducted, not in the folkmoot, but in the husting.

The chief difficulty in the history of this body lies in its name. The word Husting is certainly of Scandinavian origin, and at first, apparently, meant an assembly of a great man's dependents, meeting within doors, though it had acquired a more general sense by the eleventh century.[1] The London husting is first mentioned in a Latin translation of an Old English private document of the late tenth century,[2] which refers to two silver cups of twelve marks, 'by the weight of the husting of London.' If this reference can be trusted— and it would be a pointless invention—it shows that the London husting was in being before the conquest of England by Swegn and Cnut. It must therefore have arisen in the century following the Scandinavian occupation of London in Alfred's time, but the circumstances of its origin are still obscure. It is possible that the husting was created by the ninth century Scandinavian occupants of London. But we have no direct evidence of any Scandinavian immigration into London so considerable as of itself to produce a new form of public assembly. London passed again under English lordship as early as 886, and although little is known about its inhabitants during the next forty years, the names of London moneyers in the tenth century point unmistakably to their English origin. In these circumstances it seems probable that the Scandinavian influence which produced the husting resulted from long-continued intercourse rather than from sudden immigration, that, in fact, the husting arose to meet the needs of English citizens who were in constant association with Scandinavian traders. It is significant that the earliest references to the husting mention it in connexion with a particular standard weight of precious metal. At a later time, the husting was much occupied with matters of commercial regulation, and it may well be that this side of its activity was original.

In the twelfth century it met every Monday in the Guildhall. Like the men who attended the ancient local assemblies of the

---

[1] The word was applied, for example, to the assembly of pirate crews in which archbishop Alphege was martyred in 1012.

[2] This is a record of gifts to Ramsey Abbey by 'Athelgiva' (Æthelgifu) wife of ealdorman Æthelwine of East Anglia. It cannot be dated with any precision, but probably comes from approximately the year 990. The text is printed in the *Chronicon Abbatiæ Ramesiensis* (ed. W. D. Macray, Rolls Series, 1886), p. 58, and by Kemble, *Codex Diplomaticus*, No. 973. As we only possess a translation of the original Old English, it is possible that the reference to the husting may be an interpolation, but the authority of the Ramsey *Chronicon* is, in general, good. A document of 1032 of which the Old English text is preserved (*Cod. Dip.*, No. 745) speaks of 180 marks of white silver *be hustinges gewihte*, where the reference is doubtless to the husting of London, though the city is not named.

country, its suitors sat upon four benches.[1] It was the recognised court for civil business, for pleas of debt, for disputes about land: a wise grantee would make some formal delivery of his gift before the husting. In contrast with the immemorial duty of attendance at the folkmoot, a special summons was necessary to enforce an answer in a suit before the husting. It had cognisance of cases to which foreign merchants were parties; it controlled weights and measures. The volume of its business must have been immense. Within the husting we can just see that the aldermen form a class apart; they are expected to know the law; it is their duty to speak right. In the Norman age, it was possible, and it may have been usual, for an alderman to be followed in office by his son,[2] and in this respect, as in the matter of their legal knowledge, the Anglo-Norman aldermen of London show a definite resemblance to the eleventh century lawmen of Lincoln and Stamford. In these aldermen, who adjudicate in the husting and are at the same time in charge of wards,[3] we are most likely to find those elder citizens who from time to time appear in the twelfth century evidence.

Their memory still survives in the name of a city street. West of the site occupied by the present Guildhall, its medieval predecessor stood near to the street known as Aldermanbury already in the early twelfth century.[4] Despite some uncertainty as to the original form of the name,[5] early spellings suggest that it represents an Old English *ealdormanna burh*, a fortified enclosure[6] of the aldermen. It can hardly be a mere coincidence that a street bearing this name ran close to the hall where the aldermen of the city sat as the leading members of the husting. This local connexion at once raises a difficult question as to the nature of the gild which gave its name to the Guildhall. No certain answer can be given to this question, but

[1] For the 'four benches of the hundred,' see Round, *Eng. Hist. Rev.* X, 732. In late medieval times, the husting was considered to rank as a shire court as the wardmoots counted as hundred courts. No doubt the arrangement of suitors in four benches was once common to all forms of local assembly.

[2] Cases are noted by H. W. C. Davis, *Essays . . . presented to Thomas Frederick Tout*, p. 48.

[3] *Eng. Hist. Rev.* XVII, 487–8. For the wards of Norman London see above, pp. 185–6.

[4] See the note in Kingsford's edition of Stow's *Survey*, II, 337, and Stow's own observations, *ibid.*, I, 292.

[5] Many early sources give the name as *Aldermannesberie*. The genitive singular suggests that this *burh* belonged to a single alderman, and I took the name in this way in the first edition of this paper. But the publications of the English Place-Name Survey have shown that it was commoner than used to be thought for a genitive singular to replace a genitive plural, temporarily, in names of this type. There can be no doubt that a derivation from ealdormen in the plural, makes the name much more intelligible, and gives due weight to the situation of the Guildhall.

[6] *Burh* in London names is regarded by some scholars as virtually equivalent to 'house.' It really refers, not so much to a house itself, as to the fortified enclosure in which it stood. See below, p. 192.

the Guildhall first appears under Henry I in an incidental way which shows that it was no new thing at that date,[1] and the local connexion with Aldermanbury suggests that we may have in its name a trace of an association of aldermen, formed in Old English times, and obsolete already in the early Norman period.

One ancient association of the same kind undoubtedly came to an end in this period. A body known as the gild of English *cnihtas*, which had existed in London since at latest the reign of king Edgar, received a confirmation of its privileges from Edward the Confessor between 1042 and 1044[2]; similar confirmations from William II and Henry I prove that it survived the Norman Conquest. But in 1125 its members, in return for spiritual benefits, gave all its lands to the newly-founded priory of the Holy Trinity, Aldgate. The names of the men who made this gift have been preserved, and a comparison of the list with other London documents shows that they included some of the leading citizens of the time. Among the few members of the gild not hitherto mentioned otherwise in connexion with the city 'Wlward le Douerisshe', the second on the list, was one of the earliest benefactors to Reading Abbey, to which, as Wlward Dourensis, he gave land and houses in London.[3] The lands of the gild, united to the local endowment of the priory, formed the large tract outside the east wall of the city, which was afterwards known as Portsoken Ward.[4] But the origin and character of the gild can only be matters of conjecture. The transference of its property to the priory of the Holy Trinity virtually proves that whatever its history had been, it had become essentially an association for religious purposes by the twelfth century. Its name brings it into comparison with the gilds of *cnihts* which existed in the Norman age at Winchester and Canterbury, and the fact that the Canterbury gild is mentioned in a charter of the mid-ninth century shows that such associations existed already in the pre-Alfredian period. The *cnihtas* by whom they were formed should not be regarded as a military class.[5] The Old English word *cniht* meant a servant or retainer, not a warrior, and in a document written in English between 1093 and 1109, the Canterbury *cnihts* are expressly

---

[1] The survey of the London property of St. Paul's Cathedral, already referred to, mentions incidentally *terra Gialle*. For the identification, see Round, *Geoffrey de Mandeville*, p. 436. It is placed beyond doubt by similar forms in later records.

[2] F. E. Harmer, *Anglo-Saxon Writs*, pp. 231–5 and 466–8, where references are given to the few materials which bear upon the history of the gild.

[3] Egerton MS. 3031, f. 64.

[4] In virtue of which the Prior of the Holy Trinity ranked as an alderman of London until after the dissolution of the Priory in 1532.

[5] The social position of the pre-Conquest *cniht* is discussed in my *First Century of English Feudalism*, with reference to the various gilds known to have been formed by men of this class in towns.

called *cnihts* of the chapmens' gild.[1] There is no such clear evidence for the nature of the London *cnihta gild*. It is, on the whole, most probable that the original *cnihtas* of London were responsible servants of magnates owning property in London,[2] appointed to supply their lords with goods coming to the London market, and that, in course of time, independent traders entering the association changed the character of its membership while enrolling themselves under its ancient name. But we only see the London *cnihta gild* in the very last years of its existence, when, whatever its origin, it was a wealthy association of prominent London citizens.

The estate of the *cnihta gild* was only distinguished by its size and its position outside the walls from a great number of private franchises scattered over the whole city. The distinctive feature of London justice in the Norman age is the influence of such private liberties, the sokes. The urban immunity attains its greatest English development in London, for in other towns the landowner who held houses with sac and soc seems rarely to have held a permanent court for his tenants.[3] In part, the number and persistence of the London sokes was due to the commercial importance of the city. Access to the London market through a house in or near the city was desired by many country landowners in the eleventh century. London, like other towns, contained houses appurtenant to rural estates. The Domesday description of Surrey[4] supplies numerous instances. The archbishop of Canterbury had seventeen *mansuræ* in London belonging to Mortlake, the bishop of Bayeux had one *masura* belonging to Banstead, Miles Crispin had lost to earl Roger of Shrewsbury thirteen *masuræ* belonging to Beddington, count Eustace of Boulogne had fifteen *masuræ* in London and Southwark belonging to 'Wachelestede', now Godstone, Richard fitz Gilbert had seven *mansuræ* in London and Southwark belonging to Bletchingley, the king himself had thirteen 'burgesses' in London belonging to Bermondsey. Great monasteries like Ramsey, Chertsey, Ely, and Abingdon acquire property in London, and in the eleventh century some of them obtain royal writs which confer powers of jurisdiction.[5] That most of our early information relates to monastic properties

---

[1] Printed by Somner, *Antiquities of Canterbury* (1640), p. 365, and by Gross, *Gild Merchant*, II, 37.

[2] The predecessors of the great lords who held property in London in the Norman period, on whom see below.

[3] In Winchester the bishop's soke is recorded in the twelfth century: B.M. Addit. MS. 33280, p. 228.

[4] Translated, with an introduction by Round, in the *Victoria History of Surrey*, Vol. I.

[5] Edward the Confessor, *e.g.*, granted sake and soke to Chertsey in a writ addressed to the Bishop and Portreeve of London: F. E. Harmer, *Anglo-Saxon Writs*, No. 43.

is only due to the better preservation of ecclesiastical muniments, for the lay owner of a soke is prominent in the century after the Conquest. We read of the sokes of the honours of Huntingdon, Peverel, and Mortain,[1] the soke of Gilbert of Torigni,[2] the soke of the earl of Gloucester,[3] the queen's soke. Gisulf, a royal scribe under Henry I, held a soke of the Archbishop of Canterbury.[4] The impression is produced that most barons of superior consequence possessed a privileged estate in London; the conception of immunity so governed men's ideas of local justice that those portions of the city outside the jurisdiction of a private court are described collectively in the twelfth century as the king's soke.[5]

But London citizens might themselves possess rights of jurisdiction over their properties in the city. It has been conjectured that the Ealdred who gave his name to Aldersgate was an immunist; the same may be true of the original Billing of Billingsgate. These sokes presented a most formidable obstacle to the growth of any ubiquitous city jurisdiction. No dweller within a soke might be arrested in his house or pent-house; or anywhere except in the middle of the road. Distraint within a soke was a complicated business, only to be accomplished after invoking the soke reeve. Temporary dwellers within a soke owed nothing by way of customary payment to anyone except the lord of the soke.[6] All disputes between the men of the same soke would be settled privately, and Norman London was still in the archaic atmosphere of the wergild and the monetary emendation for personal violence. The reeve, in the London soke, plays the part of rural steward as the immunist's official. It is interesting to note that when the word sokeman appears in the London custumals it means, as in its rare appearances in West Scandinavian law, the reeve, the executive officer of a court who carries through its judgments.

The sokes of Norman London have left their impression on the later nomenclature of the city in the name of Portsoken Ward, that great extramural soke or liberty of the priory of the Holy Trinity, Aldgate, which has already been mentioned in connexion with the *cnihta gild*. It is a curious name, which has long aroused interest, and its exact significance is not easily determined. Translated strictly, 'portsoken' means simply 'town soke',[7] and it has sometimes been

---

[1] *Index Locorum* to the Charters and Rolls in the British Museum, Vol. I, article London.
[2] *Eng. Hist. Rev.* XVII, 484.
[3] *Essays . . . presented to Thomas Frederick Tout*, p. 57.
[4] *Eng. Hist. Rev.* XIV, 428.
[5] *Eng. Hist. Rev.* XVII, 492.
[6] *Ibid.* XVII, 487, 492–3.
[7] Containing the well-recorded Old English word, *port*, 'town,' familiar in such compounds as 'port way,'—not, as Stow believed, the Latin *porta*.

assumed to refer to some special authority over the city possessed by the members of the *cnihta gild*, its first lords. But the *cnihta gild* was not in any sense the governing body of the city, and it has recently become apparent that the word 'port soke' was applied to other London franchises beside the famous one outside the walls. In the Pipe Roll of 1194, William de Ste. Mère Eglise renders account of 21 shillings *de Portsocha Willelmi de Moun*.[1] A similar entry occurs in each of the following years, and in 1197 this liberty appears both as the 'soke' and the 'port soke' of William de Mohun,[2] whose lands throughout this period were in the king's hands. It would therefore seem that soke and port soke were interchangeable terms, and as there was nothing exceptional in the London liberty of the Mohun lords of Dunster, it follows that any one of the innumerable franchises in the city might have been described as a port soke. In view of this identity the chief difficulties attending the name Portsoken Ward disappear. It simply means 'the soke ward'; a description which is curiously indefinite, but agrees very well with the unique position of Portsoken Ward. Few London wards corresponded even approximately in area to sokes, and Portsoken Ward was the only one of them in which the lord of the soke became *ex officio* alderman.[3]

With the soke, the sphere of private jurisdiction, is closely associated the defensible house, the *burh*. The precincts of St. Paul's constituted such a place of defence; Æthelflæd, widow of king Edmund I, about 975, left the reversion of certain lands 'to Paul's *burh* at London, to the bishop's house.'[4] The idea of the private stronghold was familiar in tenth century society; one famous text would make the possession of such a defensible place a condition of a ceorl's advancement to thegnly rank.[5] In London, traces of the private defensible house may still be found in local names which end in 'bury'.[6] Lothbury for example, seems to mean the defensible place of someone whose name began with the Old English name-stem Hloth. The defences whose existence is implied by the word *burh* were doubtless elementary, in most cases probably little more than a walled enclosure around a house.[7] The word is, however, interesting as an indication of the type of dwelling possessed by the

---

[1] Pipe Roll Society, N. S., Vol. 5, p. 6.

[2] *Ibid.* N. S., Vol. 8, pp. 165, 166.

[3] The final *n* of Portsoken preserves the original termination of the O.E. word *socn*. It does not affect the meaning of the name.

[4] Birch, *Cartularium Saxonicum*, No. 1288.

[5] The *burhgeat* of the text generally quoted under the title, 'of People's Ranks and Law' (Stubbs, *Select Charters*, 9th edition, p. 88), refers to the gate of one of these private defensible enclosures.

[6] On the urban *burh* see W. H. Stevenson, *Eng. Hist. Rev.*, XII, 491.

[7] As distinct from the hedged enclosure, the *haga*, of which there are traces in the city in such names as Bassishaw; cf. Kingsford in *Survey*, II, 335-6, 340.

greater citizens of early London, and as one of the many Old English local terms which survived the Norman Conquest within and around the city. The Bucherelli, whose name survives in Bucklersbury, certainly cannot have been established in London before the Conquest.

Names like Bucklersbury symbolise the union of English and foreign elements which determined the character of London society in the Norman age. The foreign element has always been emphasised by historians, and, indeed, so fully that the older and stronger native influences have sometimes been allowed to fall into the background of the picture. It is well to remember that personal names of native English origin will almost certainly preponderate in any early post-Conquest list of London citizens. Even in Stephen's time, nearly half the recorded moneyers of London have Anglo-Scandinavian names. This native element is dominant in the names of the members of the *cnihta gild*, and extremely strong in the names of the witnesses to the early London charters of St. Paul's, and in those of the London citizens who presided over wards late in the reign of Henry I. In all this there is nothing peculiar to London. Native names lasted long in every ancient English borough. The London series is made important by its bearing on the early history of the greatest English city.[1] Of the two main strands in this nomenclature, the Danish element is less in evidence than the many links between London and the Scandinavian world might suggest. Most of the personal names recorded from early Norman London are Anglo-Saxon compounds of a familar type. The Danish element is by no means insignificant in numbers, after all allowance has been made for Norman immigrants bearing inherited Scandinavian names. But it represents a small minority of the population, and it has left few, if indeed any traces in the names of streets and lanes.[2] In this respect, there cannot be a greater contrast than that which existed between Norman London and Norman York, where a Scandinavian population dominant for generations in the city had given a Scandinavian cast to all but a small fraction of its local names.

It is an interesting fact that these Anglo-Scandinavian names continually appear in the lists of early canons of St. Paul's Cathedral. It is always hard to discover anything definite about the antecedents of the members of an Anglo-Norman cathedral chapter, but there is clear evidence that at London it included men having a family connexion with the city. In 1104 a woman named Thurgund

[1] A large collection of personal names recorded for London in this period is analysed by Professor Ekwall in his *Early London Personal Names* (Lund, 1947).
[2] On the local names of the city the most recent authority is Ekwall's *Street-Names of the City of London* (Oxford, 1954).

gave a piece of land to St. Paul's, 'by the advice and at the request of Thedebald the canon, whose sons were kinsmen of Thured her husband.'[1] This is a strange way of stating a relationship but it leaves no doubt as to the local associations of Thedebald the canon. It therefore increases the probability that most of the canons of English name who occur in early lists were connected by family ties with the city. Four of them—Ædwin canonicus, Ædmund canonicus, Æilward canonicus filius Siredi, Leuegar canonicus et cantor—appear as witnesses to Thurgund's deed of gift. The number is exceptional, but enough names of this type occur in other documents to show that the native elements which prevailed in Norman London were strongly represented in the chapter of its cathedral.

The impression of unbroken life given by these names is confirmed by the oldest document which illustrates the local distribution of property within the Norman City. An account of the London possessions of Christ Church, Canterbury, drawn up close upon the year 1100, reflects the Saxon past at every turn.[2] With insignificant exceptions, the properties recorded in this survey—whether churches, houses, or land—had come to Christ Church by the gift of Englishmen. The most valuable gift of all—the church of St. Mary le Bow, worth £40 each year—had been made by Lifing the priest when he became a monk at Canterbury. Some of the gifts were so recent that a son of the donor was still in occupation of the property as a rent-paying tenant of the monks. Eadwaker at Lundene stane, whose name provides the earliest reference to the enigmatical relic still called London Stone, was himself renting the land and houses which he had given to Christ Church. Even if it stood alone, this survey would prove that King William had kept his promise of tenurial security to the men of London.

Under these conditions, it was natural that when the citizens of London obtained a detailed grant of privileges from the king, many of its provisions should have a retrospective appearance. Few records in English municipal history are better known or have had wider influence than the great charter of liberties which Henry I issued to London.[3] The original document had escaped from the

[1] St. Paul's MSS. p. 61. In this group of names Thured and Thurgund are both of Scandinavian origin, and as such are exceptions to the general character of London nomenclature. Thedebald is continental.
[2] Edited with valuable notes by B. W. Kissan in *Transactions of the London and Middlesex Archæological Society*, New Series, Vol. VIII. A translation is given in *English Historical Documents 1042–1189*, ed. D. C. Douglas and G. W. Greenaway, pp. 954–6.
[3] Liebermann, *Gesetze*, I, 524–6; Stubbs, *Select Charters*, 9th edition, pp. 129–30. *See* also H. G. Richardson, 'Henry I's Charter to London', *Eng. Hist. Rev.* (1927), XLII, 80–87.

custody of the city before the end of John's reign, and has not since been found. Its exact text is uncertain at more than one point, and although it was probably granted between Michaelmas, 1130 and July, 1133, its date cannot be exactly fixed. Nevertheless, it defines not merely the king's opinion of the liberties which were the reasonable privilege of his greatest city, but also the citizens' own conception of what the relations between themselves and the king should be. The spirit of the charter is that of the earliest London custumals, demanding a real if limited degree of self-government in matters of finance and justice, and commercial privileges throughout the land. Here, as often in similar documents, it is hard to distinguish between the clauses which grant new privileges and those which merely give new force to existing custom. The king's grant of exemption from fiscal burdens such as Danegeld and the murder fine may well belong to the latter class, and long established practice seems to be receiving fresh sanction in the clauses allowing the citizens of London to take compensation from the merchants of towns where toll has been taken from Londoners, and to recover losses incurred through the default of external debtors by distraint on other individuals belonging to the defaulter's town or village. But indeed the whole tenor of the charter is conservative. The citizens are expressly relieved from the necessity of submitting to the new process of trial by battle. If it is a new thing that the citizens themselves shall hold the shrievalty of London and Middlesex at farm, the £300 at which that farm was fixed was the sum recognised in the Conqueror's day, though Henry I himself had increased it in the interval and Henry II was to do so again.[1] The citizens' hunting-rights which the king now confirmed were no new privilege.[2] The confirmation of their sokes to churches, barons, and citizens recognises existing facts. It is an innovation, and a great one, that the citizens shall appoint their own sheriff, but, in himself, this officer simply stands for the Old English portreeve. Many other individual clauses read like definitions of custom against royal encroachments. The king's promise that he will cause the citizens to have their lands, the debts owed to them, and the property which they had taken in pledge, suggests past aggressions on the king's behalf, and a definite acknowledgement that citizens have a case against the king is contained in the clause that he will do right to them in respect of the lands touching which they have made complaint to him. There is clearly a recognition of ancient rights by the king in the provisions that the individual citizen shall only be amerced for emendable offences

---

[1] On the financial relations between London and the Crown in the eleventh and twelfth centuries see Tait, 'The Firma Burgi and the Commune in England, 1066–1191', *Eng. Hist. Rev.* XLII, 321–59.

[2] *See* above, p. 181.

according to his *were* of 100 shillings, that he shall answer to pleas of the crown by the oath which shall be adjudged to him in the city, that there shall not be fines for wrongful pleading in the folkmoot or husting, and that no one of the king's or any other household shall be compulsorily entertained within the city. Privileges like these would not seem anachronistic if we read of them in texts coming from the eleventh century. Before long, the Londoners were to enlarge their conceptions of civic autonomy.

But in the Norman age proper the city was well enough accommodated with the institutions and officers it had inherited from King Edward's day: the folkmoot, the husting, the private soke; the sheriff and aldermen. The chief innovation in the government of London before the death of Henry I was the establishment in the city of the local justiciar. He was not peculiar to London; he is addressed in association with the sheriff in royal writs addressed to various counties in the second half of Henry's reign. The justiciarship of London might on occasion be held by a great noble. Geoffrey de Mandeville, at a time when nothing could safely be denied him, obtained the office from Stephen and its confirmation from the Empress Matilda. But Henry I had granted that the justiciar, like the sheriff, of London should be chosen by the Londoners from among themselves; and Round showed that three prominent London citizens—Andrew Buchuinte, Osbert Huitdeniers, and Gervase of Cornhill—held the justiciarship of London under Stephen[1].

The justiciar, in London as elsewhere, stands for a temporary royal experiment. In the Charter of Henry I he is empowered 'to keep and plead the pleas of my crown'—that is, to see that all pleas in which the King has a direct interest are properly held and determined. In London, as in other counties, he was certainly superior to the sheriff. In what must be one of the latest references to the justiciar of London, Queen Eleanor, writing on her husband's behalf, before 1161, tells the sheriff of London that unless he compels John Bucuinte to warrant certain lands to the monks of Reading, 'the king's justiciar of London' will act.[2] The justiciar, in fact, appears in the meagre evidence as the permanent local representative of the king, appointed to control the local authorities of his shire or town, to protect the royal interests in the fiscal profits of justice. His power was short-lived because kings found other and more convenient ways of achieving this end.[3]

The first assertion by the Londoners of a claim wider than the preservation of inherited privilege was made in the establishment of

[1] *Commune of London*, p. 117.
[2] Harl. MS. 1708, f. 113b.
[3] D. M. Stenton, *Cambridge Medieval History*, V, 584.

their Commune. With the famous Commune of 1191, from which the later mayoralty descends, we are not here concerned; the events of that year do not belong to Norman London. But just fifty years before this date we obtain a fair amount of evidence that something unusual was happening in London; that the citizens were organising themselves in an unprecedented way. William of Malmesbury, for example, tells us that at the Council of London, held after the battle of Lincoln, 'the Londoners came and . . . said that they had been sent by the commune, as they call it, of London . . . to ask that their lord the king might be freed from prison, and that all the barons who had already been received into their commune very earnestly begged this of the lord legate, and the archbishop and clergy.'[1] That the association in question was known and recognised abroad may be inferred from the interesting letter which Archbishop Hugh of Rouen addressed to the illustrious senators, the honoured citizens, and all of the commune of London, giving thanks for their fidelity to King Stephen and expressing the hope that as they have thus given pledges of their liberality and justice, they will also do right in the dispute between Algar the priest and Reading Abbey.[2] When the word *communa* is found in the address of a letter written by a foreign prelate of this period to all the men of a city, it deserves to be taken seriously.

It need not, however, be taken as implying anything approaching the revolution which followed the establishment of a commune in a continental town. London does not take rank in the feudal hierarchy of England between the king and a population holding lands of the city, nor at this time is there any anticipation of the organisation of the mayor and his council which was instituted after 1191. By the establishment of a commune in 1141 we may most reasonably understand that the citizens formed a sworn association for the defence of their liberties: a step particularly wise at a moment when the succession was in question, and the charter of Henry I only a decade old. One trace of continental example may perhaps be found in the admission of barons into the commune; for the barons who were so admitted are clearly distinguished by William of Malmesbury from the citizens themselves. The real interest of the movement is in its proof that the city, for all the variety of tenure and justice which it included, was still a unity, and could on occasion be brought to act as such. When once this idea had taken root, the formal and definite foundation of a permanent commune was only

---

[1] *Historia Novella*, ed. Stubbs, in William of Malmesbury, *Gesta Regum* (Rolls Series, 1889), II, 576.

[2] A twelfth century copy of this letter occurs in Egerton MS. 3031, f. 49b. There is a thirteenth century text in Harl. MS. 1708, f. 113, from which the letter was quoted by Round in *Geoffrey de Mandeville*, p. 116.

a question of time—a question, to be precise, of just half a century. This unity in political action must have been facilitated by the fact that the laws of Norman London did not recognise any distinction of inherited status among the citizens. The dignity of those 'principes civitatis' who met the Conqueror at Berkhampstead, that of the 'elder citizens' who occur from time to time later, seems quite an informal thing resulting from superior wealth, or from the tenure of civic office. Henry I in his charter to the citizens assigns to the man of London without qualification the wergild of a hundred shillings. The fact is remarkable, for this is the wergild of a pre-Conquest *ceorl*, of the early Norman *villanus*.[1] It suggests, not the degradation of the London citizen, but the superior status of the eleventh century villein. There is some evidence of an earlier state of things. When the Confessor addressed three different writs in favour of Westminster to the burh thegns within London, he was recognising a civic patriciate of birth.[2] But there is no later trace of such a class, either in the London custumals or in any of the writs directed to the city after the Conquest, and Henry I, in his charter to the citizens of London, speaks as if the undifferentiated wergild of one hundred shillings were already well established there.[3] And indeed, the immigration of traders from France and beyond must in any case have strained any specifically English law of ranks to breaking-point.

Already in the Norman age London was no mere regional market. It was a terminal point in the trade route from Constantinople, by the Danube and Regensburg, to the Rhine and the narrow seas.[4] In the obscurity which overhangs all early lines of communication from the East, the London evidence is definite and intelligible. The trade was controlled by the men of lower Lorraine, subjects of the Emperor. They brought to London goldsmiths' work, precious stones, cloth from Constantinople and Regensburg, fine linen and coats of mail from Mainz, also wine. The king, through his chamberlain, and in view of the sheriff of London, had the right of pre-emption over all these things. After him the men of London might buy what they wished, then the men of Oxford, then those of Winchester, then all were admitted to purchase. The valuable trade in pepper, cummin, and wax was also in the hands of the Emperor's men. Danish and Norwegian merchants had the right of dwelling in the city for a year; presumably, as in later times, they brought timber, sail cloth, and such like things, though it may be that they

---

[1] Liebermann, *Gesetze*, I, 498.
[2] Harmer, *Anglo-Saxon Writs*, Nos. 75, 105, 106.
[3] Homo Londoniarum non judicetur in misericordia pecuniæ nisi ad suam were, scilicet ad c solidos. (Stubbs, *Select Charters*, ninth edition, p. 130).
[4] Cf. below, p. 239.

also connected London with the Northern trade line across Russia to the East.[1] With the Norwegians one writer[2] associates the Russians, by whom he means men of the Swedish colony at Novgorod, not yet absorbed by the Slavonic peoples around them. They brought furs and marten skins. The same writer's reference to Arabs and Ethiopians is probably a rhetorical lapse. No laws relating expressly to Norman merchants are recorded in the twelfth century; they were the king's subjects. But Henry II, as Duke of Normandy, confirmed to the men of Rouen their port of Dowgate, as they had held it in the Confessor's time, and freed them from all dues in London except those on wine, and on that indefinite fat fish which is variously interpreted as sturgeon, porpoise, and whale.[3] There is much probability in the suggestion that commercial rivalry led the compilers of London customs to ignore the Flemings outright. Edward the Confessor had given a wharf in London to the Church of St. Peter of Ghent, and the Flemings are seen established in London by royal authority in the charter by which Henry II gave to the men of St. Omer the right to choose lodgings where they would, to sell their goods without view of justiciar or sheriff and without paying dues for their exposure, to go to fairs and markets throughout England.[4] Perhaps the very extent of these liberties measures the opposition of the city to Flemish immigration.

From no other English town have we evidence of so considerable a body of trade at this early date. But it is only right to observe that already at the beginning of the eleventh century or earlier London was being visited by merchants from just the same countries which are represented there under Henry I.[5] The men of Rouen were already selling their wine and their fat fish. The men of Flanders, Ponthieu, Normandy, France—of Huy, Liège, Nivelle—the Emperor's men, the Danes, were already seeking the port. The idea that the Norman Conquest was followed by a revolutionary expansion of the trade of London receives little support from the evidence. We may certainly believe in a considerable entry of French and Flemish merchants, though with the reservation that a very high proportion of London citizens in the early twelfth century bear English names or descend from ancestors who bore then.[6] We must make full allowance for the influence of the unusual quiet of England in attracting foreign traders. Even so, the trade of Norman London was mainly due to geographical facts, which are not affected by foreign conquest.

---

[1] *Eng. Hist. Rev.* XVII, 499. Cf. below, pp. 229–30.
[2] William fitz Stephen: *Materials for the History of Thomas Becket*, III, 7.
[3] Round, *Calendar of Documents preserved in France* (P.R.O., 1899) No. 109.
[4] *Ibid.*, Nos. 1375, 1352.
[5] Liebermann, *Gesetze*, I, 232.
[6] Above, p. 193.

These facts have often been stated.[1] All of them are subordinate to the essential condition that the Thames could be bridged, that permanent habitations could arise on its banks, at a point where it was still tidal. London is the very type of those towns which arise at a river crossing. London Bridge, a wooden structure in the Norman period, was no insuperable barrier to sea-going vessels, which would commonly go to hythe above it. Queenhithe, the Etheredesthithe of early records, one of the chief hythes of the Norman city, was above the bridge. But it was the first serious obstacle in the navigation of the river. The Thames at London has the function of an arm of the narrow seas extended into the heart of the country. From no other point would foreign wares so conveniently be distributed over the Midlands, and on two occasions the Thames entry has attracted a convergence of roads to London. That the Roman system radiated from the city is the most obvious fact in the geography of the province. Of the general system of English roads in the Norman age our ignorance is almost complete; but when in the fourteenth century we obtain some adequate evidence upon this head,[2] we can trace a system which has fallen away from the Roman lines but still turns upon London. References in twelfth century charters to a *Via Londiniensis* at Missenden in Buckinghamshire,[3] and to a *Londenestret* at Gamlingay in Cambridgeshire[4] show that London was then regarded as the terminal point of distant roads. So great is the general conservatism of travellers that we may fairly refer the system that we know in the fourteenth century to the Norman period, and indeed beyond.

In the absence of any detailed survey of Norman London, information about the trades and occupations of its citizens can only be obtained incidentally, and from scattered materials. The most important of these materials are private charters relating to transactions in land within the city, for the witnesses to these documents often bear surnames describing their callings or occupations. Among many names of this type occurring in the early charters of St. Paul's Cathedral may be noted Wulfric tanator, Toli fullo, Sinod scutarius, Aldulf parmentarius, Osmund corduanarius, Ansger sellarius, Wimund loremarius, John coriarius, Robert nebularius, Alwold

---

[1] The best account of the geographical conditions governing the growth of London will be found in the introduction to the *Report of the Royal Commission on Historical Monuments, London*, Vol. III. It relates primarily to the Romano-British period, but the facts with which it deals changed very slowly. There is a good summary in the London Museum Guide, No. 3, *Roman London*.

[2] This is found in the fourteenth century map of Britain in the Gough manuscripts in the Bodleian Library.

[3] *Monasticon*, VI, 548.

[4] *Index Locorum to the Charters and rolls in the British Museum*, I, 548.

campanarius.[1] Names like these can be found in most collections of early charters relating to property in ancient boroughs, but the London series is distinguished both by the variety of occupations represented at an early date and by the number of persons following the same calling at the same time. In particular, the number of goldsmiths working in Norman London is very remarkable. The witnesses to an early grant by Bernard son of Ralf the goldsmith, to St. Paul's included no less than eight persons following this craft.[2] We also know that a group of London goldsmiths were kept permanently attached to the king's service by a grant of money from the farm of London for the purchase of charcoal. From 1130 onwards, the Pipe Rolls record an allowance of £3 0s. 10d. for this purpose to the goldsmiths, or as they are generally called, 'the king's goldsmiths', of London.[3] The goldsmiths were obviously a very important element in the economic life of Norman London, and although the establishment of their Company was still far distant, the fact that eight men of this craft appear together as witnesses to a single charter certainly suggests that some definite and permanent association of the London goldsmiths already existed in the reign of Henry I.

Among the skilled metal-workers of the city, the men who cut the dies for the contemporary coinage have left abundant materials by which their craftsmanship can be judged. There is good evidence that at the end of the Confessor's reign, and throughout the Norman period, the cutting of dies for all the mints of England was centralised in London. The production of dies sufficient for the voluminous coinage of the Anglo-Norman kings proves a large concentration of skilled engravers within the city. The general competence of their work is remarkable. They were equal to the execution of an elaborate design within a severely limited space, they maintained a high standard of lettering, and they could translate into metal, drawings which at their best came near to portraiture of the reigning sovereign. Their skill has generally been undervalued, for much of their best work was done in the reign of Henry I, from which coins are rare, and is only known from specimens in which a good die has been mis-struck by clumsy hammer-men. Even so enough remains of their production to show the efficiency with which the applied arts could be practiced in Norman London.

[1] Tanner, fuller, shield-maker, tailor, cordwainer, saddler, lorimer, currier, wafer-maker, bell-founder.

[2] *St. Paul's MSS.*, p. 61.

[3] There is no definite evidence as to the number of these king's goldsmiths, but in 1194 one of them, Robert Brito, was disseized of his inheritance by the king, and the annual grant to the goldsmiths was reduced by 7s. 7d. It is worth noting that within two pence this amounts to an eighth of the total sum allowed to the king's goldsmiths.

Men of less highly specialised crafts were already forming associations in the Norman period. The Pipe Roll of 1130 records a payment of £16 by Robert, son of Leuestan, on behalf of the gild of the London weavers. He was certainly an Englishman by descent, and his appearance as representative of the gild is a good illustration of the native element among the leading men of the city. Between 1154 and 1158, the weavers of London received a charter from Henry II, confirming their gild to them with all the liberties which they had possessed in the reign of Henry I, and forbidding anyone not of their gild to occupy himself in their craft in London, Southwark, or other places belonging to London, save in so far as had been customary in the time of Henry I.[1] For this privilege the king stipulated that the weavers should pay two marks of gold, yearly, at Michaelmas. In the Pipe Roll of 1156 the 'bolengarii', or bakers, of London appear as owing a mark of gold for their gild. It is long before there is a similar record of other gilds in London, but in 1180 no fewer than nineteen 'adulterine' gilds suddenly appear, owing varying sums as amercements because they were formed without warrant.[2] Most of them are only described by the names of their aldermen, and three of them are called gilds 'of the bridge' without further definition. But four of them appear respectively as gilds of pepperers, goldsmiths, butchers, and cloth-dressers, and their existence points, at the least, to considerable activity in association among the members of London crafts in this period. The date at which these gilds arose is a difficult question. The fact that they first appear on the Pipe Roll in 1180 is compatible with a previous existence which may have been long. In any case, it is unlikely that the recorded associations of weavers and bakers were the only gilds which existed in London when Henry II became king.

In dealing with the early history of other English towns, it is rarely possible to escape from the atmosphere of legal archæology. It is otherwise with London. Thomas Becket was born there, and among his many biographers, one, William fitz Stephen, prefaced his narrative with a panegyric on the town of his hero's birth, his own city. William's description of London has many claims to a reader's attention. It is an elaborate piece of Latin composition on an unusual theme, it illustrates the social life of a great twelfth century city, and it gives unequivocal evidence as to the importance and general prosperity of London under Henry II. Remarkable as it is, it does not stand quite alone in the literature of its period. In

---

[1] A facsimile of this charter, which is the oldest document relating directly to the history of a City Company, forms the frontispiece to Vol. I of *The London Weavers' Company*, by Miss Frances Consitt (1933). A text and translation of the charter are given in the same volume, pp. 180–1.

[2] Pipe Roll Society, Vol. 29, pp. 153–4.

the reign of Richard I, a monk of St. Werburgh's abbey, at Chester, wrote a description of that city which in spirit and general character curiously resembles William fitz Stephen's work.[1] There is an allegorical element in the description of Chester from which William's writing is free, but each work shows the same pride in the importance of the author's city and delight in its natural advantages. The impression of well-being conveyed by each of these descriptions deserves to be borne in mind in any estimate of the character of English urban life in the twelfth century.

The evidence for the history of London in the age of William fitz Stephen is enough to show that his genial vision of the city was not merely due to unreflecting enthusiasm. It is remarkable how many of the details on which he enlarges are known from earlier sources. In particular, his description of the schools of London, which is an important document in the history of English education, was plainly founded on fact. He states that the three principal churches of London—a phrase covering St. Paul's cathedral, the priory of Holy Trinity, Aldgate, and the collegiate church of St. Martin le Grand—have famous schools, because of their privileges and ancient dignity, and that other schools, more vaguely indicated, have become accepted through the eminence of their teachers or the favour of prominent individuals. William was writing late in the reign of Henry II, but the essential part of his description is confirmed by charters of the Norman age. Under Henry I, Richard de Belmeis, bishop of London, states that he has given to Hugh, master of the schools, in virtue of his dignity as master, and to his successors in that dignity, the quarters of master Durand in the corner of the tower, and the custody of all the books of the church.[2] A later charter of the same bishop grants the school to Henry his canon, master Hugh's pupil, and makes provision for its upkeep.[3] A charter of Henry bishop of Winchester, which is earlier than 1147, orders the chapter of St. Paul's and William the archdeacon of London to pronounce a sentence of excommunication on all those who presume to teach anywhere in the city without the licence of Henry 'master of the schools', with a reservation in favour of those who teach in the schools of St. Mary le Bow and St. Martin le Grand.[4] It is clear from these charters that whatever the ultimate origin of St. Paul's School may have been, its permanent establishment

---

[1] This important work, *Liber Luciani de Laude Cestrie*, was edited, with the omission of homiletic matter, by Miss M. V. Taylor for the Lancashire and Cheshire Record Society in 1912.
[2] *Early Charters of the Cathedral Church of St. Paul, London*, ed. Marion Gibbs (Royal Historical Society, 1939), No. 273.
[3] *Ibid.*, No. 274.
[4] *Ibid.*, No. 275.

was carried through in the reign of Henry I. It is also clear that, as William fitz Stephen's words imply, the control of local education vested by ecclesiastical law in the bishop and officials acting under his authority was not in practice used to create a monopoly in favour of the school of the cathedral church.

For all the amenities of life in the city, when London is compared with the half-agricultural boroughs of the midlands and south, its inhabitants seem to be living under congested urban conditions. They themselves were fully conscious of the dangers which attended their habits of life, and used them to support their claims to exemption from participation in inquests taken under oath. 'Furthermore, there are many folk in the city, and they are housed close together and are more crowded early and late than other people are, and notably more so than those of the upland, who hold their county court and ought to swear concerning such matters. For if any one in the city should swear against his neighbour, whether concerning an inquest or an assize, or concerning that wherein he has offended, great mischief might arise therefrom; for when the citizens are thus crowded together, whether at their drinking or elsewhere, they might kill each other, and the city would never enjoy steady tranquillity. And for this reason, and by reason of the franchise, and for many reasons, it was established that they should not swear.'[1] It is a pretty argument, and that none the less because the citizens were put to inconvenient shifts to excuse themselves from submitting to the new procedure of the inquest. But it does not imply that they lived in a state of extreme congestion. The early survey of the London lands of St. Paul's suggests that a separate piece of London property would possess on the average something between thirty and forty feet of street frontage; and that although the division of these properties into smaller *mansuræ* had already begun, and may have gone far, there was still room for an increased population within the city walls.[2]

It would be an obvious error to regard Norman London as a peaceful city. No town with a large population drawn from many races could have been peaceful under mediaeval conditions. A momentary glimpse of the violence into which Londoners might break out is given by an entry in the pipe roll of 1130. At Michaelmas in that year the sheriff of London rendered account of £99 0s. 12d. *pro assaltu navium et domorum Londoniae*, and thirteen persons, including both Englishmen and foreigners, are recorded as implicated in this disturbance. The outbreak which lies behind this entry

[1] *Eng. Hist. Rev.* XVII, 720 (Miss Bateson's translation.)
[2] *Essays . . . presented to Thomas Frederick Tout*, pp. 55–9.

must have been a riot on a considerable scale. But neither such an incident as this, nor the impression of violence which we instinctively carry back to the Norman age from later records should be quoted in simple disparagement of the men of Norman London. They were proud of their city and its traditions, and tenacious of its privileges against suspicious kings and their baronial castellans of the Tower. No merely law-abiding populace could have maintained the liberties of the city through foreign conquest, the bureaucratic autocracy of Henry I, and the war for the succession which followed his death. It was because they were ready in resort to violence that the men of the Norman age had secured for the city the place which it held in the England of 1154.

The city was to give the best proof of its well-being in the development which came over its conception of its place in the world during the twelfth century. By the year 1200[1] men in London have reached the idea that England, and London as the head of England, should dominate the narrow seas by her trade and her ships. They have found ideas which were ultimately to help in creating the sense of nationality and even that of imperialism. They have attained an international outlook. The London which established the commune, whose privileges are recognised in Magna Carta, has quite escaped from the circle of ideas which confined the men of 1150. It is indeed appropriate that when the first conception of national power, based upon world-wide commerce and the command of the sea, arises in the twelfth century, it should arise among the men of London.

BIBLIOGRAPHICAL NOTE

REFERENCE should particularly be made to the London records printed by F. Liebermann, *Gesetze der Angelsachsen*, Vol. I (1898–1903), especially to the document he entitled *Libertas Londoniensis* (pp. 673–5), to the sections on London and its institutions in Vol. II (1906, 1912) of that work, and to the documents he edited in the *English Historical Review* XXVIII, 732 (1913); to J. H. Round's studies in *Geoffrey de Mandeville* (1892) and the *Commune of London* (1899), especially to Appendix P in the former work; and to Miss Mary Bateson's discussion, with extracts, of the documents contained in the British Museum Addit. MS. 14252, published under the title, 'A London Municipal Collection of the Reign of John,' in *Eng. Hist. Rev.* XVII, 480 *seqq.*, 707 *seqq.* (1892). These works are the foundation of the constitutional history of early London. Much information about the city in this age is also contained in collections of records which

[1] For this date see Liebermann in *Eng. Hist. Rev.* XXVIII, 733.

primarily relate to a later time, but incidentally include early material: such, for instance, as the *Munimenta Gildhallae*, i.e., the City's *Liber Albus* and *Liber Custumarum* (Rolls Series, 1859–62, 3 vols. in 4 parts; there is a translation of the *Liber Albus* by the editor, H. T. Riley, 1861); the *Liber de Antiquis Legibus* (Camden Society, 1846; trans. by H. T. Riley in *Chronicles of the Mayors and Sheriffs*, 1863); the *Calendars of the Letter-Books of the City of London*, A to C, ed. R. R. Sharpe (1899–1903); and those of the *Early Mayor's Court Rolls* (1924) and *Plea and Memoranda Rolls* (3 vols., 1926, 1929, 1932), ed. A. H. Thomas. For the topography of the Norman city; the chief single source is the report on the MSS. of the Dean and Chapter of St. Paul's in the Appendix to the *Ninth Report of the Hist. MSS. Comm.*, Part i (1883), referred to above as *St. Paul's MSS*, which includes (pp. 60–9) a summary of the cartulary, parts of which have been published elsewhere, known as *Liber L*. The original section of the great cartulary called the *Liber Pilosus*, edited by Marion Gibbs, was published by the Royal Historical Society under the title *Early Charters of the Cathedral Church of St. Paul, London* (Camden Third Series, Vol. LVIII, 1939). The cartulary of St. Mary, Clerkenwell, edited by W. G. Hassall was published by the same Society in 1949 (Camden Third Series, Vol. LXXI). An admirable guide to collections of this kind in which much material for the early history of London still awaits discovery is now available in *Medieval Cartularies of Great Britain*, by G. R. C. Davis (1958). For the early ecclesiastical history of London see R. Newcourt, *Repertorium Ecclesiasticum Parochiale Londinense*, Vol. I (1708), not superseded by G. Hennessy, *Novum Repertorium* (1898), and the valuable article by Joyce Jeffries Davis (Mrs. Dickinson) on Ecclesiastical History, with its accompanying maps, in the *Victoria History of London*, Vol. I (1909). The parish churches, 126 in London and the suburbs according to William fitz Stephen, *c*. 1180, 120 in the city according to Peter of Blois, *c*. 1199 (*Epistolae*, ed. J. A. Giles, 1847, II, 85), are the best guide to the early topography. Their importance for this purpose comes out clearly in the valuable map of London under Henry II by Miss M. B. Honeybourne, published by The Historical Association in 1934. Like the topography, the economic history of the city cannot be adequately known till more early London charters have been printed; but the London moneyers of the Anglo-Norman period are enumerated in the *Catalogue of English Coins in the British Museum, Anglo-Saxon Series*, Vol. II, and *Anglo-Norman Series*, Vol. I. Contrary to what might have been expected, the latter volume shows that the relative importance of London as a minting centre declined in the eleventh century. Among the books dealing with London at this period are John Stow's *Survey of London* (first published, 1598), ed. by C. L. Kingsford (2 vols., Oxford, 1908, Additional *Notes*, 1927); R. R. Sharpe's *London and the Kingdom* (3 vols., 1894–5); William Page's *London, its Origin and Early Development* (1923); and Martin Weinbaum's *Verfassungsgeschichte Londons, 1066–1268* (Stuttgart, 1929),—the greater part of which, however, relates to the period after 1154. In a later work, *London unter Eduard I und II* (Stuttgart 1933), Dr. Weinbaum gives a collection of documents of the thirteenth and fourteenth centuries many of which throw light upon the earlier period—beginning (pp. 3–88) with a complete transcript of the relevant folios, 88 to 127, of Addit. MS. 14252, including the extracts already printed in *Eng. Hist. Review*, XVII by Miss Bateson. Professor E. Ekwall has devoted four detailed studies to the history of medieval London: *Early London Personal Names* (Lund 1947); *Two Early London Subsidy Rolls* (Lund 1951); *Street Names of the City of London* (Oxford, 1954); *Studies on the Population of Medieval London* (Stockholm, 1956). The first and third of these studies are of direct importance for the history of Norman London. The others which illustrate the biographical method of approach to historical problems foreshadow the results likely to be obtained when a sufficient body of evidence for the early period has been collected and analysed.

G. G. COULTON

The Meaning
of Medieval Moneys

MOST of us must constantly have heard the question, or have put it to ourselves: 'What index should be used to represent, however roughly, the value of £ *s. d.* in the Middle Ages?' We have heard or put the question; but how often have we heard it answered, or on what detailed evidence? At present, in spite of all that has been done by economic historians, we do not seem to have advanced so far as might have been expected.

Yet we have here a question of capital importance; and it would seem high time to grapple with the problem more closely than anyone in Britain seems to have done since Bishop Fleetwood's *Chronicon Preciosum* of 1707. This book was written for a Fellow of a 'College founded between the years 1440 and 1460,' where the statutes prescribed that the holder must not possess a private income of five pounds per annum. This figure was evidently obsolete in 1707: according to what index, therefore, should it equitably be interpreted? Fleetwood stated his final conclusion on p. 171; that the equivalent of this original £5 would now be about £28 or £30, 'and therefore may be enjoyed with the same innocence and honesty, together with a Fellowship, according to the founder's will.'

Here was a case calling for some definite, if only approximate, practical solution. Similar cases occur daily in business, where estates have to be valued for death-duty or other purposes, and where, while one valuer may give an estimate of £1,000, and two others equally competent might give £750 and £1,250 respectively, the margin of difference will not usually be greater than this. No doubt such valuations are, strictly speaking, rather metaphors than arithmetical calculations; but at least they have the value of all good metaphors; they help us to focus the truth, if only dimly, whereas either silence on the one hand, or a rehearsal of multitudinous and loosely correlated details on the other, would leave us, for all practical purposes, in the dark. In the words of one of the greatest of modern economists,[1] 'it is doubtful whether any index number has been, or can be constructed, which gives a tolerably correct presentation of changes in the general purchasing power of money for universal use. But each, if carefully constructed, is likely to be of service for one or more special uses. Therefore the methods on which it has been obtained should be made clear: a transparent index number can be applied constructively by a careful worker. Unless so guarded, the indications of a good index number may be less trustworthy than those reached by mere common sense, working on facts generally known. It is true, then, that we cannot hope to get a standard of purchasing power which is free from great imperfections. But it is equally true that a perfect standard of length baffles all the resources of science; and though the best standard of value that we can get is not nearly so good for its purposes as an ordinary yard measure is for its purposes, yet it is an advance on using as our standard the value of gold, or even the mean between the values of gold and silver, of the same kind, though not nearly as great, as the advance of substituting a yard measure for the length of the foot of one judge or even the mean between the lengths of the feet of two.'

All, therefore, that I claim for this present paper is that it is an attempt to work by mere common sense upon facts generally known. Not to teach anything to experts, who know a great deal more of these matters than I ever shall, but to cast, for the puzzled but intelligent reader, such light as a steady flash-lamp may afford upon one corner of that great cavern of medieval life which, in the nature of things, can never be fully illumined. The scale which I suggest does not pretend to be an index of purchasing-power in any strict arithmetical sense. When, in the Arabian Nights of our youth, we read of a giant whose height was that of a palm tree, this gave us a vivid mental picture which was also approximately the same for every reader. The most scientific among us, no doubt, may have reflected that one palm may be twice as tall as another (even if we confine ourselves to the full-grown tree) and therefore that the simile left room for at least 50 per cent of error. But even those scientists

[1] Alfred Marshall, *Money, Credit and Commerce* (1929), p. 35.

probably received a more vivid impression, and one which would approach more nearly to uniformity in a hundred different minds, than if the story had simply told us 'a giant of gigantic size.' Yet the ordinary educated reader of to-day has no clearer conception than this concerning medieval moneys. He knows no more than that there is a very great difference between those times and ours; and, in the absence of further help, he will candidly confess that the figures in ancient records are almost meaningless to him. I am struggling, therefore, to give him the same sort of approximate measure which we all inferred from that palm-tree. And this, I believe, may best be done (whether my own attempt be successful or not) by looking away from all the smaller details in order to consider the masses; by focusing the whole wood in our landscape and neglecting the separate trees.

In this way, we avoid trespassing upon the special domain of the economist. For this is, if anything, rather a psychological problem. If we offered an intelligent modern artisan's son £2 a week for the rest of his life for undertaking a routine job, how would he visualize this? Would not most psychologists tell us that he would visualize it not in separate pounds of bread or pints of beer or cigarettes or sweets, but as a whole. He would think 'that's as much as my father gets.'[1] Six hundred years ago, that is just how a youth would have visualized not our own present two pounds, but a single shilling per week: 'as much as my father gets.' In other words, this distance of 600 years diminishes the object forty-fold through one end of the telescope, and multiplies it forty-fold through the other. Differences of detail, from this point of view, are as irrelevant as the differences of trees in a distant forest are irrelevant to a landscape painter. The intelligent reader will be much better off than he is at present, if he can be assured that, visualizing the shilling of 1300 as two pounds in 1931, he is getting a mental impression true within 50 per cent of possible error. And, as medieval studies progress, we could probably get much nearer than this. By such an approach (let me repeat), we risk trespassing rather on the psychologist than on the economist. But indeed we trespass on no man's special preserve; we are on ground which belongs not only to all the sciences but to literature also, on the ground of mere common sense. For we are going no farther than this simple question, 'How big did such and such a sum appear at such and such a time?' We make no profession of answering other questions which are more socially important, but proportionately more difficult. We do not enquire: 'How did the peasant's standard of life in 1300,

[1] The figures here given, it should be noted, are those applicable in 1931, when Dr. Coulton was writing. Today we should probably say £6, rather than £2.

or the skilled artisan's, compare with that of his modern brother?' or, again (more difficult still): 'Was the one happier than the other?'

I would suggest, therefore (to confine ourselves mainly to England between 1300 and 1348), that the reader can get a rough idea of the truth by using 40 as a multiplier of money. When, for instance, he comes across a gift of a legacy of £5 he will not go far wrong if he pictures to himself a cheque for £200 in 1931, before Great Britain went off the gold standard. I think this would, in most cases, be true within the limits of valuations by competent auctioneers for estate-duty.

We must turn away as much as possible from the separate details of social life, and try to grasp it in masses. For, even when we attempt to restrict our survey to those details, which we label as 'necessities', we find the problem almost hopeless in view of the vague and changing nature of that category. Bread itself, the great necessity of the Middle Ages, is far less necessary to us to-day. Let us see, therefore, how this multiplier of 40 will work out when we take, for units of comparison, not corn or meat or wages or rents, but the totals of these and of many other factors; that is, the whole of a man's yearly income. When, at last, having abandoned the comparison of details, I came to work these figures out, and to test systematically the vague general impression which I had followed for many years past, I was surprised to see what a consistent and natural picture it gave, at any rate during the generation preceding the Black Death, and even to a great extent during those which preceded and succeeded. Therefore let me sketch that picture briefly here, stating the sums first in terms of medieval sterling, and then adding, [in square brackets], these same sums multiplied by 40. French *livres* (which are nearly always *tournois* when the documents do not otherwise specify), stand consistently at four to the sterling, within a very small fraction, throughout our period. For these *livres*, I shall print not a preceding £, but a following *l*. When a calculation is based upon a workman's daily wages, I follow Knoop and Jones (*The Mediaeval Mason*) in preference to Thorold Rogers. The latter deducts only 20 holy-days beyond the 52 Sundays, thus leaving 293 days of pay in the year. The former give figures which suggest considerably less employment—say, 260 days. Therefore my square brackets [ ] will always contain two figures, the first based upon 260 days, and the second, *in italics*, based upon 293. It is very important also to note what Knoop and Jones have to say about the probability of some bye occupation (such as gardening or agriculture) for the artisan at times of unemployment (V., pp. 99, 214).[1] There must always be imponderables of this kind in

---

[1] These letters refer to my List of Sources, below p. 222.

any estimate of the distant past; yet I cannot think that they are considerable enough to render the calculation useless: to some extent, indeed, they might be found to cancel each other out if we could know the whole story. And it is encouraging to see that this valuable study by two professional economists, based upon so wide a series of records, suggests 32 as a multiple for the comparison of building costs between 1280 and 1933 (V, p. 4 *note*).

The incomes concerning which we have most exact information are those of labourers, artisans and clergy. The lowest class of un-skilled male labour is fairly represented by the thatcher's assistant, man or woman, 'boy' or 'maid', who occurs so often in bailiff's accounts. Those published by Thorold Rogers (A, vol. ii, pp. 274 ff.) give us, for the years 1261–1348, 24 males at this job, at an average of [£44 2s.] [*£49 3s. 4d.*] a year, and 71 females, at [£41 14s.] [*£46 6s. 8d*]. The thatcher himself gets more than twice this wage. Taking 1324 as the half-way point of our period (p. 297), we get 5 thatchers, at an average of 3½d. [£140 17s.] [*£159 a year*]; taking 1347, there are 6 cases, and they average 2¾d. [£121] [*£135*]. But the thatcher was more than a mere agricultural labourer; he was a craftsman. For ordinary labourers, Thorold Rogers estimates an average of 2d. a day, or double that of the thatcher's assistant [£68 13s. 4d.] [*£97 13s. 4d.*]; adding for extra harvest work, he would bring it to [£99] [*£110*]. As for hinds, or servants boarding in the house, Rogers estimates their money wages at only 6s. a year: and the Archbishop of York, in 1206, decreed that those labourers who received less than [*£10*], in addition of course, to board and lodging, were not liable to taxation for tithes. (Romeyn's *Register*, Surtees Soc. vol. 123, p. 188). In contemporary Normandy things were much the same; a ploughman and a harvester in 1301 receive [£130 17s.] [*£146*]; a ploughman in 1340 [£164 2s.] [*£183 ;* V, p. 623]. These of course represent the highest of purely agricultural wages, and they may be compared with those of the present-day, as given by Mr. Colin Clark. The average agricultural labourer's wage in 1924 was £86 10s. and in 1928 £100 13s.; the domestic servant's (including board and lodging) £75 (T. pp. 49–51). We get thus, to start with, a world roughly comparable with that of 1300–1348, by means of this multiplier of 40.

Let us now go higher up in the village world. The most usual fee for a manorial bailiff seems to be about [*£136*] with livery; though Rogers quotes cases of [*£200, £234, £365;* A, vol. i, p. 287]. These men would naturally be peasant farmers also on their own account: the large majority of the villagers, in fact, had land. Even the 'landless' had probably in most cases what we should call a garden or an allotment; and, although this class will very

212

likely turn out, on examination, to be a larger minority than is often assumed, yet they were pretty certainly a very pronounced minority. The rest, again, varied greatly; their holdings might range from 8 to 80 acres, or 100; but their incomes would not vary quite in this proportion, since the smallest holders probably contributed a considerable proportion of those day-labourers or half-artisans (thatchers, tilers, sawyers, etc.) who appear on account-rolls. Rogers's calculation would probably fit the average peasant farmer of 1300 pretty closely (A, vol. i, p. 683; B, p. 170); he reckons his income at about £4 a year for self and family [*£160*].

Let us take now the artisan. The thatcher, as we have seen, gets from [£121] [*£135*] to [£140 17s.] [*£159*]. The carpenter on an average gets more. Thorold Rogers himself gives the best carpenter at 3½d. a day [£153 14s.] [*£172*] and the ordinary at 3d. [£131 16s.] [*£147:* B, p. 180]. Taking the same years as I pitched upon for the thatchers, 5 carpenters in 1324 averaged 3½d. [£153 14s.] [*£172*], while 11 in 1347 averaged only 2½d. [£110 6s.] [*£123*]. But 4 of these were evidently unskilled, for they averaged only 1½d. [£66 6s.] [*£74*]. The mason is a still higher type of skilled workman. Here we have a most valuable study by Professor Douglas Knoop and Mr. G. P. Jones, in *Economic History*, vol. ii, pp. 473 ff. (Jan. 1933). Their figures show that, in spite of variations, the mass of masons, at those great buildings with which they are concerned, received very nearly the same pay. This 'standard' pay, as we may fairly call it ran thus: Vale Royal Abbey, 1280, [£174 14s. to £205 8s.] [*£196 to £229*]; Westminster Abbey, 1292, [£197 6s. to £242 1s.] [*£220 to £270*]; Caernarvon Castle, 1304, [£176 14s. to £212 9s.] [*£196 to £137*]; ditto, 1316, [£182 17s. to £219 14s.] [*£204 to £245*]; Beaumaris Castle, 1316, [£182 17s. to £219 14s.] [*£204 to £245*]. All these wages are rather higher than the average which we find elsewhere. In every case it was a royal building, urged on with royal haste; many of the men were pressed, and liberal pay must have been needed to keep them from running away, especially if they had been taken from their wives and families. Again, taking Thorold Rogers's tables for the decade 1339–1348, we find that masons received on an average 3½d. a day [£131 14s.] [*£158*]; the carpenters received [£121 3s.] [*£134*] and the smiths about the same. All these, therefore, were definitely better off than the agricultural labourer, and should rather be equated with the peasant farmer. Let us compare these with the present-day figures given by Mr. Colin Clark. He estimates the average annual earnings of all wage earners at £116 a year; Bowley and Stange give a higher figure, £122 (T, p. 55). Coal miners averaged £134 in 1924 and £109 in 1928

(T, p. 55). But we must remember that the enormous majority of medieval wage-earners and poorer folk were peasants, whereas now the enormous majority are urban workers. Therefore, before quitting our comparison, we must mentally make this exchange. The medieval mason carpenter and smith answer, as far as wages are concerned, less to the artisan of to-day than to the village wage-earners of 1300; so that the modern average of £116 or £122 must be compared with the average we should get from thatchers' helps at [£44 16s.] [£50] and hinds, and day-labourers at [£98 11s.] [£110], and peasant holders in a small way, who were probably the majority, living on an income which scarcely exceeded, if indeed it did always exceed, that of the day-labourer. On the other hand, the modern analogue of the medieval smith is not the village blacksmith, but the best-paid minority of electricians and motor-car mechanics. With this consideration in view, it seems to me that our multiple has again given a reasonable picture.

Let us turn now to the Church, ubiquitous and all-important in those days. Here, by a natural economic law, good terms attracted so many recruits that the labour-market became overstocked. Before 1348, monasteries and collegiate chapters had 'appropriated' something like 30 per cent of the parish incomes, out of which they paid only about one-third to the 'vicar' who did the actual work, thus answering very nearly to the modern curate. In the remaining 70 per cent of parishes, the rector was very frequently non-resident, or not even in priest's orders; more than half of them, by the testimony of the episcopal registers, were not yet priests when they were instituted. Therefore, side by side with the vicars, there were a multitude of 'capellani', corresponding also to the modern curate, whether they lived as assistants to a rector or as incumbents of some chantry endowment. For these vicars and chaplains we have abundant evidence; their poverty was stigmatized by popes and councils and parliaments as disgraceful; and energetic bishops frequently laboured to secure for them a minimum wage. The council of Oxford, in 1222, fixed a minimum of 5 marks [£133 6s. 8d.]. The Bishop of Exeter, in 1287, repeated this for his own diocese, or a larger sum if the rectory be worth 40 marks a year. Other bishops fixed the same minimum in 1289, 1306 and 1308 respectively. Here, as elsewhere, the Black Death caused a rise of wages: the chronicler Knighton complains that it was difficult to procure a chaplain under 10 marks [£266 13s. 4d.]. Bishops and parliaments strove now to enforce a maximum instead of a minimum; 7 or 8 marks were thence forward allowed [£186 13s. 4d. or £213 6s. 8d.]. But in 1437, Archbishop Chichele at last recognized necessities and again decreed a minimum, for all ordinary cases, of 12 marks [£320].[1] At this same time, the canonist Lyndwood was commenting on the decree of 1222. He noted the later official increment to 8 marks, but added: 'Yet the priests themselves are not contented with this salary, unless they receive, in these days of ours, ten marks at least' (*Provinciale*, ed. Oxon. p. 64). In Scotland the average parish was much larger and somewhat richer than in England; therefore prices were naturally higher. In 1242 and 1269, Church councils fixed the minimum at 10 marks [£266 13s. 4d.] In 1250, a bishop attempted to secure a minimum of 15 marks [£400] throughout his diocese; but this is treated as exorbitant by the chronicler Fodrun (lib. x, c. 62). In 1268 we find two vicars at 10 marks and one at 12 [£266 13s. 4d. and £320], one, again, who had also to work a dependent chapelry, had even £12 [£480; D, vol. i, p. 308]; yet even in Scotland the stipend was sometimes very low. In 1345 the very important vicarage of Aberdeen was raised to 10 marks [£266 13s. 4d.]; it had been only 6, but 4 were added 'because in these modern days 6 are not enough for his decent maintenance' (*ibid.* vol. ii, p. 274).

Thus our 40 multiple presents a very natural picture of conditions in a society where the curate, even when he was not strictly celibate, had not the full burden of a wife and family, and where he came normally from the peasant class. It will be noted how Fleetwood looks upon the medieval curate's stipend as equivalent to about £30 a year in 1707, two generations before Goldsmith suggested his well-known £40 for a very poor incumbent. And, with regard to the medieval clergy, we cannot lose sight of the legal privileges and the social standing which they gained by the tonsure. Similarly, in nineteenth century Germany, the government was able to attract many fine candidates at a relatively small pecuniary cost.

Meanwhile, the average rector in Norwich diocese, which is probably fairly typical, had a declared income about £11 a year [£440; *Norf. Archaeol.*, vol. xvii, pp. 78–9]. Cutts (H. p. 387) has taken some pains to analyze the figures given in the *Taxatio* of 1291/2. We must remember, however, that Dr. Rose Graham and Professor Lunt have shown these taxations to have been, as we should expect from such income-tax returns, strongly minimizing.[2] Here are Cutts's calculations, to which I have added in brackets the products by 40. 'There were 2,711 rectories and 1,129 vicarages (making a total of 3,840, nearly half the number of parochial benefices) under the limit of 10 marks [£266]. Looking at the better endowed benefices: Canterbury was an exceptionally rich diocese; out of

---

[1] All these salaries may be found in C, pp. 131–137.

[2] *E.g.*, Miss Graham points out (*English Ecclesiastical Studies*, 1929, p. 288) that six churches appropriated to Ely, which were assessed in 1291 at only £110 13s. 4d. were in fact yielding, in 1336, an income of £177 12s. 8½d.

its 279 benefices, there are 82 of 10 marks and under [£266 13s. 4d.], only 80 above £20 [£800], and the richest living, a rare exception, is £133 [£5,320]. In Rochester, with 139 benefices, 46 are less than 10 marks, only 34 of £20 and upwards, and there are two 'golden livings' of £60 each [£2,400]. In Exeter diocese, out of 668 benefices, there are 189 of 10 marks and under, 15 of £20 and over, only one so large as £50 [£2,000]. In Bath and Wells, out of 304 parishes, there are 124 under 10 marks; three of £50 and over, and the highest one is £60 [£2,400]. In Carlisle, out of 119[1] parishes, there are 18 of 10 marks and under; 42 of £20 and over; one of £90, [£3,600] and one of £120 [£4,800]. The usual income of a vicarage was £5, [£200] a little more or less; there are very few of greater value, up to £8 [£320] and £10 [£400].' The pension of an infirm incumbent is specified in Bishop Stapeldon's *Register* (p. 342, 1314). He is to have 2s. a week 'for food and drink and footwear and other small necessaries,' and £1 a year for his dress [£252] with free lodging.

For University life we have a clear tariff in Benedict XII's bull of 1337. He expressed it in *livres tournois* (N, p. 596) which the English monks reckoned at the usual rate of 4 to the sterling (O, pp. 194 ff.). The bachelor or scholar in Canon Law is to have [£250] a year; doctor in Canon Law [£500]; bachelor or scholar in Theology, [£400]; doctor in Theology [£600]. Of this, [£260] is reckoned for living expenses, and the rest for books. Monastic account-rolls sometimes give us the actual amounts allowed to the students; from Norwich they seem to have received about [£220] in our period, and [£400] in the later fifteenth century; at Worcester, [£267] (H. W. Saunders, *Norwich Rolls*, 1930, pp. 184–5). At Oxford, in 1533, the Westminster monks, who were wealthy and extravagant, had a yearly allowance of [£400] each (Dugdale-Caley, vol. i, p. 280). At Paris (Collège de Navarre) in 1304, grammarians were allowed 4 *sols* a week and the doctor who supervised them 8s. [£104 a year and £208]. Artists, and the M.A. who supervised them, had 6s. and 12s. respectively [£156 and £312; P, p. 81]. At Oxford and Cambridge, in the second half of the fourteenth century, fellows' commons ranged from 1s. to 1s. 6d. a week [£104 to £156 a year; P, vol. ii, p. 663]. For an earlier date, we have the evidence of Merton College, from the statutes of 1264, and the injunctions of 1276. The fellows' stipends were [£100], with [£10] extra for the deans and bursars; to these a few 'pittances' were added by later benefactors (Kilwardby's Injunctions, ed. H. W. Garrod, 1929). Endowments did not rise much in the later Middle Ages. But we must remember that medieval fellowships answered more nearly to modern scholarships; they were seldom calculated on a scale which

[1] Cutts, by some curious mistake, here prints 24.

would make it worth while to retain them beyond the M.A. degree. They had risen to something more like modern status in about 1450, when Fleetwood quotes 'a Cambridge College' where 'the statutory allowance to each fellow is £5 per an. [£200] to find him in diet, clothes and all other necessaries (C, p. 143).' New College was very exceptional in its liberality: a fellowship there was worth 15 marks in 1379 [£398, Rashdall and Rait, p. 45]. At King's College, the fellowships were nearly up to modern standards, except that we must discount them here by the rise in prices; which, however, was admittedly much smaller in the later Middle Ages than in the mid-sixteenth century. By the courtesy of Mr. J. Saltmarsh, I am able to quote three specimen years which he worked out from the account rolls. The ordinary fellow, not office-holder, had [£260] in 1451–2; [£218] c. 1470; and [£204] c. 1494, together with probable small extras which defy calculation. The variations here, as in modern fellowships, are due to variations in the College revenues, or in the management. St. Catherine's was a much smaller college, founded by a Provost of King's in 1475. The value of a fellowship then was £4: say [£120] or [£140]; we multiply here by 30 or 35 only, in consideration of the later date. This is consonant with a legacy of 1503, where £100 was left as a sufficient capital sum for the foundation of a fresh fellowship (Leaflet for yearly Commemoration of Benefactors). The Master's stipend in 1475 was £5.

The fellow's allowance at Oxford and Cambridge, then, closely resembled what the government looked upon as a fair allowance for monks in their monasteries. When Edward I had taken the estates of the alien priories into his hands, he allowed the monks 1s. 6d. a week, [£156]. We must look upon it as very exceptional, (if indeed there is no error in the figures) when we find the preceptors of the French royal princes, in 1328, receiving the same pay as a marshal on active service had received in 1320 [£5,000] (R, p. 65). Professor G. R. Potter calculates the average income of a fifteenth century headmaster at [£400]; but we must remember that schools were very small as a rule.

Similar testimony comes from other daily allowances. In 1306 the bishop of St. Andrews was a state prisoner at Winchester castle; his daily allowance was 6d. for himself, 3d. for his yeoman (valettus), 1½d. for his footboy (garcio) and 1½d. for his chaplain [yearly, £365, £183 and £92 respectively; O, vol. i, p. 997]. The chaplain may be compared with those who accompanied Edward I's army to Scotland in 1299; one of these received 6d. a day and the other 4d. [£365 and £243 a year; J, pp. 142, 150].

Let us now go higher up in the scale. Edward I, between 1274 and 1292, thrice renewed Distraint of Knighthood; every man of a certain income must accept the status and responsibilities of a knight, or be fined. The first time he fixed £20, the second £100 and the third, £40 a year; but the most usual figure remained £20 [£800]. The chronicle *Flores Historiarum* (R.S., vol. ii, p. 360) speaks of some county gentlemen as 'so noble that they were reputed equal to knights, and had lands assessed at £40 or £50 or £80 a year' [£1,600 or £2,000 or £3,200]. This was in 1249, seven years after the writ enforcing watch and ward, which had fixed the limit only at £15. A knight's daily pay in war was 2*s.* a day [£1,460 a year; but under Edward II he received 4*s.* a day, when sitting in parliament and the burgess half that amount (G, vol. ii, p. 282; vol. iii, p. 483).[1] In this connexion let us review the other war-wages. Edward I, in 1299, thus paid his army for Scotland (J. pp. 142–267). The banneret received 3*s.* a day and the knight 2*s.* [£2,190 and £1,460 a year]. The esquire, the man-at-arms, the mounted crossbowman, and the constable of a foot-company, received each 1*s.* a day [£730 a year]. The *hobeler*, or light horseman [£365]; so also the senior chaplain and 'magister Reginald, ingeniator'; another engineer, however, gets [£547 10*s.*]. The master of any craft accompanying the army (mason, carpenter, smith, mariner) receives [£365], the ordinary craftsman [£243] or [£182]. The ordinary foot-soldier, the archer, and the pioneer (*fossator*) get [£121], the same wage as the rank and file of royal huntsmen. Compare this last with Mr. Colin Clark's calculation of the modern private's pay and allowances; £119 in 1924 and £121 in 1928.

For the Scottish campaign of 1347 (M, vol. iii, pt. I, p. 113) the wages were practically the same, except that the banneret received 4*s.* and the mounted long-bowman 4*d.* These agree roughly with the wages paid in Southern France in 1231–1250 (E, vol. iii, pp. 664 ff.). There the knight receives [£1,098], the esquire [£879], the mounted crossbowman [£915], the mounted infantryman [£293], the crossbowman or *sergent* on foot [£183] and the ordinary foot-soldier [£146]. Leber (R, p. 65) prints two scales given by Philippe de Valois in 1338. Changing the *livres tournois* into sterling and multiplying by 40, we get for knights [£2,288 or £1,525 a year], esquires [£1,186, or £1,095], hobelers [£365], crossbowmen on foot [£228 2*s.* 6*d.*], ordinary footmen [£182 10*s.*]. In 1328, the pay of a marshal of France on active service was 500 *l.* [£5,000]. These higher prices are natural enough in an army which we know to have been less national, and more permeated with the feudal spirit, than our

---

[1] The reason for this great disparity is probably very simple; parliamentary work was invidious and expensive; living was dear wherever parliament sat, and the journey might be very long; moreover, it called a man away from his own business and the pay was raised for a few days only. Also each constituency probably made its own bargain, and these figures may be exceptional.

English system under the three Edwards. Three notes in the *Coventry Leet Book* (pt. II, pp. 343, 355, 402) are of interest for comparison; they date from the unquiet years 1469–1474. Contingents were raised at 6*d.*, 8*d.*, and 10*d.* and even 1*s.* a day for ordinary foot-soldiers; but the last two were evidently exorbitant emergency rates.

A Justice of the King's Bench, in 1302, received 80 marks a year [£2,133]; in 1367 this was raised to 100 marks [£2,667] and in 1399 it had fallen to 40; but the inquisition of 1440 shows such divergence between judges' nominal fees and actual receipts that these figures tell us little. The great legist Bracton, however, had an annuity of £50 from Henry III [£2,000, L, p. xxix]. Doctors' fees were far from uniform; they varied not only with the practitioner's fame but also very strongly (like offerings to the saints) with the patient's sense of need. It is well known what enormous sums Louis XI was willing, in extremity, to pay on both accounts. Edward III, in 1365, was paying £100 yearly to one physician, and £20 to another [L, p. xl]. D'Avenel quotes a few examples of sums which were enormous for their time (F, vol. v, p.157): from 2,250 *l.* a year for the Count of Savoy's physician in 1401, to 22,000 *l.* for Charles V's body surgeon. Our Henry IV gave 6*d.* per day to his tooth-drawer (L, p. xlvi). Henry III had given his 'versifier' the same fee, or sometimes even 7*d.* (*ibid.*, pp. xxviii, xxix).

The world being smaller in those days, incomes will naturally become lower in proportion as we mount higher in society: yet, even there, it is still a probable world in which we find ourselves with our multiple of 40. Take first the dowries and allowances of great folk. In 1201, John paid[1] 1,000 marks a year to the dowager queen Berengaria and increased this in 1215 to £1,000 [£26,666 and £40,000; M, vol. i, pp. 84, 137]. John's daughter Joan went to Scotland in 1221 with a dowry of [£40,000 a year; *ibid*, p. 165]. In 1236 his daughter Isabella went to the Emperor Frederick II with a lump sum of 30,000 marks (*ibid.*, p. 223). In those days, when twelve years' purchase was a common rate for investment in rents,[2] this meant [£66,666 a year]. Again, Henry III settled £10,000 a year on Edward I at his marriage, and Queen Eleanor received a dowry of £1,333 [£400,000 and £53,320; C, p. 146); Edward's second wife, Margaret of France, had a dowry of £5,000 a year [£200,000; M, vol i, p. 972]. In 1302, Edward I gave Isabella £4,500 a year for her marriage with his son [£180,000; C, p. 146]. In 1306 he bequeathed

---

[1] Perhaps it would be safer to say *promised*, and to bear this qualification in mind with all the following figures.

[2] This comes out clearly, for instance, from the many purchases of rents recorded in the Eynsham Cartulary.

to his son Edmund 7,000 marks a year [£186,666], to his son Thomas a lump sum of 10,000 marks [£266,666], and to his daughter Eleanor 15,000 marks [£400,000; M, vol. i, p. 998]; his daughter Mary, a nun at Amesbury, he had endowed with £266 13s. 4d. a year [£10,666; ibid., p. 941].

These may be compared with contemporary France. In 1271, the dowry which the Comte de Bar's daughter brought to the Count of Burgundy's son was 1,000 l. [£10,000]. In 1316 the widow of Louis X had 25,000 l. a year for her jointure [£250,000]. In 1328, the wife of the Comte de Périgord had 500 l. a year for her dowry [£5,000]. All these are from D'Avenel (E, vol. v, pp. 375 ff.); the largest lump sum for a dowry that he quotes is that of Charles V's queen, who brought him 100,000 florins; doubtless in French currency, where the florin was equivalent to a *livre tournois*. Leber gives a few figures later than the Black Death; they seem to rise gradually in amount, as one would expect at a time when money was becoming cheaper.

As for yearly household expenses, St. Louis in 1251 was spending 48,558 l. a year [£485,580]. The French Duke of Savoy, in 1279, 10,750 l. [£107,500]. In 1316, the royal household cost 36,500 l. a year [£365,000]. These sums are from D'Avenel (E, vol. v, p. 383). Compare this with some English items (L, pp. xxviii, xxxii, xxxv, xxxvii). Henry III allowed 'the illustrious King of Castile' £1 a day for his household expenses in London [£40], the dowager queen Eleanor received 10 marks daily [£266 13s. 4d.], Edward II's queen had 11,000 marks a year for her expenses in 1316 [£293,333]. In 1353 Edward III allowed to Edward Baliol, King of Scotland, 40s. daily for the expenses of his household, until he should be otherwise provided for [[£29,200 a year].] In 1358, he granted John of Brittany £26 15s. 4d. for the eight days he had spent in London: nearly [[£134]] a day, unless we allow something for the Black Death. But these figures, like the dowries and apanages, are complicated by the fact that some of the expenses were doubtless of a kind which we should reckon nowadays as political.

Among 'necessaries', perhaps the least amenable to our multi-plicand of 40 would be house-property; unless perhaps we take salt in France, under the *gabelle*. But, when we remember how small and slight the average house of that period was, seldom running even into three stories, and how relatively scanty the population was even in walled towns, so that the competition for ground-space was not comparable to that of modern cities, then we shall see that the house of to-day and the house of 1348 stand really in different categories. Here are significant instances from D'Avenel (E, vol. ii, p. 2): (1) *Prices of houses in Paris* between 1225 and 1324 (E, vol. i, pp. 2 ff.). These range from the Precentor's of Notre Dame

[£1,666] down to a butcher's [£200], a furrier's [£833] and an apothe-
cary's [£1,333]. A house with 34 acres of garden [£2,666]; a smaller
house with garden [£1,333]. As fancy prices, we may take a house,
with courtyard, on the Petit Pont—the equivalent of a spacious
tenement at the end of London Bridge or in Cheapside at that date
(1254): this sold for [£12,000]. In 1302, when Cardinal Lemoine
founded a college at the University, this cost [£16,680]. (2) *In the
provinces*. Seven houses, which seem typical, ranged from an important butcher's at Soissons [£1,660] down to village houses of
[£150] or even [£50].

Of non-necessaries, perhaps the dearest were silks, brocades,
jewels and books. The former, coming from so far, cost not only cash
but lives of men. When Edward I dowered his daughter Eleanor he
expressed the sum as 'ten thousand marks sterling, and five
thousand marks *pur son atir*' (M, vol. i, pars ii, p. 998). *Tantae
molis erat* to raise a royal trousseau. Again, 'a cloth embroidered
with pearls, for a reading-desk to be placed at the front of the
altar and tomb of Catherine, our daughter', seems to have cost
the greater part of 500 marks which Henry III paid at one time
(L, p. xxx).

Finally, books were never in sufficient demand to create a plentiful
supply. It was never worth any monk's while to imitate the ancient
classical system of dictating to a room full of scribes, by which (as
we learn from Socrates's *Apology* and Martial's *Epigrams*) books
could be produced in antiquity almost as cheaply as by modern
printing.[1] One of the busiest book industries was that which flour-
ished in Paris roughly between 1270 and 1320, and which produced
the beautifully legible little pocket Bibles of which so many still
survive. Yet prices were always enormous, compared with modern
ideas. A list of prices for Bibles may be found in D'Avenel (E,
vol. vii, p. 372 ff.) and Savage (S, pp. 243 ff.). They naturally vary
a great deal, probably according to size and condition; some probably in pocket-size, and others in from one to four folio volumes,
possibly illuminated. The average of the only three recorded before
1348 is £26 [£1,040]; they were probably all folios, and in 2 volumes.
The average of the whole lot, 25 in number, from 1260 to 1536, is
in medieval currency, £5 10s. 6d. If we multiply by twenty only,
considering the late date of most of them, we get [£110 10s.] according to modern ideas. The five pre-Black Death breviaries recorded
in D'Avenel average £7 0s. 9d. sterling [£281 10s.]; and it is unlikely
that illumination played any great part here. The average price of
the 24 scheduled by D'Avenel and Savage together, dating from

[1] The very few instances of this device are all extra-monastic: *see* Wattenbach,
Schriftwesen, (1896), p. 439.

1228 to 1518, is £4 18s. 6d. sterling. Books, however, were emphatically a luxury and, if my multiplier of 40 be generally correct, such exceptions as this will add to the interest of the subject, by substituting contrast for comparison.

It must not be forgotten that these figures take no account of taxation either in the Middle Ages or to-day. Nevertheless, I cannot feel that this question of taxation will so complicate the problem as to nullify all serious attempts at comparison. The reader may still, by means of this index of 40 or thereabouts, get a fairly true idea of what a given sum of money meant, in ordinary circumstances, to his ancestor of 600 years ago. All this, it is true, is put forward as a *ballon d'essai*. I am perfectly aware that it needs much more intensive study and a far wider basis of generalization than I have been able to command; yet it seems equally true that an effort ought to be made somewhere and somehow to arrive at an estimate. One warning, however, I must repeat. What I am trying here to express is not the values of things but their psychological scale. I do not suggest that 15s., in 1300, could buy what would cost £30 nowadays. I only mean that it would produce something of the same effect on men's minds: that a buyer would be about equally reluctant to part with that sum, and a seller about equally glad to get it. In other words, this is a psychological and social (as distinct from an economic) index.

SOURCES

(A)   J. E. T. Rogers, *History of Agriculture and Prices* (Oxford. 1866–).
(B)   J. E. T. Rogers, *Six Centuries of Work and Wages* (Swan Sonnenschein, 1901).
(C)   W. Fleetwood, *Chronicon Preciosum* (London. 1707).
(D)   D. Dalrymple (Lord Hailes), *Annals of Scotland* (Murray. 1776).
(E)   G. D'Avenel, *Histoire économique, etc.* (Paris. 1894–).
(F)   G. D'Avenel, *La fortune privée, etc.* (Paris. 1895).
(G)   W. Stubbs, *Constitutional History* (Oxford, 1878).
(H)   E. L. Cutts, *Parish Priests and their People* (S.P.C.K. 1898).
(J)   J. Topham (ed.), *Liber Quotidianus of Edward I, 1299–1300* (London. 1787).
(L)   F. Devon (ed.), *Issue Roll of Thos. de Brantingham* (London. 1835).
(M)   T. Rymer, *Foedera* (3rd ed. London. 1816–30).
(N)   D. Wilkins, *Concilia*, Vol. II.
(O)   C. Reynerus, *Apostolatus Benedictinorum in Anglia*. Appendix III (Douai. 1626).
(P)   R. S. Rait, *Life in the Medieval University* (C. U. Press. 1921).
(Q)   H. Rashdall, *Universities of Europe* (Oxford. 1895).

(R) C. Leber, *Essai sur l'interprétation de la fortune privée au moyen âge* (Paris. 1847).

(S) E. A. Savage, *Old English Libraries* (London. 1911).

(T) Colin Clark, *The National Income* (London. 1932).

(U) L. Delisle. *Classe agricole en Normandie* (Champion. 1903).

(V) D. Knoop and G. P. Jones, *The Mediaeval Mason* (Manchester University Press. 1933).

J. N. L. BAKER

Medieval Trade Routes

THE subject of Medieval Trade Routes presents certain difficulties at the outset. There is no clear definition of the word 'medieval' and, whatever period is chosen, it is obvious that trade routes within that period would be unlikely always to follow the same direction or to be of the same importance. Allowance must be made not only for the changing development of different regions, and the substitution of one form of commerce for another, but also for all the varying non-geographical factors which so frequently affect the direction and the volume of trade. It is not the purpose of this essay to discuss these political and economic factors as a whole, though it will be necessary to refer to some of them: their operation throughout the period should, however, be borne in mind.

GENERAL GEOGRAPHICAL CONSIDERATIONS

When allowance has been made for the difficulties mentioned, and assuming the existence of communities capable of maintaining commerce, there are certain fundamental, if obvious geographical considerations which, in a broad way, determine the general direction of trade and, in more detail, the lines which it will follow.

The differences in climate between different parts of the earth's surface are of themselves enough to produce crops and products of very varied character. It is true that medieval Europe knew but a small part of the world, yet it was brought into contact with several

224

regions widely differing in their products. Sometimes it was able to overcome the difficulties of carriage over long distances by introducing the commodity into Europe: this was done with success in the case of the silkworm. But in other cases such adaptation was impossible. Nowhere in Europe were climatic conditions suitable to the growth of spices, for which the west had always to depend upon the tropical and equatorial lands of south-eastern Asia. Sugar cane was another product obtainable only in the East. Rice, fruits of various kinds, Brazil wood (for dyeing) and cotton were all important products imported into medieval Europe from the warmer parts of the world. It is unnecessary to give other instances of the dependence of Europe on the extra-European lands for some of its necessities (or luxuries): Rome had long been interested in Oriental products and the supply of such articles continued throughout the Middle Ages, though different routes might be used and the amount received might vary from time to time.

Even within Europe climatic conditions were far from uniform. The lands which grew the vine to perfection naturally became exporters of wine to those parts of the Continent where no wine could be produced. The Rhinelands, southern Tyrol, the Seine valley, Burgundy and Gascony, to name a few examples, were among the more important exporting regions. In the more extreme conditions of eastern Europe the extensive forests produced not merely timber but furs, honey, and tar. If one assumed only an exchange of natural products based on climatic distinctions one would expect an east and west movement in northern Europe and a north and south movement as between non-Mediterranean and Mediterranean lands. In very broad terms this is true of medieval trade routes.

In addition to products depending on climate there were minerals, and manufactured goods. The former were not extensively worked in the Middle Ages, but the metals of Nürnberg and Dinant gave rise to important manufactures. Similarly the cloth industry of Flanders and north-eastern France provided one of the most important commodities of medieval trade. Both the assembly of the raw materials and the marketing of the finished product introduce factors which are only partly geographical, but which obviously play a large part in determining routes of trade.

A very important food commodity was fish and here the geographical conditions, which make the North Sea an important breeding ground for fish, exercised a great influence. In early times the productive fishing grounds were in the western Baltic and the eastern part of the North Sea; later the herring left those waters and were found more abundantly off the coasts of Britain. The reasons for the migration are obscure, but the consequences to the Hansa fishing towns were serious. Some of them owed most of their prosperity to the catching, salting, or marketing of fish. This great industry required salt, which was obtainable only in a few places, but its transport again influenced certain trade routes.

Finally, there are some geographical or topographical factors which have exercised a profound influence on the particular lines which trade followed (*see Fig. 1*). The routes to the Far East are strictly limited. Two are obvious at first sight. The Red Sea approaches so closely to the Mediterranean that contact between the two has never been difficult. The Persian Gulf is backed by the fertile alluvial valleys of the Tigris and the Euphrates, from which the Syrian desert could be crossed to the Mediterranean, or the mountainous border of Asia Minor to the Black Sea. A third route came overland through central Asia. Here desert or semi-desert country had to be crossed and hence oases, or some other well-watered places, which determined the stages in the journey of caravans, indicated the only practical line to be followed. These three routes ended in the west in Egypt, on the coastlands of Syria and Palestine, and on the Black Sea; and it is not difficult, if one bears this simple position in mind, to understand the long importance of such places as Alexandria or Constantinople, which from their mere situation became the media between East and West.

In Europe itself the great ranges of fold-mountains which border the Mediterranean lands on the north presented an obstacle which had to be crossed, or passed, through some obvious break. The Danube valley makes one such break between the Alps and the Carpathians, though here, for political reasons, the obvious geographical route was little used. The Mediterranean coastlands of France provide another such break, and here in particular the Rhone valley has always attracted commerce and has had its southern outlet at or near Marseille. Within the mountain belt are passes through which trade went, and the routes to those passes are clearly marked with the cities whose names are common in the annals of medieval commerce.

Inland are the mountain blocks of a Europe whose geological age is older than that of the fold-mountains. In general these old masses were, and are, less densely peopled than the lower lands which surround them and trade routes tended to run round their edges. This is particularly true of Germany and of France. From them flow the great rivers of northern Europe, which in an age when land transport was slow, difficult, and dangerous, provided natural route lines. In eastern Europe it is almost possible to cross the continent by water-ways. In the west there are no such continuous river-routes, but the arrangement of the valley lines is such that these can

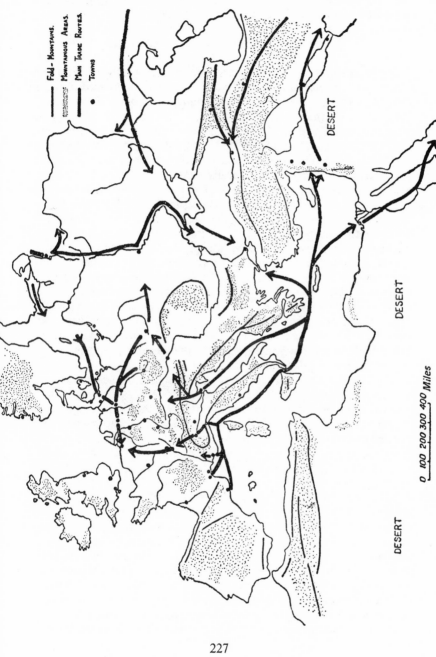

Figure 1. Europe—Genfralized Routes

be used for long distances. The Rhine, in particular, forms an important line of north-to-south communication.

THE PRELIMINARIES OF MEDIEVAL TRADE

Such are some of the elementary facts which form the basis for the study of the routes of medieval trade. We can now proceed to trace out some of these routes in more detail. The Roman Empire had been based on the Mediterranean Sea, which, for the first and only time in history, had formed a single unit. It was, therefore, natural that all commercial 'roads' should pass through, or near, that sea to Rome. With the gradual weakening of Roman power in central and western Europe trade naturally suffered a decline, but it was still maintained and it still followed the broad lines which it had taken under Roman organization. Thus, in the fifth century north-west Africa, under the Vandals, exported corn across the sea to Italy; in the sixth century Visigothic Spain traded coastwise with southern France, north Africa and Italy, and produce from central Europe seems to have come overland to the south-west corner of the continent; in Italy the cities of the south—particularly Salerno, Amalfi, Naples, Otranto—were still (c. A.D. 700) engaged in the Oriental trade with Syria and Egypt. But it was in Constantinople that the greatest commercial activity was to be found. There was some contact, through Persians, with the Far East; there was regular trade with Italy, and sometimes with the western Mediterranean; and there was regular trade with Egypt.

The Greek Cosmas, a merchant of Alexandria in the first half of the sixth century, has left a few interesting details of his activities. He sailed the Mediterranean Sea, the Red Sea, the Persian Gulf, and the Indian Ocean. He says that 'once on a time' he had been bound for 'inner' India, which may be Arabia or may be some land east of Cape Comorin; he certainly visited Ceylon, which 'lies on the other side of the pepper country of (south-west India).' This island, he pointed out, 'being . . . in a central position is much frequented by ships from all parts of India and from Persia and Ethiopia, and it likewise sends out many of its own . . . and from the remotest countries (east of Cape Comorin) it receives silk, aloes, cloves, sandalwood, and other products, and these are passed on to marts on this side, such as Male (on the Malabar coast of India) where pepper grows, and to Calliana (near Bombay) which exports copper and sesame logs, and cloth for making dresses.' The sea-route between China and India thus outlined continued westward via Sind, Persia, and Arabia to Adule, the port of Ethiopia, whither many kinds of spices and 'many other articles of merchandise' from north-east

228

Africa came for export. Cosmas claims to have seen 'most of' Ethiopia, by which he means East Africa southward to the Equator.

There was another, and important, route leading to Constantinople across Europe. This route, to which reference is made later, broke down because of the movement of Slavs into Southern Russia: it was re-opened by the Northmen in the ninth century.

From what has been said it will perhaps be clear that the barbarian invasions of Europe, though no doubt checking trade considerably, had not entirely obliterated it. But the requirements of Europe were much reduced and with them the volume of trade. Much more important from the point of view of the maintenance of the trade routes of medieval Europe was the advance of the Mohammedan peoples in the seventh century. Within 150 years the whole of the African shore of the Mediterranean was in their hands together with the greater part of Spain, Syria, and Palestine, and both shores of the Persian Gulf. Thus not only were some of the Mediterranean routes cut off but complete control was obtained of two of the main lines of communication between Europe and the Far East. As the overland route had ceased to be of importance by this time the practical result was that the Mohammedan peoples controlled all the trade routes between Europe and the Far East. Some trade between southern Italy and Constantinople remained, and gradually commercial relations with the Mohammedan rulers of Egypt were resumed though not always by the commercial classes in Constantinople itself: Levantines and Italians were playing an increasingly important part.

Meanwhile the Northmen had burst upon western Europe and brought about conditions as fatal to trade as the Mohammedans produced elsewhere. In the ninth century little real trade, apart from local exchange, was carried on. There was, however, still one line of contact between northern Europe and the Mediterranean: from the Baltic to the Black Sea (*see Fig. 1*). A glance at a physical map of Europe will show great rivers rising in the heart of Russia and flowing north and south: it was these river lines which were used by the Swedes. About A.D. 800 they set up a post on the south shore of Lake Ladoga, which was easily reached from the Gulf of Finland, and the thirty-mile stretch of the river Neva. This post commanded two routes. Southward the river Volkov led to Novgorod, and thence by the Lovat to the Dnieper, the Black Sea, and Constantinople. Eastward by the Syas and the Mologa traders passed to the Volga river, the Caspian Sea, and the eastern markets. Novgorod, and Kiev (on the Dnieper) became the most important centres of trade along these routes, which remained open until the eleventh century. Along these lines went the staple products of northern Europe—furs, honey, and slaves; in return the merchants took spices, wine, silk, and precious metals. Some of this trading activity was, in time, extended to the North Sea and thus to England, the Low Countries and north-eastern France. It would seem, then, that Europe had found a way of getting round the Mohammedan domination of the western Mediterranean Sea in much the same way as later she found a way of getting round a Turkish domination of the Red Sea.

Yet it would be a mistake to accept this generalization too strictly. The Mediterranean was never wholly closed to Europeans. The rise of Venice in the ninth century illustrates clearly how little account is taken by traders of questions of religion: Christian traders were ready to trade with infidels. The Venetian connexion with Egypt dates from the ninth century. Venice carried the timber and iron, found in plenty in her north-eastern hinterland, and slaves, to supply the needs of the Arab ship-building yards and harems. This development went on side by side with an increasing control of the Byzantine trade and, in time, with a development of trade with the ports of Syria. Thus there was re-established one of the fundamental links between western Europe and the East.

Other cities in Italy also were prominent in this Mediterranean trade. In the south Salerno, Amalfi, Naples and Gaeta traded with the lands of the Moslems, and through Amalfi in particular the goods, which had first found their way to Alexandria, were transmitted to Europe. These ports of southern Italy maintained their position until the early years of the twelfth century. In the north Pisa shared to some extent in this Oriental trade, and remained a port of some importance until the Genoese damaged her harbour in 1284. Even after that she tried to maintain her eastern trade, but after her annexation by Florence in 1406 the Florentines, through neglect of the canals and drainage works, rendered the neighbourhood unhealthy and directly prohibited Pisan commerce.

The connexion of Genoa with the Levant came later than that of the south Italian cities or Venice. Her geographical outlook was to the west and her earliest ventures were in North Africa, Spain, and France. Her natural interests lay first in defeating the Mohammedan invader, and it was not until this had been accomplished, and the crusading movement had given her special opportunities in the Levant, that she set out on that line which was ultimately to bring her into direct and serious rivalry with Venice. Indeed the Crusades which benefited all the Mediterranean ports, may be said to have made Genoese trade with the Levant.

Freedom from the Moslems also brought a renewal of prosperity to the ports of southern France and eastern Spain. Marseille, especially in the twelfth and thirteenth centuries, had important trade relations with Syria and Egypt. Saint Gilles, now an inland town west of Arles, was once the most important point of departure of pilgrims and convoys to the Holy Land and was regularly visited by Mediterranean traders. It also lay on an important pilgrim route to Compostella in Spain. Aigues Mortes had a shorter life, depending largely on the Crusades and becoming a royal port in 1248: by the end of the thirteenth century it was in decline. Montpellier traded with Egypt and Syria. Narbonne not only imported produce from Syria but carried on land trade with Bordeaux and from that port were obtained English commodities of which tin was important. Barcelona from the ninth century sent her ships to southern Spain and North Africa in the west, and to Egypt in the east. The coastal ports of France declined toward the close of the Middle Ages because the silting of lagoons rendered them too unhealthy to sustain large populations: Marseille, free from silt on the east side of the Rhône delta, and secure in its rock-basin harbour, alone remained of first-class importance.

NORTH ITALY AS A ROUTE-CENTRE

As the Moslem power was declining, and with new contacts opened up with the Near East through the Crusades, the traffic coming into the ports of Italy and particularly those of the north, necessitated an increasing use of the routes leading through the Alpine mountains to France and Germany. Here trade was, of necessity, confined to certain lines laid down by the geography of the country. Yet even here geographical features exercised no rigid control, for the importance of various routes differed with changing circumstances, and at least one new route of great value was opened up during the Middle Ages.

In the west four main routes led from Italy to France or Burgundy (*see Fig. 2*). Along the narrow coastal belt the Roman road which had connected Genoa with Marseille was still in use. This avoided the main mass of the Alps though it was connected with Cuneo and Turin by way of the Col di Tenda. In the western Alps three passes stand out in importance during the Middle Ages. Two of these gave passage from Turin, by way of Susa, to the Rhône valley. The Mt. Genèvre route led to Briançon and thence by several ways to the lower Rhône. This was a very old route and was much used from the fourth to the eighth centuries. It then yielded much of its importance to the Mt. Cenis pass, which connected Susa with the upper valley of the Arc, itself a tributary of the Isère, on which stands Grenoble, and

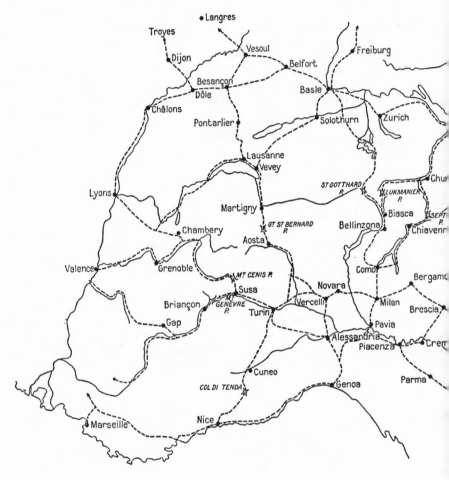

Figure

232

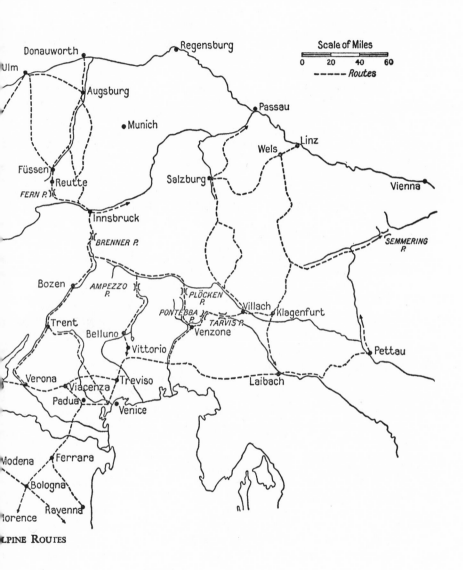

ALPINE ROUTES

which reaches the Rhône a short distance above Valence. This route was known and in use in the early part of the eighth century, but in the later Middle Ages, from the twelfth century onward, the road over this pass was of great importance and it had by that time practically displaced the Mt. Genèvre route. The Mt. Cenis pass indeed shared with the Great St. Bernard the claim to be the most important of the western passes during the Middle Ages. Yet the latter had one great advantage over the Mt. Cenis. This pass led from Aosta, on the Dora Baltea, to Martigny, on the Rhône, and so to the Lake of Geneva. From this point it was possible to travel westward to the Rhône Valley at Lyon, north-westward to the Paris basin or north-eastward to the Rhine at Basle. Thus the Great St. Bernard provided a means of communication between Italy and both France and south-western Germany. It was quite early of importance, and it retained its premier position until the St. Gotthard route was opened in the early years of the thirteenth century.

In the central Alps three passes were of importance. The route over the St. Gotthard was not opened up until the beginning of the thirteenth century, but once this pass was available its geographical situation was so favourable that it was likely to attract traffic. From Milan the route ran north to Como and Bellinzona. Beyond the pass the valley of the Reuss led northward to the Rhine above Basle. Thus the pass gave a much more direct route between Basle and north Italy than that provided by any other pass. Eastward of this route lay the Septimer. It is not certain that this pass was in regular use, though the balance of evidence seems to be in its favour: some authorities, however, prefer the Splügen. This route also connected Milan and Como with Germany. The road left the St. Gotthard route at Como, passed through Chiavenna and crossed the Alps to Chur, in the valley of the upper Rhine, and so led to the Lake of Constance, from which it was possible to reach the Rhine at Basle, or the upper Danube. Between these two passes lay the Lukmanier, opened up in the later Middle Ages. The St. Gotthard route was followed from Milan to Biasca, and the Lukmanier pass connected the latter town with the Upper Rhine and, therefore, with Chur. Beyond that point the route was the same as that for the Septimer.

Of the eastern passes by far the most important was the Brenner. There were two ways of approaching this pass. Most direct was the valley of the Adige from Verona to Trent, where the Val Sugana joins the Adige and leads eastward to the Brenta valley and so to the towns at the head of the Adriatic, and to Venice in particular. Beyond Trent, to the northward the combined route follows the Adige valley through Bozen, and beyond the Brenner leads to Innsbruck and Augsburg. There were alternative routes between Innsbruck and Augsburg, while a third route ran north-westward over the Fern pass through Reutte and Füssen also to Augsburg: from this last route it was possible also to reach the Danube crossing at Ulm. The Inn valley itself furnished yet a fourth route leading to the Danube at Passau. Thus it was possible by using the Brenner route to reach all parts of southern Germany and Bohemia.

The Brenner route was also reached by the Pusterthal. This latter was approached from Treviso and Vittorio, and by way of the Piave valley, or by a less important route up the Tagliamento and over the Plöcken pass. Of these routes that via the Val Sugana and that via the Piave were of obvious importance to Venice and go far to explain the early expansion of Venice on the mainland.

East of the Brenner were two important systems of routes. The first of these began at Venzone, where a road branched off to cross the Pontebba pass to Villach, from which point routes led northward to Salzburg and the Danube at Passau or Linz, and eastward to Klagenfurt, another road centre from which the Danube could be reached either at Linz (through Wels) or at Vienna by crossing the Semmering pass. Southward from Klagenfurt a route led to Laibach. The second route reached Laibach more directly from Lombardy, over the Birnbaumer Wald. Beyond Laibach the road ran to Pettau, on the Drave, from which point it was possible to reach Vienna. These routes were important in that not only did they give contact with Hungary but they also provided an alternative approach to the north-east of the plain of Lombardy if, through some political accident, the Brenner route was closed.

It is a characteristic of the Alpine passes that they converge on the Plain of Lombardy. Conversely they lead to all parts of central western Europe. Thus, as already explained, the most westerly passes give access to the Rhône Valley or to the upper part of the Rhine about Basle. The northward continuation of the Rhône valley is prolonged to the bend of the Rhine at Basle by the Saône-Doubs lowland in which lies Besançon, easily reached from the Lake of Geneva via Pontalier. From Besançon a route ran over the Saône near Vesoul (where the Basle-Belfort-Vesoul road joined it) and headed for Bar-sur-Aube, beyond which lay Châlons-sur-Marne. Alternatively from Pontalier a route ran through Besançon to Dijon, where it was joined by the Rhône valley route coming from Châlons-sur-Saône. Beyond this point it ran to Troyes and either Paris or Soissons (*see Fig. 3*). At the last-named town the route from Châlons-sur-Marne joined and, beyond, the Somme was crossed at Peronne and so Flanders was reached. These routes thus ran through the heart of the Champagne 'Fair' region. How old these Fairs were is not known with certainty, but they were very important in

235

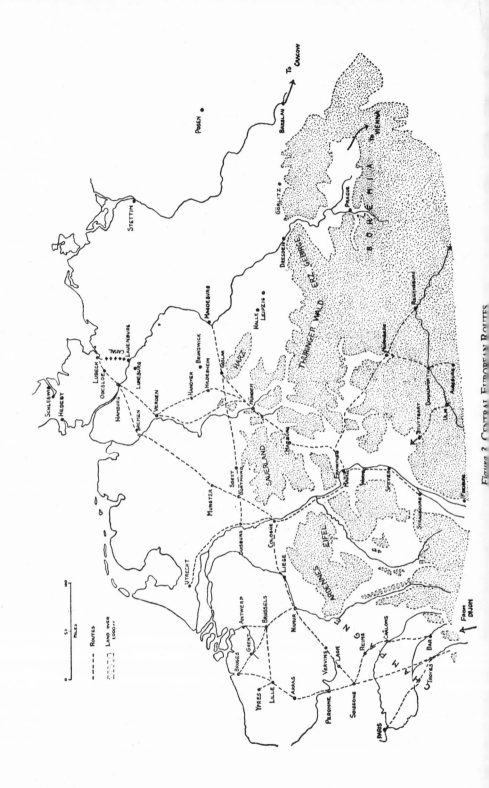

Figure 2. Central European Routes

the twelfth century, and reached the height of their importance in the thirteenth century. They performed, first, the function of intermediaries between the produce of Flanders and that of Italy, which of course included produce imported into Italy from the East. But their function was wider than this. They attracted traders from Spain, from all parts of France, from Germany, and even from Poland. They provided not merely for the buying and selling of goods of great variety but for the settling of accounts and so 'played the part of an embryonic clearing house'. Their prosperity declined in the fourteenth century with changed methods of commerce, with the opening of new trade routes, and with the disturbed political conditions that affected the area in which they were situated.

The most important articles of trade in the 'Fair' towns were cloths, particularly woollen cloths, manufactured locally, or elsewhere in northern France or, more especially, in Flanders. From Flanders also came manufactured metal goods, chiefly of copper and brass, while through Flanders came the amber of north-east Germany, and the furs of Russia and Scandinavia. The manufactures of north Italy, such as the silk of Lucca, and the eastern produce such as spices, drugs, cloth of gold, which reached Italy from the Levant or from Egypt, and more local produce, as the hides and skins from Spain and southern France, cattle, horses, cheese, and wine, were also among the many commodities exposed for sale.

FLANDERS AS A ROUTE-CENTRE

From Champagne, as has already been suggested, important trade routes led to Flanders. The lands at the delta of the Rhine had been important for their trade in Roman times when the Frieslanders had exchanged the produce of western and southern Europe for the raw materials of the Baltic lands. This trade did not stop with the barbarian invasions although there was a slight change in the importance of certain towns. The Northmen caused some interruption for a time but those same commercial instincts which, as has been seen, carried these people across Russia to the Black Sea drew them to frequent this Friesland area for trade, while the expansion of Charlemagne's empire eastward and the subsequent colonization of parts of eastern Europe by German peoples led to a similar eastward extension of the zone of influence of the Frieslanders. Thus by the end of the tenth century there were regular trade connexions by sea between Friesland and Denmark, while England was also included in the area served by the Danes.

In that region which became known as Flanders there had been, during Roman times, a flourishing cloth industry based on the wool of locally bred sheep. This industry never died out, although it received a severe check from the invasions of the Northmen, and with its revival and expansion it became necessary to import wool from England. By the twelfth century Flanders was an extremely important manufacturing region, with its centres in such towns as Ghent, Bruges, Ypres and Arras, and was sending its produce to Italy in the south and to Russia in the east.

It was along this trade route to Russia that there grew up the towns later to be associated in the Hanseatic League. We are not here concerned with the history of this league, but it is important to observe the location of its chief towns (*Fig. 3*). These fall broadly into two groups. The inland towns lie in a wide belt from Cologne to Magdeburg, though the western terminus was Bruges. Here are, in general, light, easily cultivated soils which extend along the foot of the mountain mass of central Europe into Poland and southern Russia. This belt of land seems to have played an important part in the movement, and in the settlement, of peoples and always to have contained a relatively dense population: with changing geographical circumstances it maintains the larger part of Germany's industrial population to-day. Along or near this belt lay Dortmund, Soest, Münster, Hanover, Goslar, Brunswick, and Magdeburg with many less notable places. Here communication along west-east lines was comparatively easy, avoiding the marshes and scrub-covered heathlands to the north and the mountains to the south. Moreover Goslar was in direct communication with south-west Germany through Münden, Frankfurt, and Nürnberg, while from Magdeburg the valley of the Elbe afforded a route to Bohemia.

The second group of towns lay on the estuaries of the rivers which flow to the North Sea—Bremen on the Weser, Hamburg on the Elbe, Lübeck on the Trave, Stettin on the Oder. Of these Lübeck was of greatest importance. Founded in 1158, it served as an intermediary between the Baltic and north Germany. Before its foundation trade from the Baltic went to Schleswig and crossed the narrow end of the Danish peninsula to Hedeby on the west coast; Lübeck displaced Schleswig, while beyond Lübeck German traders founded the town of Wisby, on the island of Gothland, and in the next century, the more distant Baltic ports of Stettin, Danzig, Königsberg, Riga, and Reval. Thus by this Baltic route contact was established with Novgorod, whose importance has already been mentioned.

Lübeck occupied a position of interest. It was situated on an island in the Trave some distance from the mouth of the river but where the river was still navigable. But in its relations with the Baltic it had in this respect no particular advantage over Schleswig.

On the landward side, however, it had road communication with Hamburg and when it was joined by the Steckenitz canal to Lauenburg on the Elbe at the end of the fourteenth century, it had also water communication with the latter town. Thus it was put into close touch with the salt of Oldesloe, a few miles to the south-west, or of Lüneburg, with the minerals of the Harz Mountains, and with all the cultural and commercial influences which came along the inland trade route already described. The industry of salting herrings grew to one of great importance, as did the export of fish. In addition Lübeck collected the produce of all the northern lands from towns and ports along the Baltic shores. In the thirteenth century Lübeck ships made the sea passage to Bergen while ships from Flanders sailed round Denmark into the Baltic Sea. The Lübeck traders carried grain from the Baltic to Bergen and even to Great Britain, while timber was another important commodity. When Hamburg threatened to compete with the salt imports of Lübeck the Steckenitz canal was built to secure regular supplies of this commodity, which was distributed to other ports along the Baltic. Salt was also obtained from the Bay of Bourgneuf, on the west coast of France south of the Loire, in the thirteenth century and was carried by Flemings and Lübeckers as a return cargo to the Norwegian and Baltic ports. Lübeck and the other Hansa towns were chiefly engaged, apart from local commerce, in an exchange of raw materials from the east and north of Europe for the manufacturers of Flanders.

CENTRAL EUROPEAN ROUTES

We have followed the main routes northward from the Mediterranean to Flanders and thence eastward to the Baltic and Russia. It is now necessary to look briefly at some subsidiary routes which crossed Europe to the east of the lines already described (*Fig. 3*). First comes the Rhine route which has been followed from Italy as far as Basle. Beyond that town the route ran along the Rhine valley touching at such places as Strasbourg, Speyer, Worms, and Mainz, to Cologne and beyond to Utrecht. These cities in the Rhine valley between Cologne and Basle formed the Rhine League, for the protection of commerce, in the thirteenth century; but although this League subsequently included more than one hundred members it never attained the importance of the Hanseatic League. Perhaps this was because the commerce of its towns was of regional rather than continental importance. Wine, leather goods, timber, and iron were the chief articles of trade furnished by this region. The same may be said of the Leagues organized by the south German cities in the fourteenth century, such for example as the Swabian League which, under the leadership of Ulm, included more than thirty cities in Swabia, and allied itself to the Rhine League in 1381. These cities lay on the routes from Augsburg to Ulm and the south-west of Germany or from Augsburg to Nürnberg, or from Augsburg to Donauwörth and down the Danube to Regensburg, the starting point of routes for Bohemia, or to Vienna, and were concerned chiefly with Oriental products. Another group centred round Görlitz, on the Neisse, lay astride routes which ran through Germany southward to Bohemia and eastward to Silesia and Poland. From Vienna the Moravian 'gate' provided an easy route to Cracow and, through southern Poland, to Kiev.

VENETIAN TRADE ROUTES

Enough has been said to show how widespread was the net of commercial routes in Europe in the Middle Ages. It is well therefore at this point to glance at the trade connexions of Venice which linked together the north and south of Europe. Her earliest settlers, safe on their island home in the lagoons, became fishermen and traders engaged in transport through the intricate channels, or workers in the saltpans of the neighbouring mainland. Hence they became carriers in the Adriatic and gained privileges alike from Charlemagne and the Emperor at Constantinople. The decay of Ravenna in the ninth century and the acquisition of Comaccio left Venice without a trade rival nearer than Ancona, while successful wars against the Slav pirates of the Adriatic coast strengthened her command of the Adriatic and provided her both with supplies of timber from Dalmatia and a market for her manufactures. By the end of the eleventh century she had strengthened her position in Constantinople, where she now had 'factories'. At the same time the Crusades gave her a chance to develop her trade with the Levant, while early in the thirteenth century the sack of Constantinople (1204), the acquisition of the Cyclades and Sporades, and the purchase of Crete enormously improved her possibilities for commercial expansion. There followed a severe struggle with Genoa, whose early activities in the western Mediterranean had been so increased that she too traded in the Levant, at Constantinople, and in the Black Sea. The rivalry of Genoa was ended by Venetian sea victories in 1380: Genoa never recovered and Venice remained indisputably mistress of the Mediterranean until, in the fifteenth century, she was threatened by the advance of the Turks. Even so it was not until the end of the fifteenth century that her decline was visible.

Venetian trade routes covered the whole of the Mediterranean. Her ships visited Constantinople and the Black Sea; the Morea and the Greek islands; Asia Minor and Syria; and Alexandria. From the three last came carpets, damasks, jewels, gold and silver work, spices, drugs, coffee and sugar: in return Venice sent cloth, beads and crystal. To the west her traders visited Tunis, Barbary, and Spain, and later England and Flanders. They exchanged alum, glass, sugar, silk, sweet wine, currants and spices for tin, wool, hides and cloth. By land her goods crossed the Brenner and the Septimer passes to southern Germany, France and Flanders. Whether by land or by sea she was thus brought into contact with all the most important parts of Europe. She had little produce of her own to export. Glass was manufactured locally; silk introduced from Lucca formed the basis of a valuable industry; there was some metal working, leather working and lace-making. But she was within easy reach of other industrial centres in northern Italy.

RENEWAL OF DIRECT CONTACT WITH ASIA

Extensive as is the area described above it does not exhaust the regions frequented by Venetian traders. It has already been pointed out that the Crusades gave great opportunities to merchants from Italy to develop commerce with the Levant and the Black Sea. The Crusaders' territories in Syria, using the word in its geographical sense, lay athwart the great trade routes of the Near East. The short-lived county of Edessa controlled a route from Aleppo to the Tigris: the southward extension of the kingdom of Jerusalem gave the Crusaders access to the Red Sea and so control of the route from Damascus to Egypt: the whole of the area occupied or threatened by the Christians lay beside the route from Aleppo through Hamah, Homs and Damascus southward to Egypt and Arabia, while Damascus itself was in direct communication with Baghdad, one of the most important cities of the world, and itself a great centre of commerce, as well as with Central Asia and Asia Minor. It was natural that European traders should follow up these trade routes. They certainly were visiting Aleppo and Damascus in the second half of the thirteenth century, and may even have penetrated to the Euphrates valley, though of this there is little evidence.

It has already been pointed out that one great trade route between Europe and the East ended on the Black Sea (*see Fig. 4*). This route, which had declined in importance, was revived in the thirteenth century. Venetians reached Kiev before the middle of the thirteenth century and were active in the ports on the southern shores

Figure 4. ASIATIC ROUTES

242

of the Black Sea—Trebizond, and Sinope. These ports connected with a great net-work of routes in Asia Minor, leading to coastal ports or to Syria, and were joined to two Asiatic routes: in the north to Tiflis and the Caspian Sea; in the south through Armenia to Tabriz and Persia. A third route began on the northern shore of the Black Sea at such ports as Matracha, Rosia, Sudak, Kaffa, Kherson (Crimea), Tanais, and Tana, the last built eighteen miles from the mouth of the Don about 1260. Thence the route crossed the Volga at Sarai or at Astrakhan, and passed south of the sea of Aral to the rich cities of the Oxus and Jaxartes. Beyond, through the Iron Gates in the Tian Shan, traders reached the Tarim basin and by its oases journeyed to China.

All routes to Asia had been closed to Europeans through the domination of the Turks. But in the thirteenth century a new situation arose with the spread of the Mongol power in Asia. Christians seeking an ally against the Infidel hoped to find one in the Mongol Khan: and where Christian ambassadors could go it was no less certain that Christian traders would also go. The Mongol invasions and the unification of a great part of Asia by them opened the routes in Central Asia and through the Persian Gulf: only the Egyptian route remained in the hands of the Turks.

It was along the Central Asian route that the Christian envoys, John de Plano Carpini and William of Rubruck journeyed to the court of the Grand Khan near Karakorum. They were soon followed by two Venetian traders, Nicolo and Matteo Polo, who left Constantinople in 1250 on a trading venture to the Volga region and being prevented from returning because of a local war, decided to 'go forward by way of the east' in the hope that they could find a circuitous route back. Instead they found themselves crossing a desert and finally arriving at Bokhara. There they met an envoy who was prepared to guide them to the court of the 'Great Lord of the Tartars', and in his company they 'journeyed for one year to the north and north-east before reaching the land where they had lived.' They do not seem to have done any trade, but they returned with letters to the Pope asking for 'some hundred wise men' to be sent to the Tartars to teach them that 'the Christian Law was better than their own'.

When they went back to the East in 1271, Marco the young son of Nicolo Polo went with them, and they spent seventeen years in China. To Marco Polo, aptly described as 'incomparably the greatest traveller and the most magnificent observer of the whole Middle Ages', we owe one of the most fascinating books ever written. Yet the importance of the journey lay not in the record which the Polos brought back but in the fact that they opened up two great

243

routes to the East to European traders and missionaries. They went
out through Armenia and Persia to Ormuz and then turned inland
to strike the central Asian route by which they reached China.
They came back by sea to Ormuz. Many traders followed them,
added to the information which they had collected, and exploited
the wealth of the lands previously known only through their produce. Guide books were written for the traders and one of these,
compiled for Florentines, contains the illuminating remark that 'the
road you travel from Tana to Cathay is perfectly safe whether by
day or by night, according to what merchants say who have used it'.
From Tana to Saria, that is, the most westerly part of the route, was
'less safe than any other part of the journey' and yet 'when this part
of the road is at its worst, if you are some sixty men in the company
you will go as safely as if you were in your own house.' The same
book is full of interesting information about methods of travel, food,
charges on merchandise, the conduct of merchants, and in fact most
things which would be of practical use. It is an interesting commen-
tary on the importance of this trans-Asiatic route, which was generally more used than that by sea because for trade with China it was
quicker.

The Asiatic route has already been broadly described: a few
details must be filled in. It was not a single route but a series of
routes. From Black Sea ports it could be reached northward of the
Caspian and Aral Seas, or southward through Persia. If merchants
went to the upper valley of the Oxus they crossed the Pamirs to
Kashgar and so reached the line of oasis towns lying at the northern
edge of the Kwen Lun mountains. If, however, they went to Bokhara
and Samarkand they crossed the Tian Shan to reach Aksu on the
southern slopes of that mountain range. The third route, and that
most generally used, kept north of the Tian Shan range and forked
at its eastern end to go north or south of the Gobi desert. Pegolotti's
description of this overland route was as follows :

... From Tana to Astrakhan may be twenty-five days with an
ox-waggon, and from ten to twelve days with a horse-waggon. On
the road you will find plenty of Moccols (bandits). And from Astrakhan to Sarai may be a day by river, and from Sarai to Sarachik,
also by river, eight days. You can do this either by land or by
water, but by water you will be at less charge for your merchandise.

From Sarachik to Urghanj may be twenty days' journey in
camel-waggon. It will be well for anyone travelling with merchandise to go to Urghanj for in that city there is a ready sale for
goods. From Urghanj to Otrar is thirty-five or forty days in
camel-waggons. But if when you leave Sarachik you go direct to

Otrar it is a journey of fifty days only, and if you have no merchandise it will be better to go this way than to go by Urghanj.

From Otrar to Armalec [? Old Kulja] is forty-five days' journey
with pack-asses, and every day you find Moccols. And from
Armalec to Kanchan [on the Chinese frontier] is seventy days with
asses and from Kanchan until you come to a river called . . .
[? the Grand Canal] is forty-five days on horseback; and then you
can go down the river to Cassai [i.e. Quinsai or the modern Hang-
chau-fu]. . . . From Cassai to Cambalec [i.e. Peking], which is
the capital city of the country of Cathay, is thirty days' journey.

The sea route from the Persian Gulf calls for little comment since
it had not changed since the days when Cosmas described it. It
ran first to one of the many ports on the south-west coast of India
which as well as being a wealthy region was an important collecting
centre. Beyond, the route passed through the Straits of Malacca to
Zayton (Chuan-chau in Fukien). Marco Polo described it as 'one
of the two greatest havens in the world for commerce': a later missionary said it was 'the greatest port in the world'.

One chapter in Pegolotti's book is devoted to a catalogue of goods
sold and bought at Constantinople, but chiefly at Para, the Genoese
settlement 'where the merchants are more constantly to be found'.
Nearly one hundred different commodities are mentioned. In addition to staple products such as spices, which figure largely in the list,
'France and North-country' broad cloths, oil from Italy, wine from
Greece, dried figs from Spain, flax from Egypt and Rumania, are
among the items on the list. Even so short a selection is enough to
illustrate the wide-spread character of European trade at this period.

Within a century of Marco Polo's journey direct European intercourse with the East had practically come to an end except for
isolated journeys of more venturesome traders. The conquests of
the Turks, and the fall of the Tartar dynasty, meant that security
was gone and the routes were closed. Once again the Turkish
middleman exercised his full power to take his toll of the commerce
that still continued to reach the ports of the eastern Mediterranean,
and, to quote Sir Aurel Stein, 'a policy of strict seclusion stifling
trade once again prevailed on China's marches towards central
Asia'. But European traders were already looking for new routes.
Both the Genoese and the Venetians had long been interested in
trade with North Africa and by the fifteenth century isolated traders
were crossing the Sahara to the Niger lands.

Even more significant was the fact that at the end of the thirteenth
century Mediterranean sailors were setting out on exploring expeditions to the Atlantic. Except for the discovery of the Canaries and

Madeira they seem to have accomplished little. It is by no means certain that they originally aimed at finding a route to the East round Africa, although it is very probable that this was one of the later aims of Prince Henry of Portugal ('the Navigator'). But with him and the Portuguese discovery of the sea-way to India a new epoch is reached, for the Mediterranean gave place to the Atlantic Ocean and European commerce began its modern phase. Passing beyond Cape Bojador, in West Africa, in 1434, the Portuguese completed the first stage of their progress round Africa to the Indian Ocean: at the end of the century (1498) the whole of the sea route was discovered.

NOTE ON BOOKS

The most recent, and in some ways the best books on the subject are H. Pirenne, *Economic and Social History of Mediæval Europe* (1936), and *The Cambridge Economic History of Europe*, vol. II (1952), which contain a large number of bibliographical references. Also important are the documents selected and translated by R. S. Lopez and I. W. Raymond, *Mediæval Trade in the Mediterranean* (1955). Among the older works mention should be made of C. R. Beazley, *Dawn of Modern Geography* (3 vols., 1897–1906); Sir Henrt Yule, *The Book of Ser Marco Polo*, 3rd edition, edited by H. Cordier (1903) with the supplementary volume, *Marco Polo: Notes and Addenda* (1920); Sir Henry Yule, *Cathay and the Way Thither*, new edition by H. Cordier (Hakluyt Society, 4 vols., 1913–16); the last of these contains a valuable essay on European contacts with China. The most recent authoritative discussion of Marco Polo's route is in N. M. Penzer, *The Most Noble and Famous Travels of Marco Polo* (1929). For the Alpine passes in the Middle Ages reference should be made to J. E. Taylor, *The Alpine Passes, 962–1250* (1930); W. A. B. Coolidge, *The Alps in Nature and History* (1908) is still useful. M. V. Clarke, *The Mediæval City State* (1926) is useful for the growth of towns in Italy and Germany. The whole subject is dealt with in G. East, *An Historical Geography of Europe* (1935). Much light has been thrown on Central Asia by the archæological work of Sir Aurel Stein. His 'Asia Lecture', *Innermost Asia: its Geography as a Factor in History* (Geographical Journal, LXV, 377–403, 473–501 (1925)) should be consulted. Among the many important foreign works on the subject reference may be made to W. Heyd, *Histoire du Commerce du Levant au Moyen Age*, 2 vols. (new ed. 1923); P. Boissonnade, *Le Travail dans l'Europe chrétienne au Moyen Age* (1921), translated under the title of *Life and Work in Mediæval Europe* (1927); A. Schaube, *Handelsgeschichte der romanischen Völker des Mittelmeergebiets bis zum Ende der Kreuzzuge* (1906); H. Pirenne, *Les Villes du Moyen Age* (1927) or the earlier American edition, *Mediæval Cities* (Princeton, 1925); K. Kretschmer, *Historische Geographie von Mitteleuropa* (1904); Elizabeth Chapin, *Les Villes de Foires de Champagne des origines au debut du XIVe siècle* (1937).

Index

Aaron of Lincoln, 71
Aberconway Castle, 117–18
Abernon, Sir John d', 129
Abingdon, 60, 61, 75, 80, 91, 190
Adam of Orleton, Bishop of Worcester, 74
Adam of Staunton, 69
Adam of Stratton, 77
Adige, Valley of, 234
Adule, port of Ethiopia, 228
Adulf, St., 60
Aelfric, 33
Aethelflaed, 99, 192
Africa, Corn exports to Italy, 228; Genoese and Venetian traders, 245; Route round, 246
Aigues Mortes, 231
Agricola, Julius, 6, 7, 12
Agriculture, Labourer, Wages, 213; Agricultural service, 32; Wages, 212; Pre-Roman Britain, 20; Roman agriculture, 31
Aksu, 244
Albini, Nigel de, 101
Alcuin, 59
Aldermen, 188
Aldermanbury, 188–9
Aldersgate, 191
Aleppo–Tigris route, 241
Alexander, Prior of Fountains, 70
Alexandria, 226, 230
Alfred, King, 59, 186
Algar, the priest, 197
Alien priories, 57
Allectus, 11
Allen, Ralph, 176
Alnwick Castle, 154
Aloes, 228
Alphege, Archbishop, 187
Alps, passes and routes, 226, 231, 234–5
Alselin, Geoffrey, 98, 101
Amalfi, 228, 230
Amber, 237
Ancona, 240
Anglo-Saxon, Borough, plan of, 99; Fortified posts, 98; Settlements, 2, 26
Anglo-Saxon Chronicle, 26, 60, 97, 99, 180

Anselm, Archbishop, 61, 184
Antonine frontier, 7–9
Antoninus Pius, Forth–Clyde fortifications, 8
Aosta, 234
Arabia, 228, 241
Aral, Sea of, 243–4
Arc, Valley of, 231
Archaeology, 1
Archers, 126, 132, 137
Architecture, Domestic, 177; English medieval tradition, 170; English Classical Renaissance, 173; English, Continental influence of, 161; Monastic attitude to, 79
Armalec (Old Kulja), 245
Armenia, 243
Armour, Complete suit, 128–9; Decorated, 135; Early, 124–5; Foot-soldier, 131; French, 130; Gothic, 130; horse, 126, 131, 136; Italian, 130; Maximilian, 133; Names of parts, 131; Norman and Saxon, 125; Tournament, 134–5; Weight of, 127, 131, 134–5
Armourer, 127–9, 135; German, 133; Guilds, 133; Italian, 133
Arnold, T., 185
Arras, 238
Arrouaise, Order of, 54
Arrow, 126
Art, monastic attitude to, 79
Artillery, 119
Artisan income, 212–13
Arundel, 101, 104
Asia, Central, Routes, 243; Contact with, 241; Overland route, 224, 226
Asia Minor, routes, 226
Asser, Bishop of Sherborne, 59
Assize of bread and ale, 40
Aston Hall, 171
Astrakhan, 243–4
Atlantic, explorers of, 245–6
Attenborough, F. L., 30, 32, 40, 180
Auckland, 146, 154
Audley End, 141, 162
Augustine, St., Customs, 54, 57; Life of, 60; Rule of, 54, 57
Augustinian Canons, 53–55, 58, 66

247

251